Media Rules!

Media Rules!

MASTERING TODAY'S TECHNOLOGY TO CONNECT WITH AND KEEP YOUR AUDIENCE

Brian Reich
Dan Solomon

BICENTENNIAL
BICENTENNIAL
1807
WILEY
2007
BICENTENNIAL
BICENTENNIAL

John Wiley & Sons, Inc.

Published by John Wiley & Sons, Inc., Hoboken, New Jersey.
Published simultaneously in Canada.

Blog entries have been edited for grammar and punctuation. These changes did not, in any way, impact the tone or content of the blog entry.

Quotations from individuals not mentioned in the Notes section of this text were obtained through direct interviews conducted by the authors from November, 2006 to June, 2007.

For general information on our other products and services or for technical support, please contact our Customer Care Department within the United States at (800) 762-2974, outside the United States at (317) 572-3993 or fax (317) 572-4002.

Wiley also publishes its books in a variety of electronic formats. Some content that appears in print may not be available in electronic formats. For more information about Wiley products, visit our Web site at www.wiley.com.

Library of Congress Cataloging-in-Publication Data:

Reich, Brian, 1977-
    Media rules! mastering today's technology to connect with and keep your audience / Brian Reich, Dan Solomon.
      p. cm.
    Includes bibliographical references and index.
    ISBN 978-0-470-10888-8 (cloth)
      1. Communication and technology.   2. Mass media.   3. Globalization.
I. Solomon, Dan, 1959-   II. Title.
P96.T42R44 2007
302.2—dc22

                                    2007024179

Printed in the United States of America

10 9 8 7 6 5 4 3 2 1

Contents

Foreword

This book is designed to help organizations and individuals come to terms with their new place in the world. It's a world in which everybody, including companies, individuals, and governments, has the capacity not only to consume media but to create, share, remix, and redistribute it—to *be* media.

We Media. It's a simple expression, but surprisingly complex because it means different things to different people, depending on who you think of as *we.* Some people think that We Media implies an inverse, or an opposite—that there must also be an "un–We Media." They imagine a world of us versus them—and *We* is invariably a utopian collective of amateur, open-source, bottom-up, grassroots, net roots, media freedom fighters, somehow doing battle against—well, someone else. Corporations for sure, especially big ones.

I admire that story line, because it's so simple, so starkly divided, and primed for David's inevitable triumph over Goliath.

I wish it were true, but I just don't see the world that way. I think of We Media as *everyone,* and that's a much harder notion to come to terms with—for me, at least. It means I've got to get used to having conversations with people who look at the world very differently than I do, and that I now have to figure out my place in a world that includes both Davids and Goliaths. The Goliaths remain huge and powerful, but damn, there are a lot of Davids out there too.

Dale Peskin and I first used the term *We Media* as the title for a research report our organization commissioned that accurately forecast the rise of the significance of blogging and participatory, citizen-powered media. So it's understandable that the notion of grassroots, bottom-up publishing has stuck to the term. But the idea of We Media is really much bigger. It contrasts with the traditional notion of *the* media. *The* media is a thing unto itself. It serves, informs, mediates, manipulates, or annoys us. It is out there somewhere and we use it or consume it or maybe try to get inside of it—but we aren't part of it.

We Media is different. It's here, it's everywhere, and it's everyone—all of us. In the world of We Media we are all consumers, creators, and distributors of information. And yes, big media is part of We Media, along with little media, bloggers, governments, and terrorists.

So what happens when We Media becomes the global status quo, the cultural norm, rather than an aspiration or a novelty? We get more of what's already happening around the world: The power of traditional institutions that once controlled communication through monopolies on technology and distribution is giving way to the chaotic conversation of everyone—giving way to choice. And it means all institutions must confront and adjust to their new role in the world, and to new opportunities.

The technology of media—printing presses for newspapers; broadcast spectrum and equipment for television and radio; cable studios and franchises; satellites—all these things are enormously expensive and, hence, ownership has been limited. The businesses built around these expensive, limited resources have been based on monopolistic markets and inclinations.

In place of the old culture of limitation, ours is a culture of choice.

It is a *mobile* culture. Media and the tools to create it are everywhere. And so are we. We move, we take our media with us. We make our media everywhere.

It is a *sharing* culture. We inform each other. We trust and value ideas and information from people we know. We pass along to our friends and family our favorite songs, movies, and information.

It is a *creative* culture. Technology has unleashed an unprecedented explosion of expression. We create, we imagine, we innovate—all the time.

And it is a *capture* culture. Individuals and companies capture ideas, images, videos, advertising data, personal data, and follow user movements online from site to site. So do governments, through monitoring devices installed for public safety, like cameras in the London underground, and traffic cameras to catch speeding drivers; and also through data mining and eavesdropping that violate people's expectations of privacy; and through global satellite imagery that is as easy to access as Google maps.

In the We Media culture, individuals and institutions that used to think of themselves as something other than media exert unprecedented control over their experiences with media—not only what they consume, or when, or where, but what they produce, share, remix, and redistribute with others. The idea of We Media may be complex and daunting, but it is a big deal—for everyone. The power of media institutions is giving way to a distributed, decentralized network that includes empowered individuals, empowered companies, and governments that must come to terms with a new way of communicating. Institutions that once had to go through media to deliver information are now themselves media.

This has implications for how businesses function and, really, how the world functions and becomes better, or worse, over time. Mobile, ubiquitous, pervasive media and communications technologies are spreading around the world, and these technologies will undoubtedly play a central role not only in how business functions but in any progress made in addressing problems of extreme poverty, health care, and economic disparities that contribute to global conflict and human suffering.

So yes, We Media is complex. It is a big deal for everyone. And this book provides a road map for how organizations can navigate it.

Andrew Nachison
President & CEO, iFOCOS
Managing Partner, The 726 Group
Reston, Virginia
September, 2007

Andrew helped create an annual conference called WeMedia, part festival and part global celebration for people from many different industries and professions who believe the world of We Media is rich with opportunities, not only for business, but for society. Brian Reich has been an important part of the conference from the beginning. Find out at more at www.ifocos.org.

Acknowledgments

The process of writing this book, from the time the idea was first presented to the product that you have in your hands today, took more than a year to complete. A lot has happened in that time. And we couldn't have survived any of it without a lot of help.

We would guess that many of the people listed here will be surprised to find themselves on this list—they probably didn't even realize they were adding critical insights into the organization of the book, or helping us overcome significant obstacles. But they were. They offered suggestions, took time to meet for coffee, pulled us aside at a conference, sat next to us on a plane, shared an example from their life, or introduced us to a friend. Their ideas and effort have made this book, and our thinking, much stronger.

There are also many others not listed here, not singled out, who played a critical role. And there will be many others who deserve our thanks in the months and years after this book is first published. We fully intend to continue this conversation and all those who participate will play a key role in how our thinking, and how organizations choose to apply it, evolves and expands going forward.

To all those who are reading this book, we are honored and feel privileged that you would take time out of your busy day to read our thoughts. We hope that you will continue to engage in this conversation with us going forward.

Both of us are deeply grateful to Debra Englander and the entire team from Wiley. What on earth made you think that we could write a book? No matter, your confidence from the beginning provided great motivation and your expertise has served only to make this whole project stronger. And we need to thank Helene Solomon (no relation to Dan), leader of the public relations firm SolomonMcCown, who introduced us to Debra in the first place.

We are forever indebted to the people who agreed to be interviewed for the book, including:

Jon Abbott, executive vice president and chief operating officer at WGBH, Boston

Chris Anderson, editor of *Wired* magazine and author of *The Long Tail*

Henry Becton, president of WGBH Educational Foundation

Jim Berk, CEO of Participant Productions

Charles Best, chief executive officer and founder, DonorsChoose

Corey Brown, vice president and managing director for Squidoo.

Michael Brown, CEO and co-founder of City Year

Stephen Cassidy, chief of internet, television, radio and image for UNICEF

Pat Coyle, director of database marketing and e-commerce for the Indianapolis Colts

Michael Danenberg, COO/CFO at *GOOD Magazine*

Jack Dorsey, founder of Twitter

David Dudas, CEO of Eyespot

David Gale, executive vice president, New Media, MTV Networks

Tom Gerace, CEO of Gather

Jason Goldberg, CEO of Jobster

Ben Goldhirsch, founder and publisher of *GOOD Magazine* and Reason Pictures

Phil Greenough, founder and president of Greenough Communications

Jeffrey Hollender, CEO of Seventh Generation

Jed Hoyer, assistant general manager, Boston Red Sox

Jackie Huba, author of *Citizen Marketers*

Shel Israel, co-author of *Naked Conversations*

Sumaya Kazi, co-founder of The CulturalConnect

Frank Kern, vice president of global communications for Starbucks

Alan Khazei, co-founder and former CEO of City Year

JoRoan Lazaro, former creative director for AOL

Larry Lessig, professor at Stanford University of Law

Mark Lukasiewicz, vice president of Digital Media for NBC

Dinn Mann, senior vice president and editor in chief of MLB .com

Peter Morville, president of Semantic Studios and author of
Ambient Findability

Lisa Poulson, managing director of Burson Marsteller in San
Francisco

Jay Rosen, professor of journalism at NYU

Steve Rubel, senior vice president at Edelman Communications

Edward Schmults, CEO of FAO Schwartz

Joel Schwartzberg, senior producer of New Media for NOW
on PBS

Ricky Strauss, president of Participant Productions

Jeff Taylor, founder of EONS.com

Sheryl Hilliard Tucker, executive editor of Time Inc

Rob Waldron, former CEO of Jumpstart

Ty West, senior producer for NOW on PBS

We absolutely must thank the people who helped to identify,
recommend, schedule, or coordinate those interviews—people like
Kris Engskov, Audrey Lincoff, and Valerie O'Neil from Starbucks;
Andrea Eaton and Caitlin Brooking from City Year; Allard Baird
from the Boston Red Sox and Bill Chuck who introduced us to him;
Buffy Shutt and Diana Mendez from Participant Productions; Chris
Nolan; Elaine Adolfo; Samantha Bee from Waterworks; Chrystie
Heimert and Courtney Loveman from Seventh Generation; David
Smith; Josh Cherwin; Colleen Dionne from Gather; Elinor Alexan-
der from Jobster; Jen Ringel from MTV; Michael Feldman; Chad
Capellman; Elizabeth Derczo, Caroline Traylor, and Megan Adams
from the South-by-Southwest Interactive Festival; and Jamie Parker,
Jeanne Hopkins, Komal Trivendi, and Suzy Sotmayor at WGBH.
Your comments do not appear in this book but there would simply
be no book at all if not for your efforts.

There have been hundreds of other conversations ranging from
the specific to the sublime that helped to shape key parts of this
project. Some were short, some long, some were by phone and oth-
ers over e-mail. All were important. A few of the people who were the
sources of those thoughts must be singled out for particular thanks:
Mark Cuban; Seth Godin; Morgan Spurlock; Jenny Dervin from Jet-
Blue; Scott Bauman from Greenough Communications; Joel Kotkin;
John Battelle; Mike Krempasky from Edelman; Chadwick Matlin;
Rob Cross from the University of Virginia; Henry Copeland; Brad
Berens, Masha Geller, and Jodi Harris from iMedia; Kate Kaye from

ClickZ; Graydon Carter; Andrew Nachison and Dale Peskin from iFOCOS; Jeff Nussbaum; David Mark from the *Politico*; Dorian Benkoil from MediaBistro; Michael Waldman; Ken Berard from the *Atlantic Monthly*; Lynne Johnson from *Fast Company*; and Max Schorr from *GOOD Magazine*.

You would have to live inside our heads to truly understand the impact that the media has on our thinking, and had on the writing of this book. The media is what was at the heart of all this, after all. There are hundreds of authors, reporters, editors, and thinkers whose work we consume on a regular basis. Their coverage of the happenings of the world are shared mostly with a nameless, faceless audience. We are part of that audience. We subscribe to your newspapers and magazines, buy your books, attend your conferences, download your interviews, Tivo your shows, put your blogs in our aggregators, and your podcasts and videos on our iPods. We read, watch, listen to it all. It has a tremendous impact on how we think and our understanding of the world we live in. Thank you to the people who produce media, big-M and little-m alike.

To Dan and Brian's colleagues at Mindshare Interactive and Brian's colleagues at Cone: Thank you for your inspiration, encouragement, patience, and for paving the way for many of these ideas to be born.

To Dan's family: You have long shown me the importance of being engaged in the world and embracing change. This book is another step in the tradition that you have created.

To Brian's family: I apologize for missing so many birthday parties, holidays, and other gatherings during the year-long process of writing this book. Thank you for your support.

Dan would like to dedicate his work on this book to his wife Laura, daughter Abby, and son Jacob. Thank you for being my inspirations. And to Brian: From the moment we started arguing about the title, I knew we would be longtime collaborators. Thank you for pushing to start and finish this book and for continuing the conversation.

Lastly, Brian would like to dedicate his work on this book to his wife Karen. You were exceptionally supportive during every step of this process, as you are in every other aspect of our lives. Your insights and questions served as inspiration to me and made my thinking stronger. You are, and will always be, my best friend and toughest editor. But most importantly, you are, and will always be, the most special person in my life. Thank you, Karen. I love you.

Introduction

Welcome to *Media Rules!*

This book is about media and communications. It is about helping organizations—companies, nonprofits, news providers, educational institutions, communities, individuals—to understand how a rapidly changing society impacts their operations and communications. This book is designed to provide leaders with a framework for taking action around how they manage and market themselves differently because of the impact technology has on everything we do. It is designed to be a guide to the ever-growing, always evolving audience. This book is the beginning of a conversation about the future.

It is obvious that a significant amount of our daily lives, perhaps someday the majority, will be driven by some form of interaction with technology. We talk to each other on mobile phones. We shop online. We listen to news on our iPods. We tell stories and watch events unfold on our game consoles. Organizations of all kinds are responsible for creating the information, developing the experiences, and producing the stuff which we rely so heavily. But as the world changes, rapidly and continuously, many organizations are having trouble keeping up, staying focused, and executing well.

We are here to help.

The motivations for writing this book are many. As customers, we are frustrated by products we buy and services we engage. There are endless options, but only a handful of good ones and they are often difficult to find. As the leaders of organizations, we are frustrated by the demands and expectations placed on us by the audience, with little recognition for the myriad of challenges we face each day. As marketers, a sense of chaos and confusion reigns as we try to help connect organizations and their audiences in a meaningful way. Nobody is happy. And so many opportunities are being missed.

When we started writing this book, we thought that there were fundamental insights to be had by looking at media companies and translating their best practices to all other businesses. Dan is fond of saying "Every company is a media company." But our research has proved otherwise. No one sector can be held up as the leading innovator. Pockets of excellent adaptation are emerging across industries.

How did we get here? Business owners and operators, news producers, nonprofit directors, and entrepreneurs can barely keep track of the dizzying array of communication choices available to them. The audience is no better off. No group can afford to ignore them, either. These new innovations help shape our perceptions and decision making every day. They connect us. They inform us. They support us. And they sustain us.

The goal of our book is to help provide context and a framework for people to do something with all this information and all these different things. We did not set out to highlight people's failures or criticize anyone's attempts to understand this world—and we don't think we have. There are more and more people who are investing in technology and communications programs simply because other people are doing it, with no full understanding of why or how. This book is intended to help answer the why and how. If you are producing information, experiences, or stuff, this book will be your road map to how to do it better and with a more meaningful, measurable, and powerful impact.

What Are We Talking About?

Media and communications are changing as a result of technological advancement and societal change. The lines between information, experiences, and stuff are blurring. Things that were once small and isolated can now become big and connected with little effort. How people get and share information is the product of networks and conversations—no longer dictated by a few voices or following a linear path as it once did. Everything is moving faster and farther than ever.

In the book we talk about the implications of your decisions, actions, the products you sell, the services you provide, and everything else you do as an organization, through the filter of three broad frameworks:

1. *Everything is fragmented and blurred.* It is necessary and expected that our society will evolve and the impact of those changes

will be felt by all organizations. But never has our society changed so quickly and never have organizations felt the impact so dramatically. We are all challenged to adapt in ways and at levels not previously imagined. And with little sense that the chaos will settle down any time soon, new frameworks for operating—and succeeding—must be developed and managed along the way.

2. *Small can be big.* As Chris Anderson noted in his book *The Long Tail* (New York: Hyperion, 2006), culture and economy are increasingly shifting away from a focus on a relatively small number of *hits* (mainstream products and markets) at the head of the demand curve and toward a huge number of niches in the tail. As a result, what you sell is different. *How* you sell is different. The services you offer have changed. The expectations of those who shop and share and create are shifting as well. New markets have been created, for products and ideas alike, and organizations must determine whether to participate and, if so, how.

3. *We are all connected.* Technology has fundamentally changed our culture. The online world is about connection, community, and conversation. And as the online world goes, so goes much of what the rest of the world thinks and acts on. What we know about each other is changing, or in some cases just being learned. How we think and the decisions we make are increasingly driven by many voices, not few. Total control by a few has been replaced by complete understanding and participation by many.

Each of these frameworks provides insights into the different dimensions of organizations, whether business or nonprofit management, creativity or engagement. We look to apply lessons and rules in order to help organizations leverage the frameworks to succeed. The understanding provided by the frameworks alone isn't useful. Together with lessons and rules, it is actionable.

If you don't think the world is more networked and that small things can gain great attention, stop reading. This book is founded on just these two principles and is designed to help organizations understand how to adapt to them. These two principles demonstrate that the information, experiences, and stuff that people consume are the most important and are what you, as an organization, must focus on providing in order to succeed.

Why Should You Read This Book?

Media Rules! provides the tools and insights a leader needs to understand how to survive in the new communications universe. You should read this book if you are interested in any of the following:

- *Learning how to compete.* There is more competition for the attention of your audience than ever before. Many of your new competitors already exist and are gaining new prominence; others are being revealed every day. You must be ready to move your organization ahead, understand how to compete, and respond to this challenge with a strategy that ensures success. We are here to help.
- *Understanding how to position yourself.* Customer expectations are shaped by what they read, see, hear, and experience. This has always been true, but dramatic new technologies invite information about you to travel faster and farther than ever before. How people see your organization can be shaped or reshaped in an instant—with or without your input. You must be the steward of your organization and demonstrate trust and interest to your audience. If you don't, there is someone waiting to take your audience and provide what you can't.
- *Leading a successful transition.* Your organization must change over time to meet the growing challenges of our new society. Are you ready? Information, experiences, and stuff are measured by consumption and sharing, not production. That requires a whole different operational understanding. Non-consumer stakeholders are more involved than ever before—you need to stop talking long enough to listen and engage. You will need to change how you hire, manage, organize your information flow, and spend your resources. We outline the necessary skills needed to leverage these new tools to better navigate your transition over the coming period of time.
- *Tapping into new markets.* The change in society has created new markets and supply chains for your information, experiences, and stuff to flow through. Which ones are right for you and how do you tap them? What changes does your organization need to make to succeed? The book will introduce you to some of the new realities of marketing using new media technologies and strategies.

All organizations can and should operate and communicate like media companies. Organizations that adopt a media strategy survive. Why? Audiences do not rely on a single source for content, experience, or stuff—and focusing on the media allows them to interact and find their own personal connection to something. Therefore, the same rules that apply to media organizations are true regardless of the makeup of any organizations, regardless of format, focus, or medium. Organizations must understand their audiences and change to adapt to those audiences' needs and wants.

What Will You Learn by Reading This Book?

This book does not include step-by-step instructions for how to succeed in the world today. We haven't listed eight things you absolutely must do. We don't have a blueprint for how to send more effective e-mails, participate in social networks, or build the next killer application. Why not? Because the world is changing so quickly and so dramatically that anything we suggested would quickly become obsolete.

There are plenty of books that tell you how to run a successful enterprise, what changes to make or tactics to employ to bring about the results you desire and expect. We have shelves full of them, like everyone else. What we have learned by reading them all, however, is that no one source provides the answers that address the challenges you face and will continue to face as long as our world continues to change and evolve as rapidly as it currently does.

So yes, we deliberately stopped short of making specific recommendations for how you should market or manage your organization. We don't know your specific business. We don't know what your specific audience looks like. We don't know what specific things you are trying to accomplish. But we want to, and if we did, we could help you address these issues and begin to act. Out of context, specific recommendations would fall flat. Given an opportunity to gain proper knowledge about how you operate, we can help you.

As you read through the book, consider the questions that we would ask of any client to get things started:

1. *What do you do?* Are you a business, a nonprofit, an entrepreneur? Do you write or film, collect or distribute, buy or borrow, break down or build up?

2. *Where do you do it?* Are you online or off-line? Local or global?
3. *For whom you do it?* Who is your audience? Who works with and for you? Who cares if you do what you do? What do they want and expect from you?
4. *Why do you do it?* Are you trying to make money? Do you want to make the world a better place?
5. *What do you aspire to be?* What do you want to be when you grow up? How do you measure success?

If we knew the answers to these questions about you and your organization, we could begin to apply this concept and help you rise above the chaos. Of course, as you read through the book, you should also be thinking about your organization and how to answer these questions—because a lot of what we describe can be put in place without any outside help at all.

We wrote this book to help you create meaningful and measurable change in your organization. We wrote it to help forge the link between the brilliance that these thinkers have delivered and the excellence that you must create on your own.

This book is designed to help you think through the challenges you face and begin to take the necessary actions to be successful. These are just some of the questions we need to know the answers to in order to appropriately apply the rules to your organization. If you want to talk more, send an e-mail to brian@themediarules.com or dan@themediarules.com. Or, visit our Web site (www.mediarules .com) and join the conversation that this book will launch.

How Did We Write This Book?

This book, as well as our thinking, was inspired by some of the most innovative thinkers and writers from science, design, marketing, management, economics, sports, entertainment, politics, government, and of course business. We read dozens of books, subscribed to hundreds of blogs, and debated the merits of each argument for hours on end. We sought to understand how folks like Marshall McLuhan, David Weinberger, Seth Godin, Jim Collins, Mark Cuban, David Shenk, Daniel Pink, Albert-Laszlo Barabasi, Henry Jenkins, Don Tapscott, Joel Kotkin, and the Freakonomics guys, Steven Levitt and Stephen Dubner, would address these issues. They are all powerful critics, thinkers, and theorists on the challenges that organizations face, cooperation, and execution today. They are not actively trying to shape the world. They are not burdened with having to run an organization, create a profit, cater to an audience, or report to a board.

But you are. You are a doer—every day, all the time, working toward applying the lessons you learn to ensure your organization succeeds and thrives. So in writing this book, we worked to make the theoretical immediately applicable. We tried to give you a set of tools that you could use to create real, meaningful, and measurable change within your organization.

In other words, we didn't set out to write just another business book. A big key to this book was the more than 35 interviews we conducted over the course of six months, with organizational leaders from different sectors. We talked with Chris Anderson, the author of *The Long Tail*, and Shel Israel, who wrote *Naked Conversations* with Robert Scoble. We discussed the similarities and differences between business and nonprofit management with the former CEO of Jumpstart for Young Children, Rob Waldron, who is now vice president of operations at Berkshire Partners. We met with Michael Brown and Alan Khazei from City Year and with Charles Best from Donors Choose; both organizations and their leaders are credited with helping address national and global social challenges. Dinn Mann from Major League Baseball and Mark Lukasiewicz of NBC News help guide some of the most sophisticated media companies in the world. Jeff Taylor redefined the job search market with Monster.com a decade ago and Jason Goldberg is reinventing it again today with his company, Jobster. There are dozens of others whose comments and perspectives are scattered throughout the book. Their expertise and experience were influential in how our theories and thinking came together.

And most importantly, we experimented. Every theory, every thought, every idea that we have outlined in this book mirrors what we have done, and will continue to do for our clients and the organizations we lead every day. When we fail, they fail. When we succeed, they succeed. They give us the opportunity to learn and try things that haven't been done before. It is real to us, and hopefully will be real to you as well.

Let's be honest, though. Books are a terrible medium for communicating how to make real organizational change in an environment so dramatically influenced by the outside world. The world is moving so quickly that by the time a book goes to print, at least some of what is contained is not longer relevant. That is true of this book as much as any other. There is no longer one story to tell or a linear discussion to be had. So the basic format of a book is an insufficient medium for communicating what needs to be communicated. But people buy books, and books start conversations. So we wrote a book and hope it begins a conversation.

We created this book as a starting point for a conversation we hope to have with you. It is one of several tools we have provided to you, the reader, to understand how to make choices and changes within your organization. We continue the conversation online at www.themediarules.com

Thank you for reading. We look forward to hearing from you.

BRIAN REICH
brian@themediarules.com

DAN SOLOMON
dan@themediarules.com

CHAPTER 1

The Media That Matters

The basic premise of this book is that media rules!

What exactly does that mean? Well, for starters, we believe that *media* is the information, the experiences, and all the stuff that we consume and share every day. In this sense, media is not one format more than any other. It's not the technology that delivers these things. It is the content. Media is virtually anything that we create, consume, and share in our daily lives. It might be something that you wear; it might be something that you hear; it might be something you create on a computer, or just scribble on the back of a napkin; it might be something that your audience creates on their cell phone or with a can of spray paint on the wall of a building. All these things and more are media. It's content. It's the stuff people experience. It's not a technology. It's the substance, not how it is delivered or received. And when you look at the way media is now being pushed into and embraced by the mainstream and influencing how people spend their time, money and energy, it is evidence that media rules!

Organizations, in how they operate and communicate, are confused and in some cases struggling in the wake of massive technological advancements and societal change. But there is a path to success. If organizations adopt and communicate a mediacentric strategy, they will not only survive but thrive. If they look for new ways of operating, new models to better serve their audience and live up to the full potential that technology provides in terms of delivering information, experiences, and stuff, they will distinguish themselves and the audience will follow.

Why? Audiences do not rely on a single source for information, experience, or stuff; they don't get their news from one place, buy their clothes from only one store, watch the same television show, or participate in the same activity, day after day. Technology allows each member of the audience the opportunity to find their own personal connection to something. The days of mass audience communications are over. You have to do more than just create a niche or come up with creative ways to repackage all the same things you offered in the past. All organizations, regardless of their makeup, format, focus, or function, have many of the same opportunities and face many of the same challenges now. In fact, they are your competitors, whether it's for funding or the next big idea. And, they stand between you and your communication goal, adding another voice to the mix when you know that the most limited resource your audience has is attention. It's a new ball game, a new playing field.

Organizations typically focus on the delivery mechanism and on the product they are going to produce, instead of their goals – the reason they went into operation in the first place. They are focused on that press release, or that game, or that clothing line, or that text message when they should be focused on the message they are trying to communicate, their look, or the outcome they want after someone reads their message. *Media* refers to all of the things that represent the individual's relationship with whatever that product or deliverable is—the whole of what you need to understand—and not just what you can hold in your hand or count against your bottom line.

As long as organizations focus either on the distribution mechanism or on the product, they're missing a core element, which is media. And when organizations focus on the information, the experiences, and the stuff, they succeed. If you really nail the information, the experiences, and the stuff, then everything else is going to fall into place. You will have an audience—maybe not the entire world, but a loyal, dedicated audience that is going to find what you do compelling and important. You will be able to monetize what you create. You will be able to tap into the community to help carry forward your message on its own through buzz and word of mouth. You will meet your communications and business objectives, plain and simple.

Think about how you are preparing your media—your organization's messaging, your next event, your Web site or advertising. Ask yourself, are we doing what it really takes to provide the best information, experiences, and stuff? Or are we focused on the distribution? Are we focused on the cost? Are we trying to tell our audience how to act, or integrating what we do into their lives in a meaningful way? Put your focus on creating and distributing the best possible media for your organization and your audience—the information, the experiences, and the stuff that will resonate and add value, meet (if not exceed) audience expectations, and have an impact on the environment in which that media lives and is received. When you do that, the other measures of success, things like audience loyalty, awareness and buzz, revenue and profit, will fall into place.

What does all of this mean for how organizations currently manage and market themselves? What does it mean to the audience we are all trying to reach? It means you have to do things differently.

Technology Facilitates the Transfer of Experience

When you listen to people talk about trends for the future of business, or education, or just the future in general, you hear a lot about technology. Scientists and researchers are always thinking about what the next big (or small) technology will be, what it will do, and how it will change the world. Companies race to be the one to market the next killer application or super device. They talk about microprocessors and fuel cells. They develop virtual worlds and complex simulations of real-life situations. They fuss over how to make palm-size communication devices so small that they aren't even the size of your palm anymore. They invent $100 laptops with indestructible cases and make batteries that run on solar power so they can be used in a rainforest if needed. It seems like technology is often the main focus of new product development for many businesses—technology and non-technology alike.

Well, it shouldn't be. Technology is just methods for delivering media—a tool that can be used to create or share information, develop and manage experiences, or interact with stuff. Technology is a tool to help people communicate and to learn. Technology helps to pass data from one source to the next. Technology provides context and connection to people on opposite sites of the globe, in different languages. Technology is valuable, necessary, and provides tremendous benefits. But how people use technology is more important than what the technology itself provides. You couldn't communicate like we do today without technology. But technology wouldn't have much of a purpose if we didn't want, and need, to have something to share, something to say.

And because all of the technologies are converging, blurring and synergizing from the users perspective, organizations need to focus on the user's entire experience rather than optimizing the performance of a particular channel. Messages delivered over a TV set will soon take the form of games that were formerly the province of desktop computers; billboards will "work" with mobile phones; books will be re-written in real-time so one reader's experience will contribute to the next reader's experience. There are no discreet channels in the eyes of the user, so there can't be discreet channels from the communication perspective either.

Everybody uses technology in a slightly different way, and understanding how people use technology must dictate how we, as organizations and individuals, operate and manage. How people create, consume, and share information should dictate how you prepare and distribute content, both in terms of format—written, audio, video, three-dimensional, and beyond—and what that content should be. If you think about how people use technology, you will realize very quickly that there is no single technology that they use and no single way they use all the technologies they have available to them.

Consider how a typical millennial (a mid-twenty-something person) living in a city stays informed during the day. Throughout the day, she tunes in to commercial and public radio, watches television, browses through magazines or newspapers, checks her e-mail, logs on to a social network, Twitters or Pownces (or both!) and makes calls or sends text messages through her mobile phone. Beyond that she probably shops, eats, works or goes to school, and hangs out with friends. At every turn she is surrounded by media—she is wearing and carrying stuff, information is flowing in and out, sounds and signals are creating her experiences.

Now consider how a typical parent (a mid-forties-something person for the purpose of this example) living in a suburb stays informed during the day. Throughout the day, she tunes in to commercial and public radio, watches television, browses through magazines or newspapers, checks her e-mail, logs on to a social network and makes calls or sends text messages through her mobile phone. Beyond that she probably shops, eats, works, takes her kids to school, and hangs out with her spouse, and maybe friends. At every turn she is surrounded by media—she is wearing and carrying stuff, information is flowing in and out, scents and sounds are creating her experiences. But, her media experience is very different than that of the millennial, or even that of another mid-forty-something parent.

Their differences in their activities seem minimal, but the impact in terms of communication is very significant.

Your media environment each day is different from the ones just described as well. There are some overlaps, but each person is unique and so is his/her interaction with media and technology. It varies by age, gender, and income. Geography impacts what technologies are available and what media is relevant and interesting to someone. And the designation of someone's behavior being "typical" or "average" can always be debated. What is certain is that you can't say that a particular piece of technology or content at a particular time is the way you can reach your target audience. There is no single place that people now look, online or off-line, for content. There is no single source that people view as credible or all-informed.

To this end, Mark Lukasiewicz, the vice president of Digital Media at NBC News explained one of the challenges that his news division faces when reaching out to one of their key target audiences:

> We had a group of researchers in and one of our executives asked, "Where do young women go to get their news?" And the answer was: They don't really go anywhere. They expect that if the news is important to them, it'll find them.
>
> That is a crucial insight to me, because what it's saying is In my parent's generation, informing yourself was an act of volition. You *went*. You went to buy a newspaper, you went to a television and turned it on, you turned on a radio at an appointed time. That was a choice you had to make.
>
> Increasingly, people expect that through the variety of connections they have in their life, whether it's their social networking apparatus, their e-mail, their cell phone, things that are important to them in the world will find them. They don't need to make an appointment to go find information. Some people still do it, but it's not necessary anymore in the way that it might have been to a large population 20 years ago.
>
> So that changes the exercise for us, in that I think we do have to recognize that our storytelling is much more 24/7 than

it used to be, that our storytelling and our delivery of news does not always exist in a linear context within a program that has a beginning and a middle and an end. It comes in pieces, and so we have to make sure our journalism is self-contained for those kinds of platforms, and that we need to push it out—all the platforms on which people are accessing information.

Lukasiewicz's job is to create news, to inform and educate about the current happenings of the world and what they mean to his audience. His team has more ways to collect and create the news because of technology now available to them, but that is balanced by a greater challenge in getting that audience to engage and participate as well. The good news is, technology is redefining the ways in which, really, anything is possible. The bad news is, technology is redefining the way in which, really, anything is possible.

What has happened to the information, experiences, and stuff that we already have? They have lost their way. They have begun to change. Right now it is pretty chaotic; lots of new things are being tried and lots of lessons are being learned. Keep reading and you'll see how.

Advertising is Broken ... But on the Mend

Organizations have used advertising for as long as we can remember to drive interest in whatever they do—a new product, a special service, an issue they find important, or law that they want passed. In the past, and still today for the most part, much of that advertising is done through print and television. Television, and television programming for that matter, was created to provide a mechanism for distributing sponsor ads. Millions upon millions of dollars are spent on 30-second ads, 30-minute infomercials, circulars, inserts, and displays. More recently, the focus has shifted toward online advertising, and some of those millions of dollars have been put toward banner ads and search terms. No matter the medium, however, the vast majority of that money is wasted.

Why? One reason is that most people don't spend their time looking for advertisements. They look for shows to laugh or cry at, magazines and newspapers to inform them, search results that direct them to a piece of information or an answer to a question. Another reason is that a lot of the advertising we see today simply isn't that good. People in the advertising industry would probably dispute that characterization, but when audiences are skipping more than half of commercials, that speaks volumes. Even if people were looking for an ad, what they find wouldn't be all that worth their effort.

Organizations have a job to do, and part of that job is to get the attention of the people they need to buy their product, endorse their idea, commit to their event, or take action in some way. Advertising has been seen throughout its history as an easy way to try to do that. You have a captive audience, waiting desperately to see what will come next in their favorite show or progressing page by page through a publication in search of the continuation of their article, why not force a pitch on them. But the comfort of knowing you have the space to advertise often seems to invite a mediocre response from the advertiser. The creativity, the story, the images of many ads simply fail to connect with the audience it is intended to reach. The client and agency feel good, because they can count the number of impressions they delivered and the number of references to their brand they put out there. But if the ad fails to be compelling, simply doesn't work—and increasingly technology allows people to create a personalized media environment for themselves, with the trend seeming to suggest that commercial advertisements are not going to be a big part of that media environment—then we have to try something different.

There is plenty of blame to go around. But instead of picking on anyone in particular, let's look ahead and consider an alternative. Put the people who know the most about how to communicate about an organization, and the people who know best what types of information, experiences, and stuff a target audience wants, together to solve this information problem. That is almost certainly you and your colleagues from whatever organization you represent. It probably includes the audience itself. And we suggest you also involve the people who produce the venues and tools that people use to create, consume, and share information—the networks, the portals, the blogs, the cell phones, the operating systems, the producers.

As people who work for agencies, and often contribute to advertising, it is blasphemy to suggest that the role the agency has played as middle-person may no longer be of great value. But as consumers of media, as customers ourselves, that seems like the best route to explore.

Organizations should be putting their heads together with their customers and partners to figure out how to provide a meaningful experience that benefits all involved. Make sure you understand why and how your audience uses technology and then start trying to align your communications effort. If the audience is telling us that 30-second commercials are not working, stop producing them and find another way. If so much printer advertising is required to turn a profit that the actual content of a newspaper or magazine is diminished to the point nobody wants to read it any longer, we are headed in the wrong direction. And if organizations don't think they can tell their story effectively through a standard banner advertisement online, then figure out what kind of format you need and make it compelling. Maybe you see the suggestion as radical and scary. Maybe you see this change of thinking as relatively simple. It is probably a little of both.

What are some of the things being tried? Brands are integrating their presence onto billboards, bus ads and sponsored buildings—in video games and virtual worlds instead of the real world (or at very least in addition to the real world). Advertisers are creating immersive experiences on the Web, in addition to showing ads during a television show. And they are putting products into real situations (e.g. when you get thirsty like an athlete, you think to drink Gatorade or when you see Friends sit down for a cold soda it's a Diet Coke instead of some fictional brand), but not forcing the issue on consumers. We know that people who are watching the big game or playing the video games are likely to see the ads, but the ads aren't disrupting the experience in any major way. This invites their audience to experience more than just what they can cram into 30 seconds that is squeezed between two segments of a broadcast. And just wait, because now mobile devices are extending the participation and interaction with ads after their production and distribution regardless of form.

It is not uncommon for the audience to create better ads. Do you remember the video that a fan created after Tiger Woods holed out a chip at the Masters in 2005? In real time, the ball rolled toward the hole and paused on the lip, long enough to reveal the Nike swoosh in full view of the television audience. Within hours, it was on the Web as a free ad for Nike, Just Do It tagline and inspirational music setting the right one. That was created by a guy in his living room with a basic editing setup on his computer and seen by far more people than watched the original telecast. Meanwhile, CurrentTV the television network that Al Gore founded, has made consumer generated advertising (and content) a staple of its programming—not by giving up creative control, but by supporting people who are not parts of agencies or organizations already but who have a perspective and know how to convey it. Companies like Sony, L'Oreal and Toyota were the first to experiment with this and find success—both in audience engagement and across the advertising industry.

Those are just a few examples, a handful of the new models being explored by marketers. The message is clear: the world is changing so try something different.

There Are All Types of Blogs

There is a perception in our society today that blogs represent one thing—one format, one type of voice. The stereotype, of course, is that all bloggers sit around in their pajamas and try to cut down the establishment. Nothing could be further from the truth. Every blog is unique. At last check, Technorati was tracking between 70 and 75 million blogs worldwide. More than 120,000 new blogs are created every day. There are individual blogs, community blogs, blogs that just feature pictures, and blogs that are only updated by mobile phone. Don't forget CEO blogs, some more engaging and authentic than others, blogs that offer an inside view of a non-profit organization or reveal and support plans for advocacy. The number one language in the blogosphere is Japanese—39 percent of blogs are written in Japanese at last check. And the range of topics, depth and expertise now available is staggering.

Brian worked while at Mindshare on a client, the Children's Health Environmental Coalition, (CHEC) that launched a blog while its Web site was being redesigned. The blog, called "90 Tips for 90 Days," took all the content the organization had accumulated on its Web site over the previous few years and redistributed it in 90 individual parcels, one delivered daily. At the end of the three months, the site stopped updating and the new Web site was ready to launch. That doesn't sound like every other blog you read about in the news or subscribe to in your aggregator, does it? And that's exactly the point. Even in that brief time, CHEC was able to grow its audience, attract attention from celebrities and the media, and provide a wealth of valuable information to its readers. Their success wasn't because they launched a blog, it was because of how they used it—in their case to repurpose interesting content that their audience wanted, but didn't have access to previously in a format that aligned with their needs and interests.

So forget what you have heard about blogs or think about blogs. Blogging is easy. Blogging software looks and works like the word processing software that we all use every day. It requires no knowledge of hypertext markup language (HTML) code. Once you have typed your blog post or entry, it takes a mere one or two more clicks of your mouse to publish your words onto the Web for all the world to see. Blogging has taken online communication out of the hands of the IT experts of the world and placed it in the hands of anyone with an Internet connection. You should not launch a blog, however, simply to make your content more available or to prove that you can. Like any other communication opportunity, you should look at blogging as an opportunity to add something interesting, or relevant, or timely to the discussion with your audience. And if you can't, then there are plenty of other ways to add your voice that may be more appropriate.

Everything Is Social

Online social networks are huge. The audience for social networks numbers in the tens of millions and growing. People talk about MySpace and Facebook, the big players, but there are thousands of successful niche social networks that are relevant to particular communities. There are social networks for moms, businesspeople, crafters, and communities around all different languages and cultures, sports fans and pet enthusiasts, car nuts and do-it-yourselfers.

You might not think of it this way, but Amazon.com is one of the most influential social networks in the world. They figured out long before anyone else that customers were more likely to buy a book that everyone said was good over a book that everyone said was terrible. So Amazon institutionalized rating systems and comment areas to help convey those opinions to audiences.

The concept of those rating systems and community voices has a broad reach. SixDegrees.org is a social giving site, where people come and decide, based on the recommendations from the community, to what organization(s) they should donate. And that same concept has been applied to everything from stocks to shopping to medical choices to the delivery of individual grants to school teachers. All of this is driven by social interaction, networking, and the power of people communicating with each other—facilitated by technology and the Web. All of it is reputation driven.

Phones Are for More than Calling

If you have a cell phone, and most people do these days, you probably use it for calling. But there is so much more that this one piece of technology can do. Worldwide, and increasingly in the United States, text messaging is the dominant feature that people use on their mobile phone, carrying on 140-character conversations back and forth billions of times in a year. In the coming years, the number of people surfing for information through a mobile version of the World Wide Web is growing rapidly.

Mobile phones will be the technical inflection point for deeper experience convergence. The Swiss Army knife-like technical features will allow it to interact with every other technical platform. But it is the mobile phone's inherent convenience, its portability, that makes it so full of potential for the future applications and uses.

People now use their mobile phones for basic things—a check of the weather, a search for directions. Over time, you will see people getting more substantive information, asking questions, not to mention creating and sharing content. Remember the movie *Snakes on a Plane*? The film was promoted by allowing audiences to create personal voice mail messages to be delivered by the film's star, Samuel L. Jackson, in character. The producers of Lost offer a game for mobile phone users to try to answer the question the writers have not yet: how to get off the island. And in many major sports facilities you can now use your mobile phone to order food and have it delivered to your seat, or get statistics that are relevant to what your seat gives you a view of more than anything else.

People spend more time each day with their mobile phone on and active than all other media—more than their computer, television, or radio combined. Importantly, they carry a mobile phone with them at all times, so unlike surfing the Web on a computer or watching the television from the living room, they don't have to stay in one place. Mobile redefines the importance of location in how people consume, create and share information. And that fundamentally changes communication by, and for, organizations today and going forward.

It All Begins with Search

The first thing that the majority of people do when they go online is search. They log on to Google.com or something similar and type in some keywords based on whatever they are looking for.

But *search* isn't really the right way to describe that process. The standard definitions of search suggest that people are looking for something that is missing or lost. But more and more today, we try to find things that we know exist but haven't had the need for previously. Think directions, or the answer to a question. Today we explore the contents of the blogosphere or a certain site with the expectation that the answer is there, waiting to be found. You don't have to search—you can focus on locating exactly what you need. Later in this book we talk about the concept of *findability*, which combines both what information you make available as an organization and how that information is organized, so that it can be relevant to everything else that you are doing and that your audience is looking for.

Audiences are already getting better at modifying how they seek out information online. Traditional search is getting less and less helpful, less and less efficient. The amount of information that now pours into Google and all the other search engines is so vast that even the results that pop up on the first page may not be useful or related to the original query. The searcher has to be knowledgeable in how to best use the system to get what they want or need, an added hassle to someone who simply wants to find a quick piece of information to satisfy their curiosity. Search engines are evolving to be less algorithm-based and more human-generated, more reliant on the people who use them and the contributions they can make. That's why you see Google expanding into every domain of media, even offline. As the search engines change, the information that organizations create and make available will change as well, so that users can find what they need.

Audio and Video Are Awesome

Text is really interesting. We have gotten away with writing things for a very long time, and text will never truly disappear or die out completely. But audio and video are more compelling, more interesting, more absorbing, and more enjoyable to watch or listen to.

However, not all audio and video are created equal. Look at what happened in the wake of the shootings at Virginia Tech. A student pulled out his cell phone, recorded a video, and sent it to CNN. The video wasn't even very good, mostly a blurry image with the sound of the gunshots in the distance. But when CNN put the video online for people to view, 1.8 million people downloaded it in the first 12 hours it was available. To this point, Andrew Nachison and Dale Peskin, the co-founders of iFOCOS, a think tank that helps citizens and business understand and use expanding media and communications technologies both to innovate in business and to create better-informed global citizens, wrote:

> What we experienced about the horrific events on a black day in Blacksburg owes to a savvy, social generation connected emotionally and technologically to its media. Their eyewitness descriptions, photos, video and reporting from a remote, rural Virginia town—one of the world's first connected communities—made a story visceral to the world. The ability to instantly capture and disseminate information at a time when it was most needed, as well as to communicate with each other across time and geography, has not only helped unite a community but has become a real-time example of how personal media empowers and defines communication in today's connected society. Watching events unfold, the shift in the power of media was perceptible. Traditional broadcasters and publishers competently covered the tragic events in Blacksburg. But the story belongs to Virginia Tech students. They were at once reporters, witnesses and subjects of the deadliest shooting in U.S. history. It was like watching a new kind of reality show where the stars used their devices, their social networks, and their wits to survive and to cope.[1]

With hundreds of thousands of podcasts and videocasts loaded onto the Internet for free each day, organizations must differentiate themselves and find a way to resonate. There are different formats, depending on what you are trying to communicate. There are different functions, depending on what you want the audience to do when they see your video. There are different ways of telling that story in an audio or video presentation, which you can leverage.

People will spend more time listening to a podcast or watching a videocast, if it is compelling, than they are likely to spend reading something.

Everyone Has His Own Channel

For a long time, we've all had a minimal number of dominant media channels for distributing content and information, whether that was news, entertainment, sports, or something else. Now everybody can have his own channel. There are more than 70 million blogs. Hundreds of thousands of videos are created and uploaded every day. The barriers for entry have been lowered and people are flooding in to be a part of the media environment. As people start to get and create more channels, you will see a greater differentiation in the quality. And the way to raise the level of quality is actually to help people create content for their own channels—to mentor and guide them.

This is a role that organizations can play. Recently, a company called EyeSpot partnered with the National Basketball Association to allow fans to create their own videos featuring their favorite dunks or their favorite players, all on the Web, all in a matter of minutes. The key to their success is that they provide all the raw materials and all the editing tools to the audience. Right now, most of the people who are creating their channels are semiprofessionals, people with free time who have editing suites in their homes and have some experience. But we are all creators, and we want to create and projects like this are opening this more exclusive world to a much larger audience.

Games Are for More than Playing

Video games are incredibly innovative and far-reaching, yet we have only scratched the surface in terms of what they can do to support organizations, tell stories, and engage audiences. There are all sorts of games: first-person shooters, casual games, sports and adventure games. There are also serious games and simulations that help people to learn about how the world works or understand important issues. The Army uses games to train soldiers, corporations create simulations to help managers get experience, and games have even become part of the curriculum in some schools, to help kids learn about health and wellness, get exercise, or explore complex math and science topics. These games spawn incredible communities online and off-line, some for competition, others simply for social interaction. They represent one of the most successful and fastest-growing industries in the world. And there is little to suggest that the growth or level of innovation will slow any time soon.

Everything is Syndicated

You should be pushing your content out to every available venue possible—syndicating everything you can, information, experiences, and stuff, so that people can find it. Everybody needs content, and at any given time there is a lack of really good, compelling content, in any format. But you probably have content. And you don't have enough time, enough people, enough resources, enough energy in the day to tell all of the compelling stories that you have to tell. If you did, there would be a thousand different venues—maybe a million different venues out there would be interested in taking that content.

Create content that is designed to be syndicated, to be absorbed by other venues and promoted widely. Don't just deliver prepackaged stuff. Offer information to people that can be reproduced and redelivered, raw materials that can be molded to match almost any situation. Larry Lessig, a professor of law at Stanford Law School and founder of the School's Center for Internet and Society, explained:

> Technology has exploded, meaning a wider range of creative work can be made available because the marginal costs of making that work available fall so dramatically. So anybody can get basically anything they want, and if not now, within five years electronically or digitally, and stream it to their box, or download it to their computer, and watch it whenever they want.
>
> But, at the same time, digital media is also exploding the opportunity for people to get access to concepts which they have a right not only to consume, but also to remix, and to share their remix with others. So institutions like Wikipedia are not just a resource to be read but also a resource to be revised, and lots of mash-ups that are made available through services like Google Video or BlipTV are resources for people not just to consume but also to add in their own creativity.
>
> That's just a different kind of empowerment because it's inviting not just the consumption, but it's inviting the audience to talk

back, and, ultimately, I think that's going to be the more important transformation in the way that we think about culture.

It's what he calls the shift from a read-only culture to a more vibrant, read-write culture, thanks to technology. That shift has happened and is redefining who we are.

Meaning and Commerce Have Merged as Media

More organizations are beginning to market products and services with an eye toward supporting a cause. The emphasis on simply generating revenue for your organization—and we touch on this later in the book—is no longer enough, so you are seeing a shift. This, in particular, puts an emphasis on the *stuff* that audiences want and merging it with their consumption of information and thirst for experience.

One example: A group called T-post sends out a subscription to a news source that you wear as a shirt. Several times a year you receive an updated shirt with relevant headlines and stories on them—and by wearing it around you help spread the word about an issue and inform people.

Stuff is content too—it's not just information, it's not just video, it's not just audio; it's everything you wear, everything you buy and carry around. People buy things because it says something about them, about their personality. And in doing so, they communicate their beliefs and personality for others to see and be influenced by. People may not do it consciously (though many do), but they accomplish what some marketers spend millions of dollars and years of effort trying to do, simply by getting dressed in the morning.

Putting the Pieces Together

So what are we going to have to deal with?

Media is *globalized*. More and more people are becoming connected to each other through media and all the ways described above. Add to that the vast adoption of mobile phones worldwide, and we find that people who have not had access to information and to the global audience all of a sudden have it. This fundamentally changes the way content is produced and exists online. There are more languages, more customs, and more ideas. There are fewer borders and more voices.

Media is *localized*. All of the information, experiences, and stuff that we create, consume, and share is naturally filtered through someone's individual, personal and local perspective. No matter how much you care about what is happening on the other side of the globe, you are more likely to understand and care about what is happening on your street. That puts a premium on the ability for information to be specific to a local geography or culture, not generalized for an entire population. Technology makes it that much more possible to have an impact on the things that matter to you, and your audience, most – the things they encounter every day.

Media is *nonlinear*. The audience already expects stories to be told in a new, different kind of way. Gone will be the traditional television formats—a 30-minute sitcom with 22 minutes of programming and 8 minutes of ads in between segments. Gone is the concept of a beginning, middle, and end. Welcome a flood of information, to be sorted and organized, absorbed and manipulated however the audience sees fit.

Media is getting *better*. Most of the content on the Internet is low quality. Most of the television we watch on the 500 stations we have available to us leaves something to be desired. But as more and more people are able to create more and more video, the quality is slowly improving. As technology makes it possible for people to produce audio, video, games, and everything else, we will all learn, as a society and a community, how to do it better and more effectively.

Media is *bite-size (or snackable)*. Content has to be consumable or people don't know how to fit it into their day. Either you don't have the time, or you don't make the time. Either way, content has to be consumable in a moment, because there isn't the ability to spend time processing everything we have available to us. People want little tiny pops; they want stories told in a serial format over and over and over again, not all at once when they have to sit there and focus. Media is already being packaged in a way that people can consume, wherever and whenever they are ready, and more and more will follow that path going forward.

Media is becoming *easier to find*. It isn't searched for; it is simply there. You know what you are looking for and our information environment helps you get there. No mystery, no delay.

Media is *open-source*. No single entity is able to control, create, or know everything. We are all about co-creating, Wiki-fying our lives – opening our news, education, entertainment and even decision making to the will of the masses and the cult of the amateur. Organizations and individuals are consciously deciding to welcome the voices of their community and to reflect their contributions, pushing the quality of the media to a new level in the process.

And finally, media is *transactionalized*. Individual exchanges of value are transactions, but so is every conversation, every e-mail, every experience you have. And the organizations that are responsible for those transactions are increasingly responsible for delivering a high-value experience with every transaction. There are so many options for how you and your audience interact with media that everything you do is important and meaningful. If you don't deliver value, there is someone waiting in the wings who can, and your audience will find them.

Overwhelmed? Scared? Don't be—the reaction you should be having is one of excitement, even anticipation. The organizations that will be successful are the ones that are going to have recognize that media rules. They will, you will, create relevant, compelling, timely, continually updated, bite-size, high quality, information, experiences, and stuff and when people go looking for it, you will be ready. Many organizations are already doing it. You can, too.

The audience is moving in this direction, and organizations must meet them along the way. We wrote this book to help people understand what is happening, how to adapt, and where to meet up with the audience. Being successful will take investment and commitment. Some of what we highlight is not cheap, nor is it easy to do. It certainly can't be done overnight, no matter who you are. But you can start immediately.

Follow the rules we share here. Some of what we have discussed, and will discuss throughout the rest of the book, will seem easy while some things will be more difficult. Try and fail because you are going to learn from it. You won't succeed 100 percent of the time, nobody does, but your mistakes will rarely be fatal and we will all learn from your efforts, as you will from ours. Organizations must invest and commit to operating with media at the center, because your investment and commitment when matched with others will lift us all up. And if you do not—if you choose to ignore this advice and the reality of what is happening all around you in this media environment—you will quickly be surpassed by other organizations and it will be hard to catch up.

As media digitizes, fragments, and moves closer to the audience, the information, experiences, and stuff become more a part of the audience than a product that is delivered to the audience. The very nature of how we get and share information, experience things, and consume stuff has changed, so naturally the people who create and consume, use, and share that media need to change as well. It is as much about the audience as the organizations trying to reach that audience.

Make no mistake: What we advocate in this book is not always easy. It is not immediate or singular change. It will take time, but the results will be substantial.

CHAPTER

2

Translating Transition

We are sick and tired of meaningless marketing-speak.

We hear it all the time—buzzwords, catchphrases, whatever you want to call them. We all have our favorites: *ahead of the curve, low-hanging fruit, leverage,* and the like. When you start to talk about technology it gets even more inane: What is *bandwidth,* anyway? Do you have *meta-data?* Am I an *end user?*

We are just as guilty as anyone in the marketing space. We use these words in meetings with colleagues. We sprinkle them into presentations to clients. This book is filled with them. Ask our wives and our friends—these words and phrases have probably found their way into a dinner conversation or ten over the years. You would be surprised how quickly and easily people like us can slip into ridiculous, pretentious language that has no meaning.

Sadly, we are not alone. Every business or nonprofit leader we have ever met or worked with, every political candidate or athlete we read about, even the purveyors of news on TV, in print, and now online have their own unique way of speaking. We all use some different variation on the same language. And guess who gets left out? That's right, our audience—the very people we are supposed to be talking to.

Organizations need to change the way they create relationships, explain themselves, and attract attention in the face of dramatic shifts in the way our society operates. That is no small task. And it is made more difficult by the fact that organizations are having so much trouble communicating. We are worried for these organizations. It is as if marketing-speak has replaced normal English and nobody notices, or cares to correct the situation. We all just keep on doing what we do.

The goal has been, and always will be, to find a way to connect with your target audience in a way that is compelling, relevant, and timely. You make it more difficult for yourself, as an organization, when you put a language barrier between yourself and your audience.

The people you want to engage, sell products to, get feedback and inspiration from, and who you hope will end up talking about you—they don't speak the language that you and your organizational colleagues speak. The audience wants action. Words aren't action. Mark Lukasiewicz from NBC noted, "People have access to information ubiquitously now. It isn't simply from a device parked on a piece of furniture in their homes, wired to a wall. It comes at them in all sorts of ways and all sorts of places. It's in their car. It's through a satellite radio. It's on their cell phone or some other mobile device. There are a hundred different ways to get information. So their expectation has changed in that they expect information to find them."

And part of that expectation is now that you will not only deliver good information, experiences and stuff—but do it in an appropriate context.

With that as the goal, we say the doublespeak stops here. It is time for an intervention, for all of us. Are you with us?

A New Definition of Media

As we said in Chapter 1, *media* is the information, the experiences, and the stuff that we consume and share every day. That is the definition we are using and the framework that we hope you will consider as you read this book. What we are referring to could be called little-m media. We are not talking about the journalists and news producers of the world, or the media companies that manufacture the information, experiences, and stuff we are discussing. They are big-M media. No, little-m media is not the companies or groups, but rather what role those organizations play, the things they produce, and their process for producing them.

There is lots of room in the little-m media environment. In the information category you find news and sports scores, pictures and videos, commentary—whether delivered via a blog or from a soapbox in the middle of town square—and everything else that individuals and organizations create and share. The medium is unimportant; little-m media can be found online or off, drawn from the past, happening in the present, or still to come in the future. Experiences of little-m media include video games and computer simulations, a ride at a theme park or a great play at a sporting event, a delicious meal at a restaurant and a piece of gum on the floor of a movie theater. It is the process of learning and engaging, of participating and interacting with something that creates media. Location is important, but little-m media can be anywhere or everywhere. Experience can be real or virtual, local or remote.

The rest, it seems, falls into the category of stuff. Whether we make it or buy it, borrow it or purchase it, hold it or discard it, it is all stuff. It is our clothing, our gadgets, our cars, and our homes. Sometimes the media is the medium as well, because how it feels and how it looks (think of the iPhone) is as important as the experience it delivers. For certain, media is the tools we use to frame and facilitate the information and experiences that we consume and share.

What is *not* little-m media? Emotions are not media. The act of thinking or feeling something, that process of learning you go through to understand your relationship to something is a part of media. You can convey emotion through little-m media, by showing it in a photograph you have taken or by pulling inspiration from a performance you attended last night, but that pain, or joy, fear or hunger that you experience is not media, it is what helps you understand your relationship to media.

Time is not media. It is an important element in understanding how and when little-m media is relevant to you and your audience; time provides boundaries and context. But by itself, a moment in time that just passed or has yet to pass cannot be created or shared—only its contents can, and they are all part of the little-m media.

What about the groups and experiences that fall under what has traditionally been known as, "the media"? In this context, they are what we call big-M media, the industry of people who create and share news and opinion, provide coverage and analysis of the happenings in our world. They are important—big-M media is key player in the ecosystem of information, experiences, and stuff. But they are just one part. Alongside entertainers and athletes, scholars and scientists, and increasingly the general population, they are some of the people and groups responsible for creating little-m media.

To be a part of the big-M media, people need to have special credentials or follow certain conventions. We could (and maybe should) call them journalists or newspeople. They are a special group of creators and sharers, but they can't even begin to claim that what they are responsible for runs the full spectrum of what exists, or what is needed. Anyone can create or share little-m media—you don't need a formal designation or permission; in fact you are already doing it.

Our definition is intentionally broad. Almost everything can be categorized as little-m media, and that is by design. By including it all, we can get to the important matter of understanding how to create and share this media well, and with the right audience. The definition is not important—the content, context, and application of the principles we discuss are.

Word Association

Words are used to describe different interactions with media. It is a basic concept, but in execution it becomes more complicated. There are many different meanings and interpretations for each word, and in the marketing and management of organizations, those different uses can have a broad impact.

There are more words that we can count or list that fall into this category, things like *demand* and *production, accessibility* and *value*. Don't forget *reach* and *frequency, distribution* and *promotion.* New terms are created or discovered almost every day, and nobody is solely responsible for moderating how they are used.

How do they spread? We do it. Maybe you do it also. Have you ever created a new word to describe your perspective on something, perhaps for a presentation at a conference or an interview? Your goal was to be unique, even creative, and little did you know the dominos were now beginning to fall. Someone in the audience heard that word and it piqued their curiosity so they shared it with their colleague, customer, or family. With all the different ways to distribute information today, it wouldn't be surprising if they put it in a blog post, recorded a podcast, or bought the corresponding Web address for it also.

So the word begins to spread, new interpretations are attached, and different examples start to be used to help other people understand the word's meaning. At some point, a reporter gets wind and writes an article about it. Down the line a book is published that institutionalizes the word and gives the creator of that word (or the person smart enough to take ownership and publicize it) their 15 minutes of fame. The cycle starts every day, repeats every day, and the list of words continues to grow.

Let's try an experiment. Following is a list of 12 words that have followed the path just described and become ingrained in the media culture. Read each term and record the first thing that comes to mind as you seek to define it.

1. Advertising
2. Brand
3. Channel
4. Transaction
5. Networks
6. Open source
7. Syndication
8. On demand
9. Stickiness
10. A la carte
11. Game/simulation
12. Web 2.0

Do you think you know the right answers? Here's a hint: There are no right answers, at least not yet.

Chris Anderson, author of *The Long Tail* (Hyperion, 2006), said, "I have no idea what *media* means anymore. I don't know what *journalism* means anymore, either. I basically don't know what any of the conventional words of our industry mean anymore. I don't use the word *journalism* anymore. I don't use the word *citizen* in that context anymore. Because *citizen* has a political context and *journalism* has a guild definition which I don't think has any bearings to a world of 70 million bloggers." We hear you, Chris.

Marshall McLuhan argued that words are technology, providing the common language and framework from which people can glean understanding. For that to work, however, words have to have common meaning. Without a common meaning, the words serve no function—there is no common understanding or application. If a common meaning cannot be established, the words will die.

So what about these 12 words?

Each of the people interviewed for this book, more than 35 in all, took the same quiz you just took. Not a single answer from any of the people we talked with matched anyone else's. Here is just a sampling:

Advertising. Ben Goldhirsch, the publisher of *GOOD Magazine* said advertising was about generating revenue. Jeff Taylor, the founder of Monster.com and now EONS.com said, "There's a new way and an old way." Jackie Huba, co-author of, "Citizen Marketers: When People Are The Message" said, "Yuck" and JoRoan Lazaro, the former Creative Director at American Online said, "Wow, great ideas!" when asked. Alan Khazei from City Year said advertising provided his organization a chance to, "put out our values and ideals." And Frank Kern from Starbucks said advertising was, "Generally something that we don't play in. We generally look for the experiential human connection," almost suggesting there was something bad about advertising.

Brand. Michael Brown from City Year said, "Brand is about idealism and communicating; walking the talk," while Jay Rosen, a journalism professor at NYU, said it was about marketing. Charles Best from DonorsChoose said, "people" were the core element of brand. Mark Lukasiewicz said that brand was about "credibility."

Transaction. Stephen Cassidy from UNICEF believes that transactions are, "not the end" and Steve Rubel believes they, "should be relationships." JoRoan Lazaro blurted out, "Profit" when asked. And Ricky Strauss from Participant Productions said the most important element was, "emotional."

A la carte. This term, which typically refers to a list of items that are available or priced separately, prompted Jackie Huba to think, "mashed potatoes" and Charles Best to remember, "candy at the checkout line." Steve Rubel, part of the Me2 practice at Edelman said, "We live in a bite-sized world. That's a very important thing to look at," while Larry Lessig argued it was equivalent to, "freedom," and Pat Coyle from the Indianapolis Colts replied, "choice."

Stickiness. For Jeff Taylor, the concept of stickiness is, "elusive" and about, "great products." JoRoan Lazaro said, "The new metric may be going back to the idea of democratization and giving power back to people . . . If we take what's happening online and with media, what is sticky now is less about a product than it is about a lot of people believing or agreeing that something is worth watching for ten seconds or two minutes. So in terms of looking at, say, video, which is a great example, you could say that Google video or YouTube is sticky, but it wouldn't be without the power of the millions of people that participate. And the thousands of people that contribute things for the rest of the millions to participate and watch."

Lisa Poulson from Burson Marsteller called stickiness, "the Holy Grail. It always will be. It's going to be the Holy Grail for everybody." Sheryl Tucker from Time, Inc. added, "I think the only way to achieve stickiness is when it's relevant, valuable, useful. If you're coming from the content-creative point of view, you're going to have a harder time getting stickiness than if you come from the user's point of view. And I think you have to continue to go back to that point of view to decide how you deliver it and what it looks like. That's what you pay the content people to decide, but it's got to come from some desire to have it. Books, movies, TV shows, etc. that don't do well, that's because nobody wants it."

Open source. JoRoan Lazaro associated the concept of open source with, "hippies." And when asked if the process of design could be open source, he replied, "Technically you could. That means that you would just allow a group of people big or small the ability to change the interface or the ability to change features. So you could do it. I don't know why you would except for experimental reasons. But you could do it. It's difficult to create great things if a lot of people are trying to contribute to the vision. Because what happens is there's a dilution of an idea and it rarely results in something better as compared to a smaller group of people or one person. It's not like the wisdom of crowds where people can estimate things or come up with better ideas. It just doesn't seem to work with design." This is the time for high level decision making of all kinds at organizations.

Sheryl Tucker said it was, "scary." Frank Kern pluralized it, saying, "It is about open *sources*. In my view, if a customer says 'A drive-through window would really be helpful, and there are different situations where I want to experience your brand,' we would be open to that." Mark Lukasiewicz from NBC News said, "I would say open source is a wonderful idea if creators are compensated" (and thus had even greater incentive to produce quality work as well).

On demand. For Ben Goldhirsch, the concept of on demand is, "exciting." He said, "I can't wait to have a closer relationship with our audience. I can't wait to see the market for our films as the audience, as visitors choose what they want. Right now, the market for our films includes some major studios and a few distribution points—and that stinks. One of the reasons we started up the magazine is to have a direct relationship with our audience. On demand allows for that." For Stephen Cassidy from UNICEF it means, "a whole new reality. On demand, it will never go away, just like black-and-white television's never coming back. It's done, it's dead, it's gone. Albums aren't coming back. Wax is not coming back. On demand is the new species."

There are so many ways to say or interpret things that confusion is inevitable. To avoid confusion, focus on knowing what you are talking about and who you are talking to. Using the words correctly is of secondary importance—particularly since there is no single definition, there likely will never be, and the effort to find one will tax your organizational resources far more than they will return in benefits. What is most important is to describe what you are doing as an organization in the appropriate context so that your audience finds it relevant, timely, and compelling to them.

Focus on what's important. No matter how you describe what you are trying to provide, what service you think you are offering, no matter what words you use to try to convince your audience to be interested, the most important thing will always be to deliver a terrific little-m media experience. That will always be true. So stop talking about it and just go out there and make it happen.

Be All Things

We buy all kinds of stuff. Cars, clothes, music gadgets—the list is endless. We use all sorts of services as well. We order food in a restaurant, borrow books from the library, have our car cleaned . . . You get the idea.

What is the difference between products and services? Is there one? Products provide a valuable service. They allow us to get our questions answered, our problems addressed. They deliver heat, entertainment, and communications—be it in words or pictures. We need products to serve as delivery points for these and countless other services—a TV set to watch programs or a cell phone to make a call, a special conditioner to keep our new hairstyle from losing its shape.

All around the world media is rapidly expanding and evolving, creating new challenges for organizations and forcing dramatic changes in the way they market and manage themselves. Organizations that operate online are increasingly sharing their audiences with existing brands and organizations whose presence is mostly felt offline. Online and offline organizations offer distinct and, depending on the scenario, equally compelling opportunities to engage their audiences. So, why is the story always the online audience for X increased causing a decrease in offline audience for Y? Online organizations have a lot to learn from their offline predecessors. And as more people shop, learn, communicate, and receive services exclusively online, the traditional brick and mortar businesses can take some cues from the online groups as well. They are different. Each is unique. But they impact and inform each other significantly.

"I don't think we're in a place where the culture is going to change so rapidly that everyone's going to live online and everything's going to be online forever. Television didn't replace radio. Radio didn't replace movies. Movies didn't replace anything else. We're just adding to our communications media," Lisa Poulson told us:

> Organizations want to be able to communicate with people in a specific, preferred way, in the way they believe they will impact the largest number of their preferred audience. You should do something that's appropriate based on the audience you want to reach and the offering you want to make. But you shouldn't throw your other marketing away and operate only online simply because you can!

It is important to understand how audiences form their opinions about the organizations they encounter. People use a variety of different tools, over a series of interactions, to determine what is the best use of their time and what will satisfy their needs best. For retailers and other businesses, the audience will consider far more than just a product. All the information they consume from the time they begin their search for a product—the marketing, the support they receive when they ask the store clerk a question, the return policies and customer service, the quality and reputation of the product they read about or hear about from friends, and more. Organizations that don't sell anything contend with many similar challenges—a crowded marketplace (perhaps for ideas instead of products), a fragmented audience with limited interest in truly engaging with people they don't already have a relationship with, and an increasingly time-poor world. No organization can be successful until it considers how all those interactions unfold, and excels at them all.

The goal for any organization should be the creation of a deeper, more meaningful connection between it and its audience, one that endures over time. To do that, you must be all things to your customer—a friend when they want one, a solution provider when they need one, a guide when they aren't sure what they need, and a consistent performer in all capacities.

A recent study about customer service revealed that people want organizations to do four things: (1) provide prompt, friendly service, (2) fix their problem, (3) do something a little bit extra to make up for any errors or problems, and (4) have flexible policies and consider making changes when the audience doesn't agree with the organization trying to reach them.[1] In short, customers want it all.

Organizations continue to get to know and understand the needs of their audiences. The additional learning comes as a result of increased listening and greater openness to the contributions that audiences can make—strategically, toward design, in terms of marketing and reputation building, and of course in response to a crisis. Successful organizations are able to anticipate what their audience needs and wants, then aligns their offering to meet those needs and desires. Whether this means maintaining a 24/7 call center or responding immediately to customer e-mails no matter what time of day they are received, doing whatever it takes to be responsive and attentive to audience needs is increasingly important.

Organizations need to increase the variety of communication channels they have access to and use them to engage in dialogues with their audience. E-commerce businesses, for example, have been successful to date, providing easy access to products online. But when a customer has an issue with an order, he expects to be able to reach a human being by phone—a service that most organizations don't currently prioritize or make easily available. Organizations that support a variety of communication channels—and understand how to communicate appropriately and effectively through all of them—are best poised to build relationships with an audience.

The Rise of Transactionalization

Transactions take place when any kind of good or service is exchanged for something of value. Typically, that is thought of as an exchange for money—the purchase of a product, for example. With online and offline organizations, and businesses in particular, competing for the attention of the audience, the expectation for many is that transactions will be exactly the same no matter the venue. The result is that every organization has the challenge of meeting the audience's expectations around each individual interaction. Every conversation, e-mail, visit to a store, search experience online, advertisement, and so on has to meet the audience's needs, at the speed and with the quality they expect, or audiences are likely to explore one of the countless options that exist elsewhere for them.

Organizations can't control every aspect of their audience's experience, only the ones they have direct contact with. You may be able to build up the goodwill by having a string of successes in terms of your interaction with someone, but mistakes are very costly.

That means every *interaction* between an organization and an individual member of their audience is a *transaction,* of equal importance to the one immediately prior or the one to follow. Every review, every welcome you receive when you first enter an office, every e-mail or phone call to customer service impacts the decision-making process of your audience on an equally important level. As a businessperson you have to be in control of all of these interactions.

Chris Anderson, author of *The Long Tail,* explained it as the difference between how the "Google generation engages in the world differently than the pre-Google generation." He continued:

> They expect all information to be available. They are impatient. They are able to absorb huge amounts of information very quickly. They are good at asking questions. And there is reason to imagine that they're going to apply that to the real world as well as to their online experience. What that means is that, when they walk into a store, they expect to be able to find whatever product they want, in whatever size, color, and style they desire. They expect to receive prompt and personalized service from the representative of whatever organization they have engaged.

Success for organizations comes when they are able to build relationships and build credibility with your audience. That bond of trust that is created with a business comes from providing consistent service, and credibility breeds mutual respect between you and your audience. And, if you make a mistake—when transactions go bad – you can draw on the relationship that you have built with your audience to rebuild trust.

Chris Anderson told us a story about a hotel chain that he used to stay at on a weekly basis.

> I didn't like it very much, because it wasn't very glamorous. But it was always exactly the same. I knew exactly what was going to happen. I knew what I was going to get. And it was fine. One time, I checked in and it was a mess, with pizza boxes and other debris around the room. They had to clean the room up but I

didn't care because I stayed there once a week and they were
always nice to me. It was fine. However, if I were in some other
city and it was some other hotel that I had only been to once or
twice before, I probably would never choose that hotel again.

Incremental growth in the credibility and in the relationship can
allow that kind of forgiveness. But if that hasn't been built up, there's
no second chance.

The challenge shared by all organizations is that they are judged
most by their most recent interaction, their latest transaction, and
not as much by the complete relationship with their audience. An
organization might have dozens, maybe hundreds, of successful
transactions with a member of their audience, only to make a mistake that undermines everything they have built up in that relationship. Every transaction has tremendous value beyond the exchange
of dollars for goods. More than ever, competition based on both
price and quality is increasing. Organizations can no longer build
an audience and create value simply by creating a better product or
even by holding down costs.

Customer Service versus Customer Experience

Experience is everything. From the moment someone in your audience first begins to think about you, what you offer, or even the general environment in which you operate, you are under a microscope.
If every element of that experience doesn't go smoothly in the eyes of
your audience, chances are you have lost out. That seems pretty unfair.
Much of what the audience absorbs when considering which organizations to engage is well beyond our control—because you don't operate every store where your product is sold, every channel where your
information is delivered, or every place where people experience
your brand. Even if you do, you can only do so much to put in place
standards and practices that assure a consistent offering every time.

Still, there is so much that we do control that most organizations
take for granted. Where do most organizations fall short? In the for-
profit world, laziness is often the culprit. Sometimes it happens when
the money starts to flow and management confuses profitability with
customer loyalty or a solid product offering. In some cases, the most
lucrative buyers may also be the angriest and most alienated, but
without a viable alternative to explore. Other times, your employees

don't go the extra mile to support your customers. But your audience won't tolerate that behavior—technology continues to create more and more markets for people to offer competitive services, at lower cost or with a better service attached, and your audience will go somewhere else in no time.

Lisa Poulson told us that a lot of organizations err by offering lots of interesting features simply because they can:

> A smaller business that offers one thing—say a landscape architect—should think about how she wants to present herself. She should have a marketing goal that is not attached to the "how" of online or not online. Once she knows what her marketing goal is, then she can figure out which networks and marketing tools she wants to use to reach that goal. Whether her business is online or not, her success will depend on getting and sharing as many good reviews of her landscape architecture services as she possibly can. The internet takes sharing to a new level, and lets other people share on your behalf.

By going slowly enough, organizations can make a decision based on which products are more naturally suited toward which environment. If you are going to operate online, choose offerings that you sell to audiences that are naturally online already anyway. And if you are not online, then offer things that don't make sense to sell online. There are some other considerations, for sure, but it shouldn't be that much more complicated than that.

In the nonprofit world, organizations often lose focus as they grow. They stray from their mission, losing sight of what attracted interest to them in the first place. They become heavy on programs and light on impact. There can form a sense of entitlement or a desire to separate yourself from the profit-driven world. But the audience doesn't know, or care, about the difference. It doesn't matter greatly to them whether you pull a profit for your work or don't. Like anything else, they care about the service they are getting, the product they are buying, or the work that is being done. If you aren't performing at a high level, someone else will and their cause will quickly trump yours.

Rob Waldron, former CEO of Jumpstart, a non-profit service organization that pairs college students with pre-school students from low-income backgrounds for a year of mentoring to foster literacy and social success and prepare them to succeed in school, explained:

The difference is the multiple outcomes of the social sector versus the unity of the outcome of the private sector. In the nonprofit world, people wouldn't always agree on what you were supposed to be doing. There was a lot of clarity of what you were supposed to be doing in the private sector. For example, some people viewed Jumpstart as a way for kids to get better prepared for school at four years old; other people thought its purpose was to get those children to succeed in life, so they had a view that we should work with the same children for many years. Other people thought Jumpstart was about citizenship and making college students grow up by understanding their local community. So every once in a while we'd get into battles about what we were supposed to be doing.

The definition is murkier when you're trying to solve the social needs, but the basic principles you must consider for your organization remain the same.

When that happens, what should you do? For starters, don't assume you know where you have gone wrong—find out from your audience. Jackie Huba explained:

It has always been important that organizations understand what their audiences think, always." In the past, people would use things like focus groups, or they would use paper surveys, or maybe they would have a customer advisory board. Today, there are e-mail and online surveys, customer service chat tools, and customer message boards. If you don't give people the opportunity to give that feedback, they will just give it somewhere else. And now that feedback can show up somewhere else on a blog or in a video on YouTube, or in a forum somewhere on the Web, and everyone can see it worldwide. And as it starts to spread, then you've got a problem.

James Allen, Frederick F. Reichheld, and Barney Hamilton wrote in *the Harvard Management Update* in 2005 that organizations can answer problems by following three Ds:

- D*esign* the right offers and experiences for the right customers.
- D*eliver* these propositions by focusing the entire [organization] on them. . . .
- D*evelop* their capabilities to please customers again and again . . .[2]

For each D, Allen, Reichheld and Hamilton suggest organizations encourage cross-functional collaboration so that each element reinforces the others. Together, they can help to transform any organization into one that is continually led and informed by its customers' voices. Huba says either way the pressure to listen to customers has never been greater than it is now. "The great opportunity is that there are so many tools you can use to do it now, and scale that feedback. Get more of it, and more focused feedback, and have 24/7 groups where you can ask for feedback."

Many online organizations—whether they are retailers, news services, or a non-profit group whose operations exist online only— do not provide a compelling user experience. Some sites are hard to navigate, while others fail to provide content or services that match their users' needs and expectations. To make matters worse, most organizations do a poor job of effectively assessing their audience's experiences. They don't know why their users behave in certain ways, and they don't choose to find out.

User experiences, of course, are not limited to the online environment. If you walk into a dirty restaurant, you wonder if the food you are about to be served is being prepared under the best conditions and many walk out when they decide it is not. If you are scheduled to volunteer for a worthy organization, but when you show up the organization doesn't have a clear role for you to play, activities for you to help out with—or worst of all, fail to say thank you for the time and commitment that you make to support their efforts – you wonder if your time could be better spent doing something else.

Being All Things Can't Mean Being Everything . . .

Of course, you can't just occupy a channel because it is there, in order to exist. You must tailor the method of contact to the type of audience you are trying to reach. Some will be highly engaged with technology while others prefer, or even demand, a human touch. All audiences want some kind of personalized service, no matter how difficult that might be for an organization to provide. And they are much more likely to reengage if the replies to their most important requests or concerns are consistent and quick, as well as tailored to meet their particular needs. A cookie-cutter response won't cut it (and, thanks to new technologies, it is easier than ever to avoid).

This also applies to organizations whose audience doesn't have another option, and therefore faces no competition. Those situations are fewer and farther between than in the past because technology continues to advance and our society becomes is increasingly globalized, launching new markets and opportunities in places once never possible. But even where an organization has a monopoly on the interest from an audience, there are benefits to aligning communication goals with activities, and the expectations of their audience. Organizations can maximize the involvement of their audience and the revenue or interest that interest generates, thus drawing more success from an audience even if the size of that audience does not change.

The most important thing that organizations can do is listen and learn. Customers engage more deeply with organizations that listen to their needs and respond by providing more targeted information or better value propositions. The beauty of listening through a variety of different channels is you will receive a lot of useful information about what you can improve on and where you can add more value to the interaction with your audience. Organizations must be proactive in providing customer service, not simply wait for someone to ask a question or lodge a complaint. Give information out to your audience to help them make choices or feel comfortable about their relationship with you. Offer education and training to help people learn how to have a better experience with your organization and its offerings.

Customers are unlikely to engage with organizations that send cookie-cutter replies to their most important requests or concerns. Responses that are personalized, consistent, and quick stand the best chance of attracting and retaining customers' attention. To achieve this, many companies are leveraging Web chat, e-mail, and personalized online record keeping. The online tools provide more benefits than simply scale.

Audiences have high expectations of the organizations they deal with and how those organizations should interact with them. It is about more than just products and service—it is about the total package. That is why *engagement,* one of the biggest buzz words of the online space for sure, is seen as a way to create interaction and participation by an audience.

Don't differentiate by what you do, differentiate by who you do it for—and how well you do it.

CHAPTER 4

Be Organic

To persistently take full advantage of the rapidly changing media environment, you must be organic—biologically inspired. A commitment to growth, adaptation, steady change, feedback loops, and having diverse attributes should be inherent in your work.

By being organic, your different audiences will know that you are open, trusting, and values-driven.

This chapter is about organizations operating organically. There are many words that could have been used in this context but, as discussed earlier, terminology often creates a problem. For example, the term *sustainable* is generally defined as a production method that provides a long-term profit for the producer, protects natural resources, and has positive social impact. On his company's Web site, Jeffrey Hollender of Seventh Generation cites a definition offered by Jonathan Porritt, former head of Friends of the Earth and author of *Capitalism As If The World Matters* (Earthscan, 2005), saying sustainability "is a dynamic process which enables all people to realize their potential and to improve their quality of life in ways which simultaneously protect and enhance the Earth's life-support systems. This both affirms sustainable development as a dynamic process and emphasizes the importance of social justice and equity in that it has to be made to work for *all* people."[1]

Authentic is another interesting term. One definition of authenticity is that it is real, not copied. Another is that something authentic is supported by unquestionable evidence. Applying those principles in an organizational setting can be challenging. Jeffrey Hollender offers that comes from the basic values his company was established around. He writes that being authentic is "about letting our actions be the judge of whether or not we're being the company we say we are," adding, "[A]uthenticity is not a state of being. It is a process of becoming."

Sustainability and authenticity are key philosophical concepts that organizations must embrace to be successful in an ultra-connected world. They are also the super-buzzwords of the moment. Ultimately, sustainability and authenticity are in the eyes of the beholder. One group's view of having a social impact may differ dramatically from another's. And how closely aligned an organization operates with its original mission as it grows and adjusts over time can and will be judged in part by the way that organization presents itself, and partly in the context of history in which that question is being considered.

That is why we are using the word *organic*. The fundamental definition of being organic is that something is derived from living organisms—or for our use, organizations. We are not suggesting that organizations have to operate without chemicals, produce products that have limited impact on the natural surrounding, or promote ideas that are not divisive or controversial. That is one, very narrow definition of organic, so while that would be nice, it is not the point we are trying to make here. We are suggesting that for organizations to succeed they have to make an effort to connect with their audience—they have to use the living elements of their structure to provide the energy and focus for their organization. They have to be natural, not forced or over-manufactured.

There are obviously some natural benefits to operating organically—the way you feel about your work, the way your team operates as a result of that ingrained perspective. There is also a tremendous body of research that shows that customers are interested in organizations that operate with a focus on more than profits.

In a poll of 25,000 people in 23 countries by the Conference Board, two-thirds said they want business to "expand beyond the traditional emphasis on profits and contribute to broader social objectives."[2] Cone, Inc, the brand and cause marketing company that Brian works for, conducts regular research about consumer audiences, particularly millennials (young people born between 1979 and 2001) that shows this civic-minded generation, 78 million strong, not only believes it is their responsibility to make the world a better place, but 78 percent of them believe that companies have a responsibility to join them in this effort. More importantly, the research says that millennials are prepared to reward or punish a company based on its commitment to social causes.[3]

An overwhelming 74 percent of the millennials that Cone surveyed indicated they are more likely to pay attention to a company's overall messages when they see that the company has a deep commitment to a cause. Nearly nine out of ten respondents, ages 13 to 25, stated that they are likely or very likely to switch from one brand to another (price and quality being equal) if the second brand is associated with a good cause. Moreover, the poll finds that as millennials begin to enter the workforce, they have high expectations not only for themselves but also for their employers. Nearly eight out of ten want to work for a company that cares about how it contributes to society, while more than half would refuse to work for a corporation that they believe to be irresponsible.

Millennials are not the only audience interested in organizations taking a larger focus. A recent study commissioned by Weber Shandwick revealed that a sizable 42 percent of boomers' (50+ year olds) purchasing decisions are influenced by a company's social or environmental policies. Weber Shandwick also argued that boomers' attention to social responsibility as a key factor in purchase decision making is similar to that of Gen Xers (born between 1961 and 1981)—46 percent.[4]

Jeff Taylor, the founder of Monster.com and more recently EONS, a social network focused on serving the baby boom generation, tied it together for us. He believes the challenge of reaching and engaging older audiences is similar to engaging millennials: "It's anchorman versus U-Gen. This boomer population is the TV generation and doesn't look at TV badly—in fact, they generally look at TV as a communication experience that would be the equivalent of the way a 20-year-old looks at the Internet. And I don't know many 20-year olds that feel badly about the Internet. And 'U-Gen,' or user-generated content, is a new idea—not necessarily one that is not to be embraced, just new. There needs to be a new hybrid model with a balance between both worlds."

He added, "A critical role that EONS could play would be to be the new value-oriented kind of online network solution that would be focused in on the kind of generation between Madison Avenue's interest of people ages 18 to 49, and the 65-plus population. Our sweet spot is a Web user, age 49 to around 60, and over 80 percent of our users fall in that age group."

It is not enough to know that audiences are different, or even to distinguish between what information or experience you make available to your different audiences – that is just the first step. Deep down, Boomers, millennials, and all the other groups that you can target discreetly, have different expectations regarding the relationship they will have with an organization and a different appreciation for what and how they experience things. And as time goes on, and technology and society continue to change, those expectations will change as well.

A Case Study In Operating Organically: Part Science, Part Art

Seventh Generation is the nation's leading seller of nontoxic and environmentally safe household products. They sell cleansers and detergents, paper towels, sanitary products, and the like. All the products are organic, as is everything else the company does. The company's offices are in downtown Burlington, Vermont, along the banks of Lake Champlain, in a building made from native stone, brick, slate, and copper. It is designed with dormers, awnings, porches, arches, and cupolas, "a throwback to a time when architecture engaged the eye and inspired the mind."

> It uses local wood from sustainably managed forests. Everything that can be made from recycled materials is—from the insulation in the walls to the workstations throughout the space. Even the carpets are made from recycled materials, and they don't contain formaldehyde or other VOCs [volatile organic compounds] that can pollute our indoor air. We've used non-toxic VOC-free paint and sealants. All of our lighting is energy efficient, and we might not even need it because we also designed the space to fill with natural light throughout the year. A heat exchange system assures us a supply of fresh indoor air. There are composting and recycling services. And, of course, only safe non-toxic cleaners will be used. There's even a place to plug in your electric car in the parking garage. There is a shower in the bathroom for those who want to jog to work. There is also a game and yoga room along with a space to meditate.[5]

Everything about Seventh Generation—not just the materials used to build the office space—seems inspired by a certain organic mentality. Jeffrey Hollender, the CEO, speaks passionately about how his company practices a variety of techniques to help ensure that his team operates in a manner that is in keeping with the company's core values, because developing a culture that both understands and is committed to those values is essential. He told us:

> If I try to sell you bathroom tissue and I sell you on my product at the lowest price, I won't have much of a valuable relationship with you because sure enough someone will come along tomorrow and sell you bathroom tissue at an even cheaper price. We can't win at that game and there's no point in competing. If I know you care about the environment and I can build a relationship with you because you're concerned about your footprint and your CO_2 emissions and you're concerned about global warming, and we can be a partner in trying to mitigate that impact, then it's no longer about if you can save five cents a roll. We've built a relationship at a very different level and we've become less displaceable...... Many of the things that we often buy are displaceable. And I think that that's a lousy business model, to be in a sense a commodity. So in order to be nondisplaceable, you have to really understand what it is that the person you're selling to values and you have to create not just a product but a system and a relationship.

He said in an interview that "While excellent employee benefits, community involvement, charitable donations, outstanding customer service and products that exceed customer expectations are all important, if not critical," Seventh Generation goes beyond that. Every year the company takes several days to have a staff retreat where they revisit their core values to make sure everything is still aligned with the business goals of the company. They integrate personal, community and value-based goals into everyone's job description and performance expectations. They do 360-degree reviews, use coaches to facilitate interpersonal development, provide on-site massages, take two days a year to get out of the office together—whether it is to snowshoe, raft, or just walk through the woods together—and insist that everyone in the company serves on a committee (they have a green team, a community service group, and so on).

"Generally speaking, these things get reduced to some piece of paper put up on the wall somewhere," Hollender told us. "And to a certain extent they only have meaning if they sort of exist in the life of the company and in the dialogue of conversations between people." He demonstrated his point with this story:

> A good example is how, for many years, we have celebrated Earth Day by having a contest that gave away high-efficiency washing machines. We're in the laundry business, after all, so the washing machines made sense. And these were great machines. But when you think about the value you're creating by giving away 50 or 100 machines, it's not very much. You have 50 or 100 people that are happy and probably lifelong customers and they'll tell their friends and they'll use less water and less energy. But you're not creating any kind of systemic change.
>
> So we went through this process of saying, "Okay, we're doing this promotion. How does it align with our essence, our values? What do we want to do in the world, and will those help us upgrade what we're doing?" The answer came pretty easily. First, we decided there was nothing systemic about this contest, the giveaway. It was dealing with a symptom of a problem rather than the problem itself. We used our values as a guide and it led us to some other options and other solutions. We decided that we wanted do something systemic—something that would allow our teeny company to have leverage. And it led us to this whole notion of educating college kids to be social change activists.
>
> We figured, maybe we can only educate a couple hundred kids a year, but if we do a good job they'll go out in the world and touch thousands if not hundreds of thousands of people, and they'll generate stories, they'll generate real-life examples, and they will create real change.

The program that Seventh Generation created is called "Change It." They partnered with Greenpeace to create a weeklong, all expenses paid grassroots educational training in Washington, D.C. Each year 100 students, ages 18 to 24, are invited to participate after completing an exhaustive application process. The program teaches the participants about strategy, issue selection and definition, fundraising, organizing, nonviolent action, telling stories, negotiation, and policy analysis.

As Jeffrey Hollender wrote on his blog after the 2006 Change It training, "They are learning how to make the world a better place. They are learning more about what they want the world to be and the challenges and obstacles they are likely to encounter along the way. . . . The future is in their hands and, more than most, they are willing to accept it. They do not look back. They look forward. They are less encumbered by the paths and patterns that keep us locked into the endless cycles of the despair that dissipates hope. They are curious and unafraid. They have a spirit that is infectious. I am honored to be in their presence, honored to have helped bring them together, honored to share in this small part of their journey with them."[6]

It would be easy to ignore a company like Seventh Generation because it operates in a niche category, because it is the beneficiary of a significant trend that promotes healthier living, or because it benefits from being in Burlington, Vermont, isolated from the cut-throat urban business environment. But Seventh Generation operates like any other major business. The team members face the same challenges associated with growth, competition, and availability of talent, and so on. They don't just benefit from a movement promoting healthy living, they have actively helped to *define* it—not as a marketing ploy (though it certainly does benefit the company) but as a member of the world community. And as a result, they have grown about 25 percent per year for the past five years; they are profitable and have become the nation's leading brand of natural, nontoxic household products.

Another Way to See Success

There are two very important elements of Seventh Generation's success that all organizations can model. First, Seventh Generation is driven by a core vision and philosophy that is about the world community they are a part of, not the business they are in. The Seventh Generation vision includes the concepts of leadership, inspiration, and positive change as well as sustainability, justice, and compassion. Their mission explains that they are "dedicated to setting the standard for superior service and to providing our customers with the resources and inspiration they need to make informed, responsible decisions" as well as "becoming the world's most trusted brand of authentic, safe, and environmentally responsible products for a healthy home." The company knows there is always a risk in educating consumers about their choices, but it is confident that its service and products will align with people's informed views—it doesn't need to manipulate that decision-making process.

The second element of Seventh Generation's success is that it is measured on more than just the financial return of the company. According to Hollender, Seven Generation considers "how honest and complete is the communication between staff members as well as with customers and other stakeholders; how safe is it to challenge your boss (how many people are willing to show up and sit across from me and let me know that they feel that my own behavior seems to conflict with our stated values?); what's employee turnover like, and why are people leaving; to what extent do our products and our entire company deplete the planet of nonrenewable resources, create greenhouse gasses, or produce solid waste; and so on." Hollender, and anyone else you talk with at Seventh Generation, is confident that if the company meets or exceeds expectations in these areas, its customer base will expand and its bottom line will continue to grow.

By contrast, look at how most major consumer goods companies talk about their core operating principles. Most of them speak of their "commitment" to the community, devoting sections of the annual reports and Web sites to demonstrating all the ways they are good corporate citizens. But for the most part they talk and act through simple donations made to charities or support for issues that relate to their core business (publishing companies focus on literacy, food companies try to tackle hunger). They don't live their values in everything they do.

We are not questioning whether the commitment these companies make is real or meaningful—they give away hundreds of millions of dollars a year that serve a lot of people and groups who are in need of support. However, by failing to fully integrate the concept into every aspect of their organizations—from who they hire to how they are structured, to the products, services, and marketing programs they create—this commitment becomes just another department in the operation and not a core operating principle.

Do food companies consider the impact they have on childhood obesity when they roll out a new flavor of sugared cereal? They see a huge market for young kids desperate for something that tastes good to start their morning off. And when they do market a healthier alternative, is that because of their commitment to the consumer interest or because they see a marketing opportunity driven by a trend to fight childhood obesity in our society (that they may have inadvertently, or in some cases deliberately, helped to create)?

We are not blaming the companies who operate with profit in mind. And we work for many companies that fit this model. Businesses do not need to give up their commercial agendas. In fact, companies that don't operate with an organic perspective in mind, have been more financially successful to date than their organic competitors. For many companies that measure of success is enough and we make no judgment on them. But companies can act organically and still make considerable profit. And beyond profit, there are many reasons that operating organically is an appropriate long-term strategy for organizations. First: the audience is increasingly shifting its perspective and valuing a more sustainable set of business principles – because of increased awareness about the impact of organizational activities on the environment, local communities, and individuals, That makes the long-term success unknown or at least redefined. Second, a commitment to these practices will create new markets and new opportunities for organizations to enter and have an increased impact.

More and more, we see restaurant and grocery chains like Whole Foods founded on the idea that when you walk through their doors, you don't think about it as just a market. The intent is to establish a place that will help customers feel better physically and emotionally. There's a connection that goes beyond what tastes great or what is needed for dinner.

To do that, the foundation of your organization has to be about more than just short-term success. The reason for its existence cannot be merely to launch an IPO to sell off to somebody else. It must not be focused solely on profit in its purest form but rather based on an agenda that has credibility with the audience. John Mackey, the founder of Whole Foods, addressed this very concept in an essay about what he calls *conscious capitalism*. He wrote:

> Have you ever asked yourself what is the purpose of a business? It is an interesting question that most business people never ask themselves. If you think about it, what is the purpose of a doctor or hospital? Is their purpose to maximize profits? Well, this is

certainly not the purpose that they teach in medical schools or most doctors advocate. The doctor's purpose is to help heal sick people. What about the purpose of the teacher or the school? Do they exist to maximize profits? No, of course not. Their primary purpose is to educate the young and prepare them to live successful lives in society. What about the purpose of lawyers or law courts? All lawyer jokes aside, the purpose of a lawyer would be to pursue justice and our law courts exist to settle disputes in our society and to bring wrongdoers to justice. All of the other professions put an emphasis on the public good and have purposes beyond self-interest. Why doesn't business?[7]

All organizations should, regardless of their function, think this way. For an organization to do that, the guidance and leadership must come from the top and bottom at the same time. Mackey writes: "While the capital from investors is obviously very important to any business, there is one participant in business who has the right to define what the purpose(s) of the business will be in the world—the entrepreneur who creates the business in the first place. Entrepreneurs create a company, bring all the so-called 'factors of production' together, and coordinate them into a viable business. Entrepreneurs set the company strategy and negotiate the terms of trade with all of the voluntarily cooperating stakeholders—including the investors." And of course, it must be lived and exemplified by all who follow in his or her footsteps.

For many organizations, operating organically will require a pretty significant change in perspective and potentially some serious investment of time and resources. The effort required to make those changes offers reasons enough to keep most organizations from acting. But the real changes that need to be made can happen over time, and even the smallest of efforts can have a dramatic impact.

There are examples to follow. Jeffrey Hollender, John Mackey, and others like them are often called *social entrepreneurs*—leaders who recognize a social problem and use their business knowledge and principles to organize, create, and manage a venture to bring about meaningful change. Many companies can't stomach the thought of shifting away from their core business objectives to tackle social problem. And even many nonprofit organizations, educational institutions, and other groups find the success they have had and the prospects of profit growth in the near future a pretty comfortable and safe place to be. But success is not about being safe; you can't change the world without taking some risks.

Success can be about more than just replicating what has worked in the past. It should be about continual renewal and change, evolving opportunities, and pushing the entire environment you are in to align with your organization's values. Entrepreneurs have always changed the face of business, being the risk-takers who were able to pursue a small innovation in a market so that other companies could replicate their model in a different vertical or scale. Social entrepreneurs set out to find what is not working and solve the problem by changing the system, identifying new opportunities and solutions, and persuading entire societies to take new leaps. They aren't satisfied with the status quo of their industry or their organization. They are personally committed to, and believe their audience is interested in, making institutional changes and not just achieving personal or organizational success. And you should be, too.

CHAPTER

Be a Guide

The average American is exposed to nearly 5,000 advertising and promotional messages per day. Those pushing products, services, and ideas hope that their message is one of the few that actually resonates with a target individual, resulting in a purchase, a donation, or commitment of any kind, no matter how small.

The chances are pretty slim. Why is that? Marketers—and make no mistake, we are all marketers at some level, whether selling a product, pushing an idea, or simply trying to convince a friend to join us for a cup of coffee—do not fully understand the increasing difficulty that people have in making choices. Instead of supporting the natural process that people must go through each day to make choices, we continue to bombard our audience with options. Most marketers overwhelm their target audience with so many options it becomes paralyzing.

To be successful, you have to be a guide. The current media environment mandates that you create the benchmarks and assistance to help people find what they need. Some of those benchmarks may be in the support of fewer choices, or you may utilize information technology to help them identify appropriate choices and come to a decision.

So Many Choices . . .

How many different products, styles, and options do we have to filter through before making a decision? Two? A dozen? A thousand? A million? It is personal to each one of us, but for everyone, even the simplest of decisions now requires sorting through a near-endless number of options.

Start with the online experience. Tens of millions of people go online every day to find information, shop, talk to their friends, and do their work. The opportunities they have available to them with just one click of a mouse are mind-blowing:

- The iTunes Store features more than 3.5 million 99¢ songs, 65,000 free podcasts, 20,000 audiobooks, 200 TV shows, movies, and iPod games.
- Amazon.com offers millions of different products in at least 35 separate categories, things like: Music, DVD & VHS, Magazines & Newspapers, Video Games, Electronics, Audio & Video, Camera & Photo, Office Products, Musical Instruments, Bed & Bath, Furniture & Décor, Gourmet Food, Pet Supplies, Automotive, Tools & Hardware, Industrial & Scientific, Apparel & Accessories, Health & Personal Care, Sports & Outdoors, Exercise & Equipment, Toys & Games, Baby, and, of course, books.
- Netflix, the online movie company with the familiar red envelopes, stocks more than 70,000 movies, television shows, and how-to videos in more than 200 genres.
- Technorati, the leading blog search engine, is now tracking over 70 million weblogs, and about 120,000 new weblogs are created worldwide each day. That's about 1.4 blogs created every second of every day.[1]
- YouTube currently has more than 100 million videos available—with 65,000 new videos being uploaded daily.
- And of course, if you search for something on Google you will be handed tens of thousands, maybe even millions, of results of varying length, specificity, and accuracy.

Offline, the number of choices is more modest but far from reasonable for an average person to be able to thoughtfully process.

- There are 55,000 possible drink combinations at Starbucks.
- A typical supermarket stocks 30,000 to 40,000 products.
- A Wal-Mart Supercenter has more than 100,000 products on the shelves.

- Local ice cream stands boast upwards of 40 different flavors (and long lines, because nobody knows what they want when presented with that many options).
- A company in San Diego offers 200 different varieties of replica male sex organs.
- Procter & Gamble had plans to launch a project, Reveal, which would produce 10,000 different shades of lip gloss, but it was cancelled.

And the multitude of choices extends well beyond just products. Groups that offer services are offering too many choices as well.

- Copyshops, like Kinkos offer dozens of different weight and color of paper around their basic copy service.
- XM and Sirius Satellite Radio each offer more than 300 channels of music, talk, sports, and other programming. If and when their merger becomes official, they have the potential to double that.
- Predictions are that we could have 500 separate cable television channels available to us within just a few short years, and satellite services are already there.
- On the nonprofit front, organizations like The Nature Conservancy offer a dozen different ways to help—donate online, become a member (or renew your membership), give a gift membership, sign up for monthly giving (which entitles you to membership in the elite "Friends of the Nature Conservancy" group), coordinate workplace giving, make a stock donation, include it in estate planning, make a real estate donation, "Adopt An Acre," support the Rainforests Fund, "Rescue the Reef," or volunteer. You can also become a conservation buyer and pursue a number of different everyday activities—assist in bird conservation, improve the quality of rivers, combat invasives, and help coral reefs.

These are just a few of the areas where too much choice exists. It's true for cars and other automobiles, mutual funds, hair care and other personal hygiene products, electronics, upholstered furniture, clothing—you name it. There is no escaping these choices.

Why Are There So Many Choices?

What could possibly compel an organization to overwhelm their audience to the point of being paralyzing? It's not that people have to make more choices than in the past, but that they have so many more options available to them so each choice is more difficult to make. For example, someone still chooses to purchase a caffeinated beverage to help them wake up in the morning, but now, instead of milk and sugar, she is deciding between more than 50,000 combinations. Those options are now more available and accessible at a lower transaction cost as well. Think about it: you don't fly around the world to get the best, hand-made pair of shoes—just log on and buy it. You don't have to seek out the perfect shirt to match your outfit—you can go design it yourself and have someone make it and ship it to you.

Now, back to our question—why make it so hard for your audience to find exactly what they want? Our guess: Either organizations don't realize what they are doing is causing confusion and anxiety in customers, or they are so afraid to miss an opportunity that they do whatever they can to cover their bases, even if it means making so many varieties of something available, they are hard to distinguish from each other. In our view, the latter is the case, but there is some truth in the first option as well.

The more options that exist, the more likely people are to buy something. And it is not just when you are selling something. Stephen Cassidy, the chief of internet, television, radio and image at UNICEF, says, "It's a little bit like playing roulette. The wheel goes round and round, there are many numbers on the wheel. The audience is the ball. The numbers are the platforms because we live in an on-demand, multiplatform world, and the audience is using those to gather, to organize, and sort of disperse around various ideas on these various platforms. I can win at roulette every time if I put a chip on every number. Wherever the ball falls, I'm there to meet the audience with my message."

But does it work that way? There is an old tale told in business schools about a lady selling preserves at a farmers' market that demonstrates the impact of choice on our society. There are many variations, but the one that David Kiley wrote on the *BusinessWeek* "Brand New Day" blog in June 2005 sums it up nicely. He wrote: "She had 5 flavors and sold more than she thought in just an hour. Wow, she thought. If I offer 15 kinds of preserves, I'll clean up. So, she came back with 15 flavors. It took her longer to sell less product. The farmers' market customers, it seems, were just stymied by all the choices and moved on to the bread table instead."[2]

In the consumer marketing space, even with 30,000 to 40,000 products offered, the reality is that there is a constant battle for the limited shelf space in most grocery stores. If you are ConAgra, you want to have more shelf space in a store so customers have the opportunity to buy more of your product than one that General Mills or Kraft offers. Product developers will tell you that if your competition comes out with new sizes or flavors, you feel you have to keep pace so you will do the same. So companies create and market more and more products in more and more varieties.

On a routine shopping trip to a local chain grocery store, Brian stopped to ponder his options in the pasta category. The local Shaw's Supermarket devotes one-third of one side of one aisle to pasta products (there are 14 aisles in this supermarket), not including sauces or other accompaniments. In that one relatively small area alone there are a dozen different brands of just pasta, a floor-to-ceiling display of everything from Barilla, Buitoni, De Cecco, and Hodgson Mill to Prince, Nature's Promise, Mueller's, Ronzoni and of course the Shaw's generic brand. There is angel hair and thin spaghetti, linguine, macaroni, penne, ravioli, rotini, farfalle, and elbows all with white flour and some made with whole wheat flour. There are also frozen, prepackaged (like Kraft Macaroni and Cheese or Chef Boyardee), and kosher (Manischewicz noodles) options sprinkled through other sections as well. Does your own experience sound familiar?

That same challenge is being put on your audience for everything and if the thought of having to select any of those options is keeping you out of the grocery store, it surely is doing the same for them. And in response, most end up buying the same thing every time so they don't have to make a choice. The decision making process around a project goes right back to the strength of the relationship and the additional value—beyond the product itself—that an organization offers to its audience.

For nonprofit organizations, the challenge is finding as many ways as possible to compel supporters to make a financial or similar contribution to your organization. Once a supporter makes that initial leap from consuming your information to actively supporting your organization, you've got them for life. The Red Cross, for example, invites you to contribute via cash, stock, in-kind, spare change, airline miles, bequest, life income gift, gift of life insurance, pooled income fund, charitable lead trust, gifts of retirement plans, as well as the option to volunteer your time, give blood, make a tissue donation, donate your goods and individual items, coordinate bulk donations of product from manufacturers or distributors, or donate medical equipment and supplies. Rather than try to convince a prospective donor that making a contribution using a credit card is the best option for them, nonprofits like the Red Cross have decided to offer every conceivable option in hope that donors will find one that is comfortable or interesting to them. There are now so many ways to show support for an organization that donors aren't clear on which one is most valuable to the group they want to support. What is important, instead, is not the number of choices but making people feel compelled to give in the first place, engaging them in a meaningful way so they want to give at all.

Some organizations have felt pressure from consumers who are terrified of making choices and curbed their enthusiasm for new product releases. John Gourville, a Harvard professor, noted that Honda at one point decided to offer its popular Accord in only one of three models—the DX, the LX, and the EX—which he calls "a good, better, best strategy." Titleist, the leading golf ball maker in the world, has cut the number of golf ball varieties to only five.[3] In both cases, this greatly reduced the number of choices a consumer would need to make.

Although an explosion of choices may mean we sometimes get exactly what we want, too many choices can also overwhelm the audience to the point where choosing nothing at all seems like the best option. We don't believe organizations have to limit the number of choices they provide or in any way put a curb on creativity or variety. We don't think walking into a Starbucks and seeing a menu that simply reads "Regular or decaf" is better than being able to customize your experience. But, to appropriately support that kind of choice, organizations must do a better job of supporting their audience and the process they go through every day when making choices. Moreover, the dramatic increase in available options for people to choose between doesn't just create anxiety—it drives up your audience's expectations that the quality you provided when you had a limited number of offerings will continue when your inventory dramatically expands.

Wagging the Long Tail

Is it possible for so many different products and services to be created and supported effectively? Can all those pastas be good, or good for you? Does each of the methods for donating to the Nature Conservancy provide enough support to the organization to justify its niche? Stephen Cassidy from UNICEF argued that "the wheel's always spinning, it never stops, right? The ball's always dropping in—it never stops. Go back to the beginning, tell the story well, and have faith that they will find you. And the people who are genuinely interested in what you have to say will find you, probably in big numbers."

Our belief is that organizations trying to satisfy the individual needs of their entire audience ultimately gravitate towards providing support to a niche segment of their audience anyway, because that segments responds more (or more loudly) than another segment. The challenge arises when the organization proclaims that it supports all audiences equally, but in reality the offering they give to one comes at the expense of providing overall good support to all.

New York Times columnist Tom Friedman wrote in his book, *The World is Flat* (New York: Farrar, Straus, and Giroux, 2005) that globalization allows organizations to offer more of just about everything at lower cost (to them, with the reduction presumably passed along to the audience) and greater efficiency by extending their workforce around the globe. He says this has the potential to drive innovation, economic prosperity, and business excellence in still-developing nations on every corner of the earth. But has anyone asked whether the products and services that these globalized organizations are offering are still living up the quality standard they did when their efforts were less spread out?

The argument goes something like this: The greatest beneficiaries of globalization are consumers because globalization expands the range of choice, improves product quality, and exerts downward pressure on prices. Customers who had been victims of poor service and overpriced, low-quality goods because there was no real competition to spur domestic producers to meet the demands of their consumers are once again in the driver's seat. The biggest challenge that these companies now face, however, is how to raise standards of total quality in all areas of production, sales, and service at all locations. In a manufacturing environment, quality improves reliability and increases production. Fewer defects translate to fewer warranty claims and increased customer satisfaction. Process improvements also eliminate waste, improve flow, and enhance workplace safety, all contributing to the bottom line. And this is not limited to product manufacturing.

In other words, any cost you incur that would not have gone up if quality work had been present in the first place contributes to your underlying costs. The measurement of those costs, besides the loss of potential investment dollars, is the loss of loyalty and the increasing amount of frustration that audiences feel with the delivery of low quality products and services.

When the concept of "the long tail" was introduced by Chris Anderson, the editor of *Wired* magazine, first in an article in 2004 and later in a 2006 book of the same title, it showed how the distribution and sales channel opportunities created by the Internet are enabling businesses to tap deep into specific markets successfully. The long tail demonstrates how the Internet (or, more broadly, technology) invites you to offer nearly unlimited choice to your audience in whatever area you specialize.

There is a long tail for music, for movies, for books, and even for beer. Because all these different long tail markets exist (and Anderson can make a case for just about any market having a long tail component), audiences are increasingly able to find exactly the thing they want, be it a niche product or a unique experience. That is why online rental giant Netflix can offer a movie like *Heavy Metal Parking Lot*—a two-hour cult classic documentary about a most devoted group of metalheads gathered in a parking lot in Maryland before a Judas Priest concert—even though it has an extremely small base of interest. Or, as Anderson puts it, online retailers can offer seemingly infinite inventory, and the result is the "shattering of the mainstream into a zillion different cultural shards."[4]

Study after study has shown that more choice does indeed mean people are more likely to find exactly what they want. But choice has its limits. Barry Schwartz, author of *The Paradox of Choice: Why More Is Less* (New York: Ecco, 2004), argues that the bewildering array of choices for everything from health care plans to college classes, even to buying a pair of jeans, floods our exhausted brains, ultimately frustrating us instead of satisfying our want. Schwartz goes so far as to show that the massive amount of choice that consumers face each day actually works to erode our psychological well-being. But do we still buy?

Why does this overabundance of options have such an impact on our psyches? According to Schwartz, having many choices raises expectations. If there are 10,000 shoes on Zappos.com, the leading online shoe warehouse, you expect to find the perfect pair. Schwartz argues that most people wind up disappointed if (or when) they do not. The reason Schwartz calls this process a paradox is because if there were limits put on the choices you were given, your brain would begin to believe that you were being deprived of something you might have found enjoyable, and you will be back looking for unlimited choices. When unlimited choice is offered again, it breeds the same worry that you made the wrong decision. The reality is, that perfect pair of shoes almost certainly exists on Zappos.com, since they have almost every conceivable style, size, and brand available, but the consumer can't find it. Reviewing all those options takes a lot of time and energy that in most cases the customer is not willing to commit.

So while globalization and the long tail create the opportunity for consumers to find exactly what they want among the unlimited choices offered by organizations, customers need help to understand what choices are most relevant to them. Organizations are having trouble supporting outsourced global operations while retaining the high-quality service that the audience expects. Either way, the audience is getting the short end of the bargain, with the long-term impact still largely unknown. This is why online search function ability and ease of use are incredibly important. But it goes beyond that as well. The audience doesn't just need choice. They need some guidance.

Growing up, Brian used to visit the Tower Records store on the post road in Westport, Connecticut, at least twice a week. The manager of the store was a young guy, maybe mid-20s, wearing a standard uniform of a concert roadie: T-shirt with ripped sleeves, arms and neck covered in tattoos, piercings everywhere. This was almost certainly not the presentation that Tower Records, a corporate music giant at the time, would have expected in a place like Westport. But he remained manager for more than a decade at the same location, and the reason was obvious. Whenever Brian visited the store in search of a musical purchase, he would ask this young man's guidance on what to buy. Sometimes Brian would supply the genre—heavy metal, for example (he was a Metallica, Guns 'n' Roses, and Poison fan growing up)—and ask what CD he would recommend. The clerk's answer would typically reference something available in the store as well as less mainstream offerings that Brian could order to satisfy his musical curiosity. His expertise was evident and his advice could be trusted. He not only delivered valuable information but also helped Brian to understand which choices were best for musical interests. The quality shopping experience resulted in a lot of purchases over time and a diverse love of music.

Customers still want this personal guidance, even in an online environment. That explains, at least in part, the reliance that people put on customer reviews when they visit Amazon.com or the Best Buy Web site. It is the same factor that has differentiated Tivo and its ability to 'know' what programming you are interested in based on your behavior, from regular television.

Good advice and a trusted voice are sometimes not enough. Over the past 10 years Anheuser-Busch, [which is a client of Mindshare Interactive Campaigns, Dan's company], has expanded the number of beers, coolers, and other alcoholic drinks it offers, from 26 brands in 1997 to 80 brands in 2007. The company now offers organic beers, drinks targeted to women, microbrews such as Bare Knuckle Stout and ZiegenBock (available only in Texas), and even a nonallergenic beer selection.[5] Chris Anderson calls this, not surprisingly, the Long Tail of Beer. Anyway, to market these niche offerings, Anheuser-Busch began offering unique experiences for their audience to sample these beers. One such example is a beer-pairing dinner. Modeled after wine-pairing dinners commonly offered at vineyards and fine restaurants, these events are intended to introduce various beers as a core element of the food experience.

Brent Wertz, the chief executive chef at Kingsmill Resort in Williamsburg, Virginia (an Anheuser-Busch property), is one of the innovators in offering beer-pairing dinners and organizes them regularly for groups visiting his resort. He plans his menu around beer, marinates and cooks with it, and passionately recommends beer as a component of every course. His advocacy of beer is not simply a sales pitch for his employer; the dinners actually allow Wertz, and Anheuser-Busch, to introduce beers in an ideal context. By doing so, they help customers understand the wide array of products and their even wider number of appropriate and recommended applications or uses. And, it builds or solidifies a customer base for both companies, by creating an environment where people can get together, share good food, good beer, and good conversation, and expand their knowledge of both food and beer in the process.

Please Hold for the Next Available Operator

Almost everybody, it seems, has at least one story, about bad customer service. Media critic Jeff Jarvis has recounted his frustrations on his blog, BuzzMachine.com, about issues he had getting a faulty Dell computer to function properly. Jarvis' story has become infamous, known online and offline as 'Dell Hell." Further, a whole movement now exists behind Web sites like www.ihatedell.net to collect and help promote stories. In response, Dell was forced to invest upwards of $100 million to address issues with its production and customer service operations.

As Louise Lee wrote in *BusinessWeek* in October 2005, Dell created a whole slate of new support offerings, including "remote assistance so technicians can take control of the customer's PC to fix problems . . . and a series of one-year memberships so customers can opt for various levels of help, at various prices." One of the options Dell offered was a quarterly PC tune-up, in which a techie would remotely clean up the hard drive and check security settings, presumably to preempt any major issues (which would be much costlier for Dell to fix and more frustrating for the customer to deal with) from occurring. "All of this adds up to a quiet attempt to reset customer expectations in the PC industry." (*Hanging Up On Dell?* by Louise Lee and Emily Thornton. BusinessWeek. October 10, 2005)

This not only suggests the importance of excellent customer service but the growing power of the consumer to do something about it.

Seth Godin, the business and marketing guru of *Purple Cow* (New York: Portfolio, 2003) and *Small Is the New Big* (2006) fame, suggested in a blog post last year that "Customer service is broken."[6] He cited three reasons:

1. *The Internet has taught us to demand everything immediately (and perfect).* As a result, we expect that every single time we pick up the phone or deal with someone in a retail setting, we'll be dealing with the Senior Vice President of Customer Satisfaction, the head of accounting and the chief of quality control, all at the same time. We expect instant results and undivided attention.
2. *The rapid proliferation of choice has taught us to demand that everything should be cheap.* As a result, we won't pay extra for superior service, which means companies need to hire cheap.
3. *The availability of blogs and other public histories means that it is harder than ever to treat different customers differently.* Word gets out.

Godin continues: "As a result of these three inexorable trends, companies are on the defense. They are forced to add a new layer to their pyramid, and yes, it's on the bottom. This layer consists of lots and lots of people, the cheapest the company can find. These folks are ill-trained, poorly supported and under lots of pressure. There is a lot of turnover (what a surprise) and most are working with nothing more than a simple manual and a lot of metrics."

Right on, Seth! Providing a high level of training to manage most complex customer service challenges requires extraordinary investment of both money and time—not exactly what most companies who have chosen outsourcing to save money want to hear.

The Solution: Guided Choice

The solution is for organizations to help guide the choices that customers make. Making all the options available to a consumer may be possible because of the growth of technology, the dominance of the Internet, and the cost-effectiveness of globalization, but customers need help to understand how to differentiate between millions of choices. And organizations can help with that.

Consider how newspapers function. For much of their history, newspapers seemed to just throw together words and pictures. Then along came Edmund Arnold, a consultant in graphic arts design and former typographer, editor, and publisher, and brought about dramatic changes in newspaper design. As his obituary (Arnold died February 2, 2007) read: "At his peak in the 1960s, Arnold helped implement changes that have since become standard, including bigger type and a shift from eight narrow columns to a more legible six columns of print. He also pioneered the use of a modular layout in which stories were packaged in squares instead of long, haphazard chutes of text that might jump unexpectedly to the next column. He argued for photographs that enhanced a story, rather than those plopped in as meaningless decoration, such as obligatory head shots."[7] Those changes remain in effect to this day.

Now consider what Jakob Nielsen, a user advocate and analyst of online design who is often called "the king of usability," wrote about the design of Amazon.com:[8]

> Amazon's product pages are littered with extraneous features, ranging from a "Gold Box" over a "wish list spree" to promotions

for reading glasses and other irrelevant products. A single book page I analyzed contained 259 links and buttons. It was so cluttered that key product information—like publication date, page count, and average review rating—was three full screens below the fold (on a standard 1024 x 768 screen). Cluttered pages might work for Amazon because its users are typically long-time customers who know the features and can easily screen them out. Although first-time visitors are no doubt overwhelmed, by now they account for a tiny percentage of Amazon's revenues . . .

Try buying a Mozart concerto or a plasma TV on Amazon. Unless you know in advance the exact product you want, Amazon's category pages make it basically impossible to identify the best offerings. Using a single e-commerce engine for thirty-one different product categories has fueled Amazon's tremendous growth. The cost to customers, however, is poor support for each product type's special requirements. If you're selling classical music, you're better off studying the best classical sites rather than copying Amazon's design. Something that works for popular music fails for a genre in which a single composer can be represented on thousands of CDs.

The comparison is striking. As the Internet has gained prominence in our daily lives, the conventions of programmers have replaced the commonsense elements that support good customer support and marketing. Amazon.com has proven itself with its core audience of middle-age, high-income, educated online users. While these repeat users are very likely to find what they are looking for using the search function, they may not be aware of the full range of products Amazon.com offers—several hundred thousand products in all. The home page spotlights a variety of items, based on user behavior, popularity of items, and so on, but with an unlimited number of choices, what is the likelihood a site visitor will stop there? To help expand the interests of customers, the introduction of a tour guide to the site that engages visitors directly to help personalize their shopping experience would go a long way.

For example, the guide might ask visitors about their specific interests or ask them some questions related to current events within a certain vertical (books, music, food, etc.). While the order tracking and other customer recognition tools record all the activity a certain user has completed on the site, they don't recognize which were gifts, what your purpose for visiting at a certain time might be (and whether it is different than another time), and so on. The guide could take the collected knowledge and show results, highlight key areas, even make product recommendations based on the data the visitor provided. We understand that much of the Amazon.com product presentation process is already driven by data, but we believe engaging customers directly during their visits, instead of relying primarily on historical shopping behavior, would present a different set of options for Amazon.com to build customer relationships.

And it shouldn't be limited to online organizations. Forth & Towne, a retail concept by Gap Inc., was formed to tackle a similar challenge off-line. The stores catered to female consumers, described by the *Seattle Times* as "women who have outgrown Banana Republic but aren't ready for Talbots." (*Gap's latest venture wants every woman to have a style consultant. By Melissa Allison and Monica Soto OuchiSeattle Times. February 2, 2007*) Each location was equipped with at least one style consultant. The style consultants were trained to recommend pieces in the most flattering silhouettes and to point out styles and products that an average shopper might not otherwise be aware of. At the center of each store was a circular fitting salon that helped focus the energy of the shopper on her fitting experience, and simultaneously allowed her to receive total focus from the store's associates.

This level of service shouldn't be limited to organizations that are selling something, either. On the Web site for DonorsChoose, an innovative not-for-profit organization, teachers submit project proposals for things their students need to learn. These ideas become classroom reality when concerned individuals choose projects to fund. The idea for DonorsChoose was born out of a unique opportunity that Charles Best, who launched the non-profit organization and continues as its CEO today thought of one day in the lunchroom.

"I taught at a high school in the Bronx for five years and it was just during my first year of teaching that my colleagues and I would be in the teachers' lunchroom, always having the same conversation about books that we wanted our students to read and art supplies that we needed to do an art project and a field trip we had just conceived of," Best told us. "And, you know, we couldn't bring any of these ideas to life. Most of us would just buy paper and pencils for our students out of our own money. And then on the donor side it was really just common sense, it wasn't any careful study of the landscape that made me figure that people are just getting skeptical about writing a $100 check to a charity and wondering if it went into a black hole and not really knowing where the money went." Donors were most concerned with having an impact, and having a choice. "Actually, what they really emphasized was: I can choose where my money's going and I can direct my own dollars."

DonorsChoose doesn't operate like a traditional nonprofit organization—writing lots of grant applications to foundations and the government, sending out direct mail solicitations with a picture of a kid or a puppy on it, or holding a bunch of black-tie dinners. "We're really about marketing citizen philanthropy to the general populace. We are about marketing citizen philanthropy via the internet and via some viral methods to the general populace," Best told us.

According to the DonorsChoose Web site (www.donorschoose. org), "Proposals range from 'Magical Math Centers' ($200) to 'Big Book Bonanza' ($320), to 'Cooking Across the Curriculum' ($1,100). Any individual can search such proposals by areas of interest, learn about classroom needs, and choose to fund the project(s) they find most compelling." DonorsChoose then makes sure that "donors receive a feedback package of student photos and thank-you notes, and a teacher impact letter," as well as an expenditure report showing that their tax-deductible gift was spent as directed.

The concept of guided choice focuses on helping an audience move toward the decision that is best for them (and that may happen to correspond with what you are offering). Organizations typically believe they can control every element of an experience—in most cases by offering every conceivable option for an experience with the expectation that everyone is going to find something they like. This is not as helpful as it seems. The focus should be on the overall presentation that organizations give to their audience, and on making sure that the resultant experience has met the audience's expectations.

An alternative to reducing variety would be to help consumers navigate the variety that exists. Sometimes this can be done by identifying alternatives by their use rather than their features. As Harvard business professor John Gourville wrote, "Dell sometimes identifies their desktop computers in terms of who they are intended to serve. The result is a 'gaming' desktop, a 'home office' desktop, an 'Internet-ready' desktop, and so on. Rather than worry about what specs you require, you get the desktop that meets your profile." Most companies do this at least implicitly in their marketing, but naming it makes the impact stronger—your audience knows you are talking to them.

Other manufacturers take this a step further and actually walk you through the decision-making process. Gourville says, "At one point Titleist asked potential purchasers a series of questions, the answers to which would result in the recommendation of a particular golf ball. By saying you tended to hit far but off line, you'd have one ball recommended to you. By saying you tended to be good around the green but short off the tee, you'd have another ball recommended to you. In all these cases, by either reducing the number of alternatives or helping consumers through the decision-making process, a company can reduce the complexity of the choice and reduce the consumer's feeling that they might be making the wrong choice."

The proliferation of technology certainly makes it easier for you to offer more, and cheaper, choices to your audience. But that does not mean you should make the choice to go in that direction simply because you can. Is that what your audience wants? Use new technology to help improve your communication with your audience so that they recognize the effort you have expended and return it with their investment in your long-term relationship. Be a guide.

CHAPTER 6

Be Choosy

Innovative thinkers and doers instinctively say yes. But "no" is a necessary option.

Richard Branson, the founder and chairman of the Virgin Group, is a billionaire, world-class traveler and adventurer, and, a global business genius. Despite all the things he does well and has had success doing in his life, there is something he struggles with: saying no. In fact, he told *Business 2.0* magazine the key to being a successful person was to "Learn How to Say No (Even If You're Known As 'Dr. Yes'). He said he turns people down with extreme difficulty sometimes, becasuse the people he is saying no to "are people I don't want to discourage." He adds, it should be difficult to say no, and you have to be good at it to be successful. "I often used to dodge doing it myself, and hide behind other people and delegate it, but if you're the boss, that isn't the right thing to do," he wrote.[1]

The Business Culture of "Yes"

Whether it's out of politeness, fear of rejection, the desire to seize every opportunity, doers and connected people have a habitual need to say yes all of the time. We've even created a business mythology around it.

When you walk into the flagship store of Stew Leonard's, the "World's Largest Dairy Store," located in Norwalk, Connecticut, the first thing you see is the company's corporate policy carved into a piece of rock. It reads:

> Rule #1: The customer is always right!
>
> Rule #2: If the customer is ever wrong, reread rule #1.

The origin of this concept that the customer is always right, known more commonly as the Golden Rule of Business, dates back to the early twentieth century and is most commonly associated with Marshall Field's, the famous Chicago-based department store. Either Harry Gordon Selfridge, the founder of London's Selfridges store (opened in 1909), or Marshall Field himself, for whom Selfridge worked from 1879 to 1901, was the first to utter the phrase, though nobody knows for sure which one did. Either way, Marshall Field and Harry Gordon Selfridge changed the way organizations thought about their relationship with customers—and not necessarily for the better. They were trying to make the customer feel special by giving their staff the disposition to behave as if the customers were right, even when they weren't, but in doing so they have created a monster.

And the current media environment, which amplifies the voices of consumers, makes it more compelling to say "yes" all of the time.

A key part of the evolution of our media culture is the integration of user-generated content—or, more generally, the role that the audience plays in how the work of organizations is now conducted. Jackie Huba, who co-wrote *Creating Customer Evangelists* (New York: Kaplan Business, 2002), told us, "I think that the pressure to listen to customers has never been more than now. The great opportunity is that there are so many tools you can use to do it now, and scale that feedback. Get more of it, and more focused feedback, and have 24/7 groups where you can ask for feedback." It has everyone, corporations, nonprofits, even the individuals who are now being invited to join the conversation, scrambling to adapt and accommodate. We are witnessing a radical shift of control.

Huba made clear that she thinks the audience understands that a company can't do everything its customers want. "What they want is a company that's responsive. Let your customers tell you why you are not able to meet their needs on certain things, and then think together about other ways that you and your customers can work together to help address that issue that you have. It's about feedback, it's about getting insight that you, the organization, can use. And these are people who want to participate. But they wouldn't be there and be giving up the time if they didn't feel something towards the company, that they want to help them."

When an organization listens and releases some of its tight controls, there are potential risks. In March 2006, Chevrolet introduced a Web site allowing visitors to take existing video clips and music, insert their own words and create a customized 30-second commercial for the 2007 Chevrolet Tahoe. Users were given a series of video clips depicting the Tahoe in natural settings, like driving through snowy mountain ranges or perched at the edge of a rushing waterfall, along with eight different soundtracks and an option to add text to narrate the commercial. The campaign successfully compelled online users to forward videos to their friends online, but the most popular videos were critical of the Tahoe for its fuel efficiency. The *New York Times* cited two critical ads. "Our planet's oil is almost gone," said one. "You don't need G.P.S. to see where this road leads." Another commercial asked: "Like this snowy wilderness? Better get your fill of it now. Then say hello to global warming."[2]

Chevy deserves credit for handing creative reins over to its audience in such a public way. Unfortunately, the lesson most organizations took from that episode was that consumers couldn't be trusted with much, if any, control. *BusinessWeek* noted:

> Most companies are wholly unprepared to deal with the new nastiness that's erupting online. That's worrisome as the Web moves closer to being the prime advertising medium—and reputational conduit—of our time. 'The CEOs of the largest 50 companies in the world are practically hiding under their desks in terror about Internet rumors,' says top crisis manager Eric Dezenhall, author of the upcoming book *Damage Control*. 'Millions of dollars in labor are being spent discussing whether or not you should respond on the Web.'[3]

We think the opposite is true. The lesson that organizations should have taken from the Chevy Tahoe incident, and dozens of other experiments like it, is that there is an appropriate balance for an organization to provide control to its audience as long as it has a plan in place to respond when things don't go as expected. As an organization you have to figure out what that means for you.

The demand from the audience is for an organization to always say yes. The appropriate thing for the organization to do is only saying yes. The rest of the time you have to come up with another answer.

"Just Do It. . . Differently."

Starting in 2001 stay-at-home activist, Noah Peretti, who tried to make a point about Nike's work with overseas sweatshops, applies here. In 2001, Nike offered customers the opportunity to buy a pair of its shoes and, for a fee, the company would personalize your shoes by stitching any name, word, or phrase you want under the Nike swoosh. It was called the "Nike ID" program, which the company Web site advertises as being "about freedom to choose and freedom to express who you are."

The goal, of course, was to have people put their name, a personal motto, or a motivational word on the shoe. Noah Peretti sent in his money and the word he wanted—only to get back a form letter stating that his personal ID was rejected for one or more of the following reasons: (1) it contains someone else's trademark, (2) it contains the name of an athlete whose name is not licensed to Nike, or (3) it contains profanity or inappropriate slang. What was the word that Peretti had hoped to adorn his shoe with? *Sweatshop.*

Peretti resubmitted his word choice to Nike. He politely pointed out the word is not a trademark, an athlete's name, or profanity. He wrote: "I chose the ID because I wanted to remember the toil of the children who made my shoes. Could you please ship them to me immediately? Thanks and Happy New Year."

Nike sent another rejection letter, this one asserting that *sweatshops* was inappropriate slang. This conversation went back and forth for a while. Peretti wrote back, saying that in *Webster's Dictionary* "I discovered that sweatshop is in fact part of standard English, and not slang. The word means, 'a shop or factory in which workers are employed for long hours at low wages and under unhealthy conditions.'" Again Nike said no, claiming that small print on its Web site allows it to reject any "material we consider inappropriate or simply do not want to place on our products."

Nike has an obligation to protect its brand and its relationship with customers, two things that—in this situation and many others like it—are in conflict with each other. Nike had positioned itself appropriately, listing which types of messages were not appropriate. Its failure came on two fronts: Nike was not able to sync the explanation of its policy with the wider belief, particular among activists, that it was using sweatshop labor to produce its shoes; and it did not make the effort to truly connect with Mr. Peretti to negotiate a reasonable resolution to the issue.

In this case, Nike met a challenge with which it was not prepared to engage in a serious battle. Peretti sent the e-mail chain to 10 friends, who forwarded it to 10 more friends, and so on, until the exchange became something of an Internet legend, transforming Peretti—who had never protested against Nike and swears he was just goofing with the company's lofty marketing rhetoric—into a hero of anti-Nike crusaders. The news spread on the Web and will forever be associated with Nike—and continues to this day to be referenced in articles and case studies about how corporations should and should not engage online.

"No."

Your clients, your customers, your audience are always right about their needs, wants, and perspectives. They are not always right about you and what you will do. "No" is important. Survival depends on your ability to say it at the right time.

In the new media world, the concept of personalization or customer ownership can go too far. Organizations have the option to say no when that happens, to protect both themselves and the consumer. More than an option, it's a necessity. When customers are abusive, disrespectful, or fail to take any of your suggestions or recommendations, all they do is absorb valuable resources that could be applied toward customers who would clearly appreciate it more. Fire them. Politely decline to do business with them. Refer them to your competitors. Take them off the mailing list. Don't make promises you can't keep. Don't be rude—just move on.

Imagine someone going to shop for a pair of pants. They need something that is simple and comfortable, dressy, yet easy to clean (without having to go a dry cleaner)—the kind of pants you could wear to work, out socially, or on the weekend to take in a movie without being over- or underdressed for any occasion. In all likelihood, you can't find that pair of pants—the size, the color, the fit, something just won't be right. Why not? There simply isn't a market for a pair of pants that is perfectly suited to you only. And for good reason: The perfect pair of pants is a one-of-a-kind offering. The customer won't value a simple pair of pants enough to pay one-of-a-kind prices. And in all likelihood, the company producing such pants would have trouble making a profit by catering to the needs of customers one at a time.

So organizations standardize and generalize, and segments of the audience are left out. Some businesses succeed with their one-of-a-kind items, but they are small, niche enterprises. The rest of the companies produce something fit for a larger audience, and the customers adapt to whatever is available. And everyone settles—on a color that isn't their favorite but still looks good, on a size that is close but not as flattering as it could be, or on a business that is interesting, but doesn't serve the greatest customer need in the end. This is the old way of operating—this is changing.

With advances in technology, customization on a mass scale seems possible now. In the past, a few major retailers or organizations defined what was popular and should be sold on store shelves or similar, and the whole production capacity for organizations flattened. Now groups are able to offer services online at a fraction of the cost. On the Internet, information becomes more of a commodity and users are empowered to find, or create, exactly what they want. In an interview, Chris Anderson told us:

> Brick and mortar businesses cannot compete with the Internet in terms of choice and variety. That is no longer what brick and mortar business is for. Brick and mortar is for convenience, for tactile, equalities, experiences. It's broadly to provide the most popular products. Wal-Mart is for the head and the internet is for the tail. Supermarkets are for the head and internet is for the tail. This is a pretty natural division of labor. Brick and mortar is largely for the most popular items that turn the average store often enough to pay the rent on the shelf-base. Only popular items can do that, and there's nothing wrong with that—that's what retail's for. There are other elements involving service and again the tactile qualities that maybe in certain categories, such as clothes, remain important; and obviously perishable goods,

like milk, will remain a classic [item] for bricks and mortar. You
can't do something that isn't done on the Internet. You cannot
beat the internet in terms of variety.

Naturally, the long tail changes the relationship between organizations and their audience. The audience has expectations of what
they can get, how, and when. If you want a single song instead of a
whole CD worth of music, you can buy it at iTunes. If you want to
rent an independent film on DVD that your video store doesn't keep
stocked, you can find it through Netflix. Now you can have things
your way.

Some organizations try to offer this off-line. Frank Kern, a senior marketing officer at Starbucks, told us the global coffee chain is
structured to offer the same personalized opportunity to its customers. If you want your double tall, half-caf, extra hot, skinny latte with
room at the top, you simply walk up to the counter at Starbucks (or
a dozen other coffee places nearby) and order it. Frank said:

> Customization is very much what the brand is about, and how we
> truly are somewhat unique. We are a space that can be utilized
> however our customer sees it. And in our product offering, it is
> a very personal experience. A customer can create anything they
> want—that's part of the enjoyment of Starbucks, that it is a very
> customized, very personal experience. So in so many ways, it's
> not a matter of us defining the brand for the customer. It's the
> customers defining the brand based on how they choose to use
> us, whether it's the creation of product, a customized beverage,
> or whether it's through the space and how they use it.

Audiences increasingly want to customize their information and
experiences so that they only have to consume the data or spend
their time on things that are most interesting and relevant to them.
Think of a MyYahoo page. This shift works online because there are
vast amounts of information online that can be sorted and categorized to fit any user's need. Customization by users saves them time
and fits the individualized lifestyle of today's modern society where
people have several very special interests and hobbies. It also puts a
premium on how good or relevant that information is to a user.

In short, people expect to get what they want, when they want
it, and how they want it. There is a strong demand for localized,

specialized, and individualized content with high quality and additional value like shopping assistants. Technology has made so many of these options easier to provide and more available, their value in the eyes of the audience has decreased. The audience demands something of an organization, is not interested in paying extra for the personalized attention, and it is left to the organizations to determine how to respond.

It is simply not possible for an organization to cater to the specific demands of every individual audience member at a reasonable price. There are little additions or changes, extra services, that any organization can provide to satisfy the demands and expectations of its audience. But when each and every individual customer or member starts to demand something specialized about their product or service, organizations can't keep up. So, when the customer's demands make it impossible for a business to provide high-quality service or sell products at a profit because of the expectations the customer has of them, it is time to say no.

Audiences, customers, clients have learned how to game the system. They know that organizations are desperate for their support and are afraid to offend them. So, when an organization promotes a policy of catering to customer desires—as virtually every single one does—customers try to take an unfair advantage.

Southwest Airlines knows how to balance this well. As its history explains, "They began with one simple notion: If you get your passengers to their destinations when they want to get there, on time, at the lowest possible fares, and make darn sure they have a good time doing it, people will fly your airline."[4] They were trying to do all the things that the rest of the airline industry wasn't willing to do. And they were extraordinarily successful doing it. They built a brand and business on the foundation of a strong relationship with their customers and the extra level of service they provided. Herb Kelleher, the company's CEO, described some of the letters he got:

> A guy has a heart attack at Love Field [in Dallas]. He goes to the hospital. Our ticket agent stays there all night, calling his wife to let her know how he's doing. I got a letter from a passenger on another airline who said: "Herb, I couldn't believe it. I had gotten off the airline, went to the parking lot, and I had a flat tire. And one of your people came along and changed the tire

for me, and I said: You know I didn't fly Southwest Airlines. He said: I don't care. That has nothing to do with whether you fly Southwest Airlines." That's the kind of folks that we want.[5]

Their customers, however, quickly learned to expect that the airline would do almost anything to make them happy. There is a story, some say an urban legend, about a Southwest Airlines customer nicknamed the "Pen Pal" because after every flight she wrote in with a complaint. She complained about the absence of seat assignments, a first-class section, and meals. She didn't like the boarding procedure or the flight attendants' sporty uniforms, she disliked the casual atmosphere, and she abhorred peanuts! Her last letter, reciting a litany of complaints, momentarily stumped Southwest's customer relations people. Southwest has a policy of answering every customer letter, so they sent it to Herb Kelleher for advice and inspiration. In sixty seconds, Herb Kelleher penned the response: "Dear Mrs. Crabapple, We'll miss you. Love, Herb."

There is no excuse for a customer treating you or your employees with anything less than respect and courtesy, presuming that you are offering the same first and in return. Southwest Airlines goes above and beyond the call of duty for their customers and the majority appreciate it and respond with loyalty and admiration for the airline. For the few that don't, including Mrs. Crabapple, the moment they crossed that line, Herb Kelleher had permission to kick them to the curb.

How to Say No

Many organizations know deep down that it is appropriate to say no to unreasonable demands. In a lot of cases they aren't sure what qualifies as being unreasonable. In other cases they just don't know how to say no. It is certainly different for every organization and type of organization. For some it relates to profits and loss while for others it has to do with reputation and loyalty. In all cases it is more about common sense and reasonable behavior than anything else.

If any member of your audience is being rude, you have permission to say no; there is never any excuse for someone treating you poorly—never. If it is a client, even a lucrative one, and they don't treat your people well, show them the door. If someone in your audience requests something that gives them a special advantage that nobody else is entitled to, don't do it. The last thing you want is to create an obvious inequity that will cause widespread frustration or resentment.

Here are some other situations in which it is appropriate for organizations to say no.

Don't Offer Unreasonable Choices in the First Place

Have you ever talked a prospective customer out of buying something from you? Have you told a donor that their money would be put to better use in another organization? It seems unnatural, but in some situations it's the right thing to do. It is probably better not to make a sale, or take a contribution, if that person is ultimately going to be unhappy with his decision. That's part of the reason he contacted you in the first place—to get your input about what the best option was for him. Saying no is a lot better than committing to something that isn't right.

You have lots of options in a situation like this. You can simply suggest that the service or product you offer is not the right one for him and end the conversation. You can recommend an alternative product or service, giving the person the sense that you are fully committed to his well-being. Sometimes just offering information that helps the person decide whether a purchase is right for him, even if it doesn't come out in your favor, is the best thing.

Organizations have the right—an obligation even—to say no when the situation threatens the focus of the organization or its relationship with its audience. But organizations must also make clear what levels of control they are going to try to have, when, and where, and can't simply make up the parameters on the fly (or at least not without some criticism).

Here are some solid reasons to say no:

- *The project isn't something you have the resources to do right now.* Alan Khazei and Michael Brown, the co-founders of City Year, a national service program, told us, "When we first started launching new City Year programs around the country, we had some loose guidelines. What we've learned over time, through a lot of trial and error, is we need these ten things and if those ten things—which don't guarantee success, but make it more likely—aren't in place, it won't be sustainable. It takes funding up front, over a multiyear period (everybody wants to fund something for the first year, but then the next new thing comes along), and if we don't have broad-based community support up front, we struggle."

- *The level of effort and the return don't line up.* Ben Goldhirsch, the founder and publisher of *GOOD Magazine*, a publication that balances news with an interest in the social good, told us, "I would say no probably 99.9 percent of the time when the problem is that the resources, the capital, aren't available. We might have the greatest story to tell, the greatest artist or writer to tell that story—a person who really deserves our energy and support. But with all the energy that we have to put into producing a good magazine, a great film, and supporting great people, we can't do everything. We have to be very careful. And I don't mind—as long as we respect everyone who's asking, I have no problems saying no."

- *It's distracting from your core objectives.* Frank Kern from Starbucks told us, "I think that it's really important that as we grow, that we, at the end, are true to our core. We're very mindful of that, and at the core, we're a coffeehouse. So I think we're comfortable in expanding the brand into those areas that still accentuate the coffeehouse experience, if you will. And I think music, books, for instance, would fall within that. We have an internal policy that says 'Just say yes.' Part of the connection that we want to have with our customers is that we always want to be able to serve them in any way we can, including being a part of the community. We're asked to provide coffee service at parties, or we're asked to provide donations to some local raffle, or something like that. And we always try to. We always want to be open to their point of view and any of their suggestions. I think whenever possible, we would always say yes, or we would always try and do whatever we could for our customers. But if it doesn't fit, if it doesn't help reinforce that core, then we will say no."

- *You disagree with the audience about what is best.* Tom Gerace from Gather.com, a social network, told us, "We will have conflicts with subsets of the community, for sure. We already do. But I think the bigger decisions are product decisions where it's impossible for us to please everybody because there's a huge breadth of opinion. And we walk a difficult line. And frankly I think the most important thing we can do in that case is to have a dialogue with the community. To hear and discuss all perspectives, then after we've considered them fairly and had the long debate, to show them the respect back and let them know what we agree with, disagree with, and what we're going to do. And for the most part I think we earn the respect. You know everybody knows they can't get their money 100 percent of the time. For the most part, I think in a community there are going to be folks that go away, or that strike, and we've got a unique platform because people can strike. But I think that we can navigate—you know, we can get 80 percent of the world to be happy because they'll get their way enough of the time and respect when they don't if we engage them in the process."

There are exceptions to the rule. Consultants routinely take a loss on a project with a new client in the interest of building a relationship or developing a unique case study. Similarly, organizations will pilot programs at the request of a particular donor or investor, or to engage only a very small audience, because they value the learning and relationships that will come from that effort. But you don't want to make a habit of stretching your resources or putting up with overly demanding elements of your audience as a matter of practice.

Protecting your employees is an important element of saying no. It is not hard to imagine that employees who are happy at work provide better service. They care more about other people, including customers, and they put more energy and focus into their work because they want to excel. When they aren't happy, employees stop caring about service. When they feel like they are being abused, taken advantage of, or hung out to dry, it may be even worse. Some customers are quite simply bad for your operation because they drive down the morale of your team or consume resources that could be better spent on the rest of your audience.

Every organization faces these types of challenges, in person but especially now that more and more information can travel freely—and anonymously online. But each organization must determine what the appropriate response should be for its space and its interests. When it comes to saying no, a standard response, while easy for you, is not enough. Unlike needing to personalize your product line or organizational mission to suit everyone, making sure that your customer understands the reason why their request was denied is absolutely key.

Exclusivity Is the Most Polite Way of Saying No

If you say no enough, you become exclusive. And if you are good and exclusive, you are definitely more valuable.

Mark Lukasiewicz at NBC News practices this, explaining,

> Almost all of our work appears in ways that we control. We decide. We try to make it as widely available as we can. But, I am not currently putting our news content, on a regular basis, on YouTube. I don't feel I have a need to. Our news is on MSN, one of the most widely distributed portals, on a free Web site, well served, well enabled by technology. It is not any problem for anybody to find our content freely any time they want to. But it is also an environment that we help to control, and ensure presents the best news content. So I don't have a problem with that.
>
> Now, I don't yet—*yet*—enable people to share our content in a way that YouTube has enabled people to share. Do I want people to be able to randomly re-edit a three minute report from our Baghdad correspondent? To take out that which they don't like and reassemble it in a way that fits their view of reality better? No. I don't want them to be able to do that.

Lisa Poulson says that the concept of exclusivity works to build trust as well. She explained, "Consider the relationship you have with a reporter, or a partner. You say 'I will give you this small thing as an exclusive, but you can't source it back to me.' You continue this, giving them more, and more, and more. And over time, you build up a pretty significant trusting relationship, because you have helped them do their job and given something to them that nobody else can claim." And then, what do you get in return?

Exclusivity does not mean scarcity. For example, NBC News releases hours and hours of programming, some of which appears on their daily broadcasts, but much more that is valuable and compelling because it hasn't appeared on the broadcast news. You can be exclusive with lots of competitors as well, offering slightly different and unique versions of whatever you create. But giving up control, allowing any audience to simply adapt your content without your knowledge or participation, has its limitations. In the end, saying no to the right people at the right time in the right way can be great for the bottom line, or to add credibility and generate interest in what you produce to the point you gain an even larger audience.

As an organization, you must plan and execute your efforts so that you remain in control and focused on your core goals, while still giving an appropriate amount of input and deference to your audience. There are numerous pieces to the relationship you have with your audience—how you initially engage them, how each individual transaction is handled (whether that is a purchase or some sort of other exchange or conversation), how you deliver your product or service, and how well you follow up and connect between cycles. You won't always get all the pieces right, but knowing which ones are wrong and how to say no when they are is a key element to ongoing success.

CHAPTER 7

Be a Fighter

Conflict with your audience is inevitable.

You have your plan for how to manage your organization. Your audience has its own ideas and expectations.

You set the vision and expend blood, sweat, and tears to make your organization run. Your audience gets to make a snap decision about whether your idea is solid.

You create the products, provide the services, and create the experiences. Your audience chooses whether to invest, become members, or make purchases.

You have big plans and goals. They think its all about them.

You have made the choice to say no or to be exclusive. They don't like being told no.

Again, conflict is inevitable.

Managing a dynamic organization is challenging enough. When you consider the need to win approval, build loyalty, or monetize a relationship with an audience on top of everything else, it is no surprise that things get more complicated and more confusing. Add in the fact that the audience's expectations of quality, speed of delivery, and price competitiveness have become so high, as a result of the advances in technology and the rise of competitiveness in the marketplace, it may not be possible to fully satisfy your audience all of the time anymore (if it ever was possible).

All the more reason that you should never give up or stray from your mission of offering valuable information, a compelling experience, or high-quality stuff to your audience. Trust that your instincts, experience, research, and the effort you put in every day will carry your organization forward to success.

That's not easy to do when you have a frustrated customer standing in front of you complaining that your product is not what she wanted. It is not easy to do when you have a donor or investor on the phone and they want to hear that you are committed to a program they think is important, but you don't necessarily see playing a key part in your strategy. More often than not we try to defuse these situations by giving people what they asked for—bending over backwards sometimes to make it happen and make them happy.

But giving in to your audience, delivering exactly what they want, when and how they want it, is a short-term strategy. You may make a sale or win support that one time; you might survive that phone call or face-off. But, as your organization grows and your relationship with your audience progresses, doing whatever it takes to please your audience will become increasingly difficult and you will find yourself unable to do what is best for your organization.

What should you do when that conflict arises? Pick a fight.

It seems counterintuitive. But if you expect loyalty and attention from your audience, you have to fight for it. Besides, it is dramatically more expensive and time consuming to acquire a new audience than it is to manage an existing one. It doesn't benefit anyone to have an audience that isn't in line with what you are trying to do. So, rather than just managing them, satisfying them or coddling them, show them you want their support and their loyalty. Demonstrate to them how important they are to your success. Tell them things they don't always want to hear. You need to show your audience that you are working hard, with their interests in mind, but that sometimes you are right and what you are doing is worth fighting for.

If you do, the good ones will come back.

There will always be situations, like the one Southwest Airlines faced with Mrs. Crabapple, where fighting will have no impact, and thus isn't worth it. There is also a difference between picking a fight and issuing an apology. Organizations make mistakes all the time, and someone in your audience is likely to be one of the first to notice. Before the press, before your investors, even before most of your colleagues and employees find out, someone in your audience is likely to know the story and is ready to talk. Why? They were probably affected—the indiscretion happened when they were in your store, on the phone with your customer service team, or using one of your products or services. It doesn't matter what went wrong, big or small: any attempts to cover up a mistake, gloss over it, or try to explain it away are almost certain to fall short. So apologize. And don't delay—particularly in the connected age when bad news can travel so quickly. When you screw up, say you are sorry. Your audience knows when a mistake was made and they will forgive you (in most cases) if you acknowledge it.

Again, if you do, the good ones will come back.

Where Conflict Comes From

Do you know where conflict comes from? There are plenty of obvious candidates. Bad communication can turn a seemingly innocuous situation into a major conflict. A lack of information—when the people involved in the decision-making process are in the dark about what they have to do—always seems to lead to a bad result. And the need for control and predictability, particularly right now, when those things are hard to come by, make any situation more challenging than it really needs to be. The short answer is, conflict comes from a lot of places, and more often than not we bring it on ourselves.

The environment that organizations operate in today is changing dramatically. What we have always known about how to operate businesses, manage nonprofits, or even conduct ourselves as individuals has shifted. It is scary not knowing what you are dealing with, and in some cases even scarier to *know*.

Of course, in any situation, you are dealing with an audience—*your* audience. Audiences have expectations. They have ever-changing wants and needs. They expect to get what they ordered, no matter what it is you offer. Like everyone else, they want the best value for their money. In the end, whether they are a core part of your audience yet or not, each segment of an audience has specific wants and needs that must be addressed and prioritized if an organization is to serve it successfully.

With the rise of technology and the reach of the Internet, an organization is at risk of having any member of its audience—knowledgeable or not—become a powerful critic. The Bivings Report noted:

> In the past when a company goofed up with a patron, the snafu remained relatively unknown. The customer likely was disgruntled and either never turned to the company again with their

business or thought hard before doing so. Very few people initiated a vicious word of mouth campaign since they have plenty of other things to do besides dissing a company. However, the Internet enables people to spread their wrath towards a company unhindered by their social network and geographic constraints, and disgruntled customers have harnessed the Web to spread their displeasure.[1]

Conflicts don't happen because of the Internet, but there have been numerous situations where one person with a simple connection was able to take a routine issue and make it into something that gained massive public awareness.

As we noted earlier, in June 2005 media consultant Jeff Jarvis bought a new computer from Dell. When he received the computer in the mail and began to set it up, he realized it didn't function properly. A regular blogger, Jarvis naturally found an outlet for his frustration on his blog, Buzzmachine (www.buzzmachine.com). Jarvis explained in a series of posts that he had paid extra for the machine so that Dell, if something were to ever happen to the computer, would arrange for an engineer to repair it at his home. But when Jarvis called to arrange the appointment, Dell proved unable to provide the service it had promised. The first post the Jarvis put up on his blog read:

> Dell lies. Dell sucks.
>
> I just got a new Dell laptop and paid a fortune for the four-year, in-home service.
>
> The machine is a lemon and the service is a lie.
>
> I'm having all kinds of trouble with the hardware: overheats, network doesn't work, maxes out on CPU usage. It's a lemon.
>
> But what really irks me is that they say if they sent someone to my home—which I paid for—he wouldn't have the parts, so I might as well just send the machine in and lose it for 7-10 days—plus the time going through this crap. So I have this new machine and paid for them to F***ING FIX IT IN MY HOUSE and they don't and I lose it for two weeks.
>
> DELL SUCKS. DELL LIES. Put that in your Google and smoke it, Dell.[2]

One one hand, Jarvis's complaints were routine and justified. The tone of his commentary was unnecessarily harsh and combative, but his frustration with the promise that Dell had made being broken was understandable. Not surprisingly, they were also very similar to those shared by other Dell customers. Over the next few days and weeks, dozens of equally frustrated Dell customers and interested bloggers discovered and responded to Jarvis's comments. After all, Jarvis was not the first person who had experienced an issue with a piece of Dell technology nor the first to post a complaint online about the computer company—a simple Google search reveals hundreds of frustrated customers with similar, and in some cases worse, complaints. The information spread online as you would expect it to—to other bloggers, to tech discussion boards and so on—until finally the story got picked up by mainstream media including *BusinessWeek* and the *New York Times*. Jarvis's timing, the influential nature of his blog audience, and a host of other factors had come together to trigger a firestorm of activity online that came to be known as "Dell Hell."

Conflict between audiences and organizations unfolds online quickly and dramatically nowadays, and organizations must figure out how to handle it. Dell did what you would expect most organizations to do when faced with a crisis with a customer such as this one—they reached out to Jeff Jarvis directly and offered him a refund on the computer, trying to appease him by making the situation go away. That might have worked in the past for Dell, but it wouldn't this time and it certainly wouldn't work for Jeff Jarvis. It didn't work because Jarvis' expectation of what he would receive from Dell included a visit by a qualified engineer and nothing short of that would suffice. He had created a relationship with Dell when he bought his computer and he fully expected Dell to live up to its end of the bargain.

There are plenty of other ways that Dell could have responded in this situation. The Bivings Report notes, "when this happens, it is important for companies to remember that when a customer attacks online, nothing prevents the company from participating in the discussion. Further, such involvement could help alleviate any PR problems associated with complaints aired online. The Internet has changed how customer complaints can spread throughout society." Dell could have joined the online conversation that was taking place on Jarvis's blog and across the rest of the Internet. But more than that, they should have picked a fight.

We don't mean to suggest Dell could or should have challenged the claims that Jarvis had made or targeted him as being an inappropriate spokesperson for the audience of disgruntled customers. Fighting is not about injuring or insulting your audience. But they shouldn't have sat on their hands either, or delivered the company line. Simply engaging in the conversation was not enough, however. Jarvis and other customers needed to see that Dell was concerned about the issue and ready to fight with its customers, to show it is also ready to fight for them. It wasn't a matter of solving the problem. Dell needed to work on the relationship that its audience had with it. Its response failed to do that.

Dell Hell has become a case study in customer service, blog management, and media relations. But long before Dell Hell ever surfaced, everybody knew what conflict between an organization and its audience looked and sounded like. The only things different about Dell Hell is the venue through which it unfolded.

Nobody sets out in business to provide a bad product, but with information moving as quickly as it does now, news travels fast when you do. Nobody invests their time and energy so they can fail to serve their audience well. But it happens, and when it does, the audience gets upset. Dell needed to show its audience that it was committed to fixing the problem, not just having it go away. It took years, and hundreds of millions of dollars in lost sales and bad PR, before they were able to demonstrate that and recover from the impact of Dell Hell.

Fast-forward a couple of years to February 14, 2007, when a massive snow and ice storm blanketed much of the eastern part of the United States, shutting down airports and making travel in all forms a challenge. For JetBlue, a low-cost alternative to the major airline carriers, the weather proved to be a major headache and a defining moment for the company. Dozens of JetBlue flights were cancelled because of bad weather, and because the three-year old airline had never experienced this type of situation the decision making became muddled, the communication confused, and the failures very public, very quickly. In one high-profile situation, passengers were left stranded on a JetBlue airplane, on the tarmac away from the gate, for 10 hours.

JetBlue wasn't the only airline that had to cancel flights that day, nor the only airline that trapped passengers on the tarmac for an extended period of time. But JetBlue had a customer, Genevieve McCaw, who went to the Internet to make her complaints public. McCaw launched JetBlueHostage (http://jetbluehostage.blogspot.com), a blog, to document her complaints. She quickly became a rallying point for other stranded customers and fodder for the mainstream media. Just like Jeff Jarvis before her, the media pounced on the opportunity to use the customer complaints to pin a major, well-respected company with a high-profile failure. CNN and Fox News interviewed McCaw, and hundreds of articles and blog posts cited her efforts. Genevieve McCaw became the de facto spokesperson for an audience of people who were upset about not only JetBlue's response to the Valentine's Day storm, but also the state of the airline industry in general.

JetBlue responded differently than Dell. JetBlue went on the offensive. They picked a fight. They couldn't, and didn't try to, challenge McCaw's claim that her delay was the result of poor management by Jet Blue in the face of the crisis. They couldn't, and didn't try to, suggest that JetBlue should not be held to a higher standard by their customers than other airlines. But they also didn't roll over and let people complain, make assumptions about the capabilities of the company, without weighing in on the discussion.

JetBlue CEO David Neeleman posted a video apology on the JetBlue Web site in which he talked personally and honestly to customers about JetBlue's failures and their desire to address them appropriately. The company issued a Passenger Bill of Rights within days of the crisis which both compensated customers for their troubles on Valentine's Day and established a solid policy for dealing with future crises. And the airline gave McCaw some time with Neeleman so that he could answer questions from her and others who submitted questions via the blog. In the days and weeks that followed the Valentine's Day storm, JetBlue returned to normal operations and the vast majority of its customers returned.

There were some passengers, including Genevieve McCaw, who have said publicly they will never fly JetBlue again. That is a fact of life in the airline business and for any organization. But others, pleased with the penance that JetBlue had paid, decided to give them another chance. Steve Rubel noted on his blog, Micropersuasion (http://www.micropersuasion.com): "This is a great model for anyone in PR or customer service." Calling it "the cold french fry syndrome," he explained "If you go into a fast food restaurant and you get cold french fries, you're mad. So naturally, you start to complain. If the worker behind the counter takes the time to (a) hear your complaint and (b) try as best he or she can to solve it, there's a good chance they can win you back." You can't please everyone, all of the time. But putting up a fight dramatically altered the way that this situation unfolded for JetBlue and possibly saved their business.

Despite appearances, conflict originates with the customer, typically as a result of some action that an organization took. The challenge is that the way conflict is communicated, on the news or through the rumor mill to cite a few options, reflects and distorts the origin of the problem. Blame is quickly placed on whatever organization is associated with a bad outcome and not the circumstance that actually created the problem. You can get upset, deny the problem, work to address the issue—and your effort will be appreciated and in many cases rewarded. But no matter what, conflict will sometimes exist between you and your audience and there is nothing you can do to stop that completely. So instead, embrace conflict when it happens because you will learn a lot from it that will make it easier to deal with the next time.

Why Fighting Pays Off

An organization could offer the best prices and services around, the most unique product, or even have a personality that is different than anything else an audience has ever seen, and still not be successful. There is no way to control what your audience thinks or how they will respond to your efforts. But if your organization fails to make your audience feel wanted, you can know for sure that you are unlikely to build a strong and loyal audience.

Your audience likes to feel appreciated. When people invest time, money and energy in something they want their effort to be recognized; they want to become part of the organization they believe in. Ben Goldhirsch from *GOOD Magazine* argues: "I think that brands become part of the way people identify themselves. People identify themselves as Apple users and that becomes a part of how they see themselves and part of how they kind of explain themselves to other people. Apple carries with it a certain intelligence and creativity and a certain iconoclastic nature—and that creates a certain loose community of Apple users. I think really strong brands do that."

As for the challenge for many newer organizations, particularly those looking to engage younger audiences (as *GOOD Magazine* is trying to do), Goldhirsch says:

But at the same time, this audience that we're appealing to doesn't just belong to one brand. There's a certain degree of skepticism always, you know, and they are careful about the brands they choose. I think it's an interesting thing to note because we can't be everything to everyone and we also need to recognize other brands like Apple that are appealing to this audience and align ourselves with them. I think we're doing that naturally but . . . it's a sensibility. It is a sensibility that's represented by the people here. We're finding touch points that are not just in the content of the magazine but also in our other efforts [such as their partnerships with nonprofit organizations]. That's not job-specific or even budget-specific or anything. They're going to run into *GOOD* and they're going to be attracted to it and then hopefully, they'll become a *GOOD* reader.

Here is another example: Brian's cousin, David, really likes eating sardines. When he lived in Baltimore, he shopped regularly at a variety of markets near his house, including a Whole Foods. None of the stores, including the Whole Foods, regularly stocked fresh sardines. One day David shared his desire for fresh sardines with the fish manager at the Whole Foods and his frustration that none of the local markets stocked them. The fish manager explained fresh sardines were hard to come by in Baltimore, but offered to take his phone number and call if he ever came across some. David didn't think much of it, until a few months later the phone rang and the fish manager from Whole Foods said he had a shipment of fresh sardines that had just arrived. David rushed down to the store, bought the fresh sardines, and to this day talks about all the recipes that week he was able to include them in.

It is a simple story, and probably not one that most of us can relate to (fresh sardines? No, thank you). But it is similar to what you will hear a hundred times when talking to people about what they expect from an organization they support and the reasons why they are loyal to some groups and not others. We all want to be recognized for our support—we all want to feel that without our patronage the organization will suffer. David, like all of us, knows that the occasional order of sardines is not going to make or break the fish business at the local Whole Foods, or the company as a whole for that matter, but it was clear that his loyalty to the fish counter was important to the Whole Foods team in Baltimore and that was meaningful to David. He still talks about it, even years later. Now living in Providence, Rhode Island, he hasn't found a regular outlet of fresh sardines, but he is looking for a local fish manager who will take his number.

David, of course, is not alone. People choose where and when to spend money and time based on the level of support and effort shown by an organization. Perhaps customers expect it. Perhaps we are so pleasantly surprised by good service these days that our loyalty to an organization that treats us with respect, like the kind David was shown, is that much stronger. Either way, any organization can adopt a customer-centered response today. And every organization will benefit, from the standpoint of audience loyalty and engagement, if they do.

Make it a Fair Fight

There are books, manuals, training courses, and workshops devoted to managing conflict and defusing tense situations. Entire departments of major companies focus just on this important concept. Organizations of all kinds go on retreats in the hopes they will come back better prepared to deal with difficult situations. Save your money and your weekends. We can sum the core lessons of all of them up like this: Treat your audience like a human being.

Dell responded to Jeff Jarvis, and the thousands of people who shared his frustration, like customers. JetBlue responded to Genevieve McCaw, and the thousands of customers who shared her frustration, like people—like an audience they appreciated and valued. David Neeleman's video was personal, his voice pained, and his body clearly tired from hours of dealing with the stressful situation. Dell's outreach to Jeff Jarvis followed protocol, including a call from a customer service spokesperson, a standardized response that would have left anyone feeling cold.

The more you know about your audience, the more personal touches you can make to show you care—not just about their business, but about them as people. JetBlue didn't need to read the complaints on Genevieve McCaw's blog to know that they had messed up big-time. They are passengers of their own airline as well and operate every day with the motivation that they are providing a different experience than the other airlines. They were concerned about the situation on Valentine's Day long before the media got involved.

The next time JetBlue was faced with a situation where weather threatened their flights, JetBlue was better prepared. Three weeks later when a second major storm blanketed the northeast, disrupting air travel, JetBlue made decisions about its actions based on what their customers needed, not what was easiest for the airline. The *Wall Street Journal* wrote of one example, "JetBlue . . . analyzed the itineraries of the passengers on its flights. Planners noticed that nearly all the passengers on a Burlington, Vermont to New York flight Monday intended to make connections there to fly on to West Palm Beach or Orlando, Florida. So that plane didn't stop in New York at all. It traveled to Orlando, dropped those passengers off, then continued to West Palm Beach."[3]

It wasn't a major change or disruption to their service, but it had a major impact on their customers' travel plans. JetBlue was better prepared to respond with their customer's best interests in mind, and the results showed.

A few months later, David Neeleman was forced out of his role as CEO by the Board of Directors at JetBlue. The reasoning was because his failure to respond appropriately in the face of significant weather delay on Valentines Day cost the airline valuable revenue. Customer response was mixed, but the consensus among many—us included—was that the board made a mistake. David Neeleman's public and seemingly genuine commitment to provide high-value customer service to passengers on JetBlue, in the immediate aftermath of the weather events, and in general, was important to customers and a distinguishing characteristic in the airline industry. JetBlue is a different kind of airline and David Neeleman was a different kind of CEO. By measuring Neeleman's effectiveness on financial performance alone, the board failed to recognize that JetBlue is a special airline because of David Neeleman's commitment to the customer and what allowed it to recover, and thrive, in the months afterward.

Meanwhile, sadly, for an organization to get public credit for waging a battle with its customers, to preserve the best interests of all customers, will take some additional work. And that is part of the reasons to do it–because the benefit will be seen in the relationship with your customer, and not simply for PR benefit.

In the current media environment, it is almost a given that your fight with a customer or other member of your audience will go public. In some cases you will bring the fight—choosing to make your position known by launching a blog or posting a video on YouTube. In some cases, however, you might find a complaint lodged through a chat room or gossip site before it ever makes it through the official channels you have set up at your organization to handle such issues. If that happens, you are on the defensive.

While you don't want to fire off a response too early, recognize that there is a benefit to going public and being out front in a fight. You control the dialogue, set the tone, and establish your credibility in the medium on your terms, not theirs. That takes preparation (having your materials ready to go in anticipation of a potential challenge), careful planning (including a fundamental understanding of how the particular channel or venue you want to utilize really works), and the ability to make quick decisions. There are few, if any, organizations that we know who have all three of those conditions working for them.

If you opt to fight early, or fight at all, be prepared to stick it out to the finish. You can't leave before the action is over, and sometimes that means investing a significant amount of time and energy in the conversation. A couple of years ago, activists from Seattle's Ethiopian community, local group Fair Trade Puget Sound, and Oxfam America teamed up to post some videos on YouTube criticizing Starbucks for unfair labor practices related to coffee growing in Ethiopia. The videos were part of a campaign that activists claimed generated 70,000 faxes to Starbucks CEO Jim Donald demanding the company support Ethiopia's ownership of its coffee names, a move intended to boost payments to farmers who produce world-class coffee but live in poverty. Starbucks responded quickly, posting its own video two days later. The video featured Dub Hay, Starbucks' head of coffee, answering questions about the company's position on the issue.[4]

Posting the video response was like poking a hornet's nest—it raised Oxfam's profile, generated thousands of additional responses, and set an expectation that anytime an activist launches a video campaign against the coffee giant, they will be prepared to respond as needed. Points for Starbucks—they responded quickly and substantively to an attack, in the appropriate medium, and showed their customers and the activists who were criticizing them they were ready for a fight. But they should have been prepared to keep fighting, not to mention staying ready for any fights that followed.

How and where you fight are equally important. In the Starbucks case, a video criticism deserved a video response. And that is almost always true in the online space. If someone wages a response through a particular venue online, you must engage them through the same venue or risk your response going unheard by your audience. Many organizations we have worked with have chosen to respond to an attack through the channels they know best, regardless of where the fight was brewing. They might get the results of an online petition and decide it makes sense to send out a press release or schedule a series of interviews to offer their side of the story. But if your audience spent its energy online, you cannot be sure they are going to read the newspaper or watch the news? That works if your audience is the media, or all you care about is what your investors are thinking—but it doesn't show your audience that you have heard their concerns or are interested in hearing from them.

When You Don't Need to Fight

Just because you have an opportunity or invitation to fight doesn't mean you should. In the cacophony of voices, many will not be heard. There will always be comments floating around online or complaints about how your organization did something wrong. They should be tracked, and as an organization you should make it a practice to listen and try to address the feedback that you hear. But not everything needs a full-scale fight. Remember, there is no use in fighting back if the criticism is true. Instead, put your energy toward fighting for your audience to give you another chance, then show them you deserve it, or explain why you are doing the thing that is being criticized, so they understand and appreciate the time you took to discuss it with them.

More importantly, don't fight if nobody is interested. You could invest an endless amount of energy fighting every little comment and critic, only to find they are just an army of one. You should never ignore what people are saying about you, online or offline, but choose the battles that will have the most impact.

Your ability to resolve conflict successfully is one of the most important skills you can have. You can always compromise or acquiesce, bow to your audience's demands no matter how unreasonable or outlandish. Organizations do it all the time and continue to be successful. You can also fight—show your entire audience, not just the vocal few who complain or find a channel for expressing their anger, that you want their support and are willing to do whatever it takes to get it. Your measure of success is your ability to effectively balance the needs of your organization with the needs of your audience over the long term. Reaching a high level of satisfaction among your audience as well as for you and your team will pay dividends for a long time.

Being prepared to deliver information through a variety of different venues, online and off-line, will help to raise awareness of what you are doing, blunt any potential criticism that is being waged against you, and establish credibility for your organization among the part of your audience that gets this kind of information online. Fighting will win you points, but only if you fight well and your audience knows you are doing it.

CHAPTER 8

Be an Expert

Even with all the innovations in technology and opportunities for each of us to control our own flow of information, experiences, and stuff, it is not uncommon to want to talk with someone who knows more, has greater experience, or offers a different perspective than ours—a teacher, a coach, an executive, even a reporter. When we are looking for something—to make a purchase, to plan a trip, to solve a riddle, or to answer a question—this is even truer.

Looking beyond our own personal knowledge and perspective is a critical part of our daily survival. When we pick up a prescription, we ask the pharmacist about the side effects that might be caused by the medication we have been instructed to take. When a pipe leaks, we call on a plumber (or maybe in Brian's case, his father-in-law) for assistance.

Why do we ask these people? They are experts at what they do.

There are tools that exist, online and off, that allow us to answer all these questions ourselves. We can go to the library and read one of the thousands of books on whatever subject we are seeking to understand—aeronautical engineering, art, architecture, business, criminology, drama, the earth, fashion, human rights, mathematics, and hundreds of others. We can visit one of the millions of Web sites, blog posts, chat room discussions, and access white papers, transcripts, and other online resources that might reveal some important detail. If you are walking around and want to get a cup of coffee, you can send a text message with the ZIP code of your location to 697289 (MYSBUX), and receive a text message back with the addresses of the three nearest Starbucks locations.

Each of these options will provide you with access to information. The next step is to decide whether it is good information that will help you make a decision and move on during your day, or if it is just information.

Imagine you are hosting a dinner party for four people and you want to prepare steaks for your guests. Before you head out to the grocery store you log on to Google and type "pounds of steak per person for dinner average" or something similar. It is a pretty basic question: how much meat you should buy to make enough steak to feed four people? But your search reveals 678,000 results in 0.21 seconds. On the first page of results you find resources that tell you the average annual meat consumption per person in 2002 (200 pounds—including red meat, poultry, and fish).[1] You learn that eating vegetables for a week will save about 19 pounds of CO_2.[2] You also find recipes for cooking goat meat, cooking meat in water, grilling with dry rubs, and instructions for the best way to barbecue boneless or bone-in pork butts on a grill. There are hundreds of thousands of pages of results that follow, and none of them seem to answer your question.

You spend some time clicking through the results and reviewing the materials. Whether you spend 30 seconds or 10 minutes looking for the answer, it seems more often than not you come away still not having found the information you need. You have found that when purchasing a turkey you should estimate one pound of meat per person.[3] When planning to serve lobster, one and a half to two pounds per person is in order.[4] But not a single site, or chat room, or anything revealed in your search provides a quick answer to what feels like a simple question.

If you are like most people, you will hop in your car, head to the grocery store, and when you get there you will hope that a butcher is available so you can ask him the same question. If you are so fortunate to find one, your butcher will likely tell you that 16 to 24 ounces per person of meat is a reasonable serving and you will buy between five and six pounds of steak to cook your dinner. Depending on the store, you might walk away with some helpful tips on how to prepare the steaks to get maximum flavor as well.

The advances in technology have changed our expectations as consumers of information, experiences, and stuff. We believe that we can do everything ourselves, that the answers we seek can be easily found by punching in a simple question on a search engine. But it is not always true. Finding the answers to most questions takes time; we are increasingly short on time.

As our society increasingly relies on technology to get and share information, each of us needs to devote substantial time to the quest for information. All of us have to search and review the information we find. For some, there is also a need to produce and promote the information to satisfy those searches. In essence we all quickly become authorities on the subjects, products, or services that we seek to utilize.

Why We Rely on Experts

Your expertise is other people's solution to confusion.

There wouldn't be so much talk about expertise if people didn't need help. The audience wants top-notch, quality, relevant information—and beyond that, they want to know what makes that information important, both generally and specifically to them. Most people want a go to an expert for a specific need—a doctor for medical advice, a mechanic for car service, a hair stylist for a cut and color job, for example. They want to get the benefit of the credibility that an expert can provide instead of doing it for themselves.

And what will the expert offer? Experts can point you to the right information, experiences, or stuff more quickly and with greater focus. Experts can offer their opinions, based on real experience with a certain subject. You can find news anywhere but you can never have enough good analysis, evaluation, synthesis, or informed predictions.

There are lots of choices and decisions that need to be made every day, and each person has his own expectation of how much time he reasonably wants to devote to a task. Technology provides us all with a gateway for getting and sharing information and experience more quickly and from more sources. It is a tool for attaining expert status in something. But for the most part, it puts all the activities we pursue on the same level, instead of recognizing that there are some things we are good at and some we are not.

There are lots of people who can, for example, change the thermostats in their house from manual to programmable. There are an equal number of us, maybe more, who cannot, no matter how much help we get from a user manual or a good Internet connection. Brian spent three hours on a Sunday afternoon recently trying to do this, ultimately calling both his stepfather and his father-in-law to tap their experience and expertise on this subject. Was that three hours on a Sunday worth it? He felt like there were better ways to spend his time.

Either one of us could probably change the oil in our cars, file our own taxes, or build our own computers from component parts we purchased at the local technology store. But there are experts in each of these fields on whom he can rely, and in exchange for a certain fee, we can get back the time that we otherwise would have spent and focus it on something else. Given the choice to do it again, Brian would call an electrician and asked their help to install his thermostats.

There are, of course, limits to expertise. Being an expert in one type of problem does not increase your ability to understand or comprehend another subject. Experts may have a better process for addressing related issues, but they do not know everything about everything. Moreover, expert knowledge sometimes goes too deeply into an issue, providing answers way beyond what is needed. Less experienced people, by contrast, do not differentiate between important and unimportant aspects, so they are more likely to remember many details that were not crucial to the problem—but possibly stumble across something that makes everything much simpler.

What Makes You an Expert?

Knowledge makes you an expert. Your experience makes you an expert. Your network makes you an expert. Your notoriety makes you an expert. Expertise in the current media environment is in the eye of the beholder. But to be an expert for the long term takes a bit more.

Expertise comes from the skills and knowledge that someone possesses, distinguishing them from a novice or less experienced person. People become experts because their expertise is recognized and because they become a member of a community of practice— a group or partnership around a specific issue or service. You can become an expert simply by being the only one who has experienced something. Being an expert is a social designation.

Writer and consultant Clay Shirky argues that "society typically recognizes experts through some process of credentialing, such as the granting of degrees, professional certifications, or institutional engagement." He continues, "We have a sense of what it means that someone is a doctor, a judge, an architect, or a priest, but these facts are only facts because we agree they are."[5]

There is obviously a need for formal education of some kind—in part to expand your expertise, but also to help validate it in the eyes of the audience. But a degree—an MBA or law school degree, PhD, or certificate of achievement from the Boy Scouts—is not a measure of expertise alone. Many people get formal training as lawyers to help them understand better how to think and approach problems. Some business leaders began as artists, musicians, or computer programmers and went on to earn millions and redefine their fields.

You probably consider yourself an expert in something, at some level, and you probably are. The larger question is what role that expertise might play in our society as a whole. Seth Godin wrote an ebook entitled *Everyone's an Expert (about something),* in which he argued:

> Think about the way you shop—online or in the real world. Unless the item is a staple or the store is quite familiar, it's unlikely that you buy the very first option you come across. Instead, you circle the store, putting off the salespeople ("I'm just browsing"), or you click around the Web, poking and exploring and searching until you understand your options. You're not seeking the answer at first—first you want to understand the meaning behind your choices.
>
> Before you download that software or buy that product, you might want a better understanding of how a technology works. Or you might want to find three or four choices for your budget before you book your hotel in London. You might want to be more comfortable about the ways to persuade your school board not to ban a certain book, or you might want to know how Moby's new album is coming along. . . .
>
> Sooner or later, you'll figure out whatever it is you're trying to understand. Sooner or later, the picture will snap into focus, and then you'll stop investing your time on *researching* the issue and take *action* instead. After that, maybe you'll take your newfound understanding and use it to teach and persuade others (after all, now you're an expert). Or maybe you'll move on to discover something else.[6]

When you do figure it out, you will have become an expert – perhaps narrowly in only the field that you view to be important. But with some investment of time, you may be able to offer your expertise to others with similar interests as well.

Sounds exhausting, all that time and energy spent trying to answer a question. And for what?

But *can* anyone be an expert? Kathy Sierra, a best-selling author and thinker says "the only thing standing between you-as-amateur and you-as-expert is *dedication*." She writes:

According to some brain scientists, almost anyone can develop world-class (or at least top expertise) abilities in things for which they aren't physically impaired. Apparently God-given talent, natural "gifts," and genetic predispositions just aren't all they're cracked up to be. Or at least not in the way most of us always imagined. It turns out that rather than being naturally gifted at music or math or chess or whatever, a superior performer most likely has a gift for concentration, dedication, and a simple desire to keep getting better. In theory, again, *anyone* willing to do what's required to keep getting better *will* get better.[7]

According to Sierra, people will typically fall into one of the three categories when it comes to knowing something: expert, amateur, or dropout. She notes that the dropouts decide during the "I suck at this" phase that it isn't worth continuing and they give up. The amateurs are the folks you overhear saying, "Yes, I know there's a better way to do this thing, but I already know how to do it *this* (less efficient, less powerful) way and it's easier for me to just keep doing it like that." In other words, they made it past the suck threshold, but now they don't want to push for new skills and capabilities. And then there are the experts, who push past that threshold where there's a much greater chance they'll become passionate about a subject, and get to the point where they can attain expert knowledge.

It takes hard work to be a recognized expert over the longer term.

A Network of Experts

You will never come close to knowing everything, and there is a good likelihood you will get many things wrong along the way. Since you won't be the only expert in your space, you will face competition and in many cases you will lose. But failing should provide both motivation and valuable learning. All the best are continuously learning—reading, asking questions, listening for clues about what makes people tick. So if no single individual can be competent in everything, maybe a group of experts working together can.

Expertise is personal. You have to know what makes your approach to learning and sharing information different from someone else's and gravitate toward your strengths. The path to expertise begins when you first discover the thing that you are passionate about, where you retain the detail most easily and communicate about it most fluidly. Most people who try to become expert fail because they try to force it. Expertise requires a certain level of obsession, but one that comes naturally, as well.

Peter Morville, author of the book *Ambient Findability* (Sebastopol, CA: O'Reilly Media, Inc., 2005) and an expert in information architecture, noted in an interview:

> If you take an educational setting for instance, the old model is that the professor knows best. That there is a teacher that is going to define the curriculum, and the format, and the way that the course proceeds, and that the students sit here an empty vessel to be filled. And you know, in the educational field, there's this notion of constructivism. Learning is really more about engagement with issues and challenges and redeveloping more of conversation and discussion. And we have this whole kind of cultural move toward this notion that the user is always right, and we should be bending over backwards to figure, "Well how do our students want to learn, and what communication channels work best for them?"

The right answer is in the middle. You can look at it as bringing together old and new, or simply recognizing that experience, expertise, and authority have real value, while at the same time, some of the new technologies, trends, and ways of communicating and interacting are pretty exciting. You can also expand and apply your expertise through a strategic network of other experts who can address certain key aspects related to your expertise. Having this type of network does not make you a one-stop shop but you do serve as a trusted source of good information and access to people, which will help build loyalty and keep them coming back to you for support.

The developing of expert networks is nothing new. In fact, many large businesses apply expertise location systems, or ELSs, to help tap the best available knowledge within their organization. ELS is a natural by-product of the advances in our society. Greater bandwidth, plummeting storage costs, and communications tools like instant messaging and wikis help foster collaboration and knowledge sharing like never before. Organizing and applying that knowledge, however, is a major challenge.

Of course, getting people to share information sounds a lot easier than it really is. Some people are afraid to share what they know because they fear they won't be needed anymore. But true experts don't really worry about holding on to their information because what they are expert in is a particular field of knowledge, and they're discovering new things all the time. And while having knowledge is key to being an expert, how you attain that knowledge—and continually enhance it—is even more important.

Expertise should not be an isolating experience. Expertise should be shared. Chances are, you will never be the only expert in any area, or know everything there is to know about a subject. Get to know the other experts in your niche, collaborate and communicate with them openly. Expertise is not about recalling facts and information alone; it is also about understanding the impact and importance of things.

Communicating Your Expertise

To be valued, expertise needs to be applied. More importantly, it needs to be expressed and recognized. This social dimension of expertise is well suited for today's media environment.

There are lots of ways to promote your expertise. You can write your own authoritative nonfiction book and travel the country promoting it to all who will listen (we'll let you know how this experiment works out—we can assure you it is a lot of work to pull off). But why go to all that trouble when there are easier ways that can be more appropriately targeted to the audience that will appreciate your expertise the most? Here are two examples:

1. *Search and engage.* Search online for venues that are aligned with your expertise. Chances are you already have a list of sites, blogs, and online newsletters in mind since understanding

how your subject is handled online is a key part of being able to demonstrate your expertise in today's technology-infused world. If you want to get their attention, propose a unique partnership that benefits all involved—something that shows your understanding of their audience and what it would enjoy. Every venue needs content, particularly from an expert, so you can make a natural exchange of energy for audience. But to pique their interest you want to offer to distribute unique commentary through their site in return for some much-needed promotion and the ability to leverage the credibility of their brand, with their audience.

2. *Start talking.* There is nothing keeping you from launching your own podcast or videocast and distributing it far and wide. Mignon Fogarty, aka Grammar Girl, launched a daily podcast of grammar tips after becoming fed up with the routine mistakes she was finding in her job as a technical document reviewer. A few months into her experiment she was reaching millions of listeners a week, getting references in Supreme Court decisions, and even making an appearance on the Oprah show.[8] The key to a successful podcast is the same as producing any other content for online distribution: Make it relevant, keep it interesting, and keep the production value high. Promotion will be your challenge, but if your expertise is sound, there are countless venues just waiting for something that will add greater understanding to your audience's experience.

You don't need to focus on the opportunities that are made available only online. There are panel discussions, coffee klatches, and other gatherings of people where your voice and experience will be welcomed. No matter the venue, the most important thing you can do when showing off your expertise is reveal your personality at the same time. It sounds basic, but most organizations think that sending a standard e-mail to a contact online or repurposing some content from a previous effort will be seen as compelling or unique. It won't. It may be more efficient to send a form letter to a wide audience of people online, but efficiency doesn't equal effectiveness. The thing that is most compelling about your expertise is you, so show your personality and begin to build an audience one person at a time.

Putting Your Expertise to Work

What can organizations do to support expertise within their ranks? Imagine a system that helps its audience identify where the gaps are and then augments that knowledge. For example, as more and more questions come up—and the expertise of someone is called upon regularly—an organization recognizes the trend and prepares itself, by training others on how to respond or adapting their policies and offerings to satisfy the demand.

Take eBay for example. eBay boasts more than 25 million items for sale through its online auction system at any one time. In 2005 it processed roughly $24 billion worth of sales to more than 40 million active buyers.[9] Out of this massive network came a whole cottage industry of professional sellers, entrepreneurs who account for more than 95 percent of that $24 billion in gross sales.

Many of the sellers are part-time, operating out of their living rooms, while others operate full businesses, opening storefront shops in towns across America. But finding new sellers and keeping existing ones happy has gotten tougher lately. While eBay was once the only auction commerce site online, several new rivals have popped up.

Individual sellers—people who have become experts in how to manage the complex eBay environment—have an interest in knowing what tricks and tips will make them even more effective. So it is not uncommon for veteran sellers to huddle with eBay leadership to exchange tips on how to raise sales. The company is also increasing efforts to train its sellers in the eBay way by continually expanding and improving its eBay University program, which runs a one-day series of classes in 30 cities around the country to coach both beginners and veterans in everything from listing items to advanced photography techniques. Within a month of taking the class, eBay has found, sellers double their selling activity on the site.

Apple does something similar. When Apple stores launched back in 2001, the company installed a series of Genius Bars where people could go for advice, insight, and hands-on technical support for their Mac products, including iPods and other accessories. CNET wrote about the Genius Bars when they first opened that "This is where perplexed Mac owners can pull up a stool, lean on the bar, and spill their woes to the nodding guru, or 'genius.' . . . And for truly baffling troubles, a red 'hot line' phone—a concept borrowed from an old Batman episode—connects the genius to presumably higher-level geniuses at Apple's headquarters."[10] The idea was the brainchild of Ronald Johnson, the chief of Apple's retail efforts. He told *Fortune* magazine that the group in charge of launching retail operations for Apple came from a variety of backgrounds. When the group met, as an icebreaker, he asked team members to describe the best service experience they had ever had. "Of the 18 people, 16 said it was in a hotel," he said—which was unexpected. But he later made the connection: "The concierge desk at a hotel isn't selling anything; it's there to help." And with that revelation, the idea of the genius bar was born, driven by the goal to create a store experience for Apple customers that had the friendliness and support provided by a Four Seasons Hotel.[11]

Not all organizations are in the retail business, and even the ones that are don't have to follow eBay's or Apple's models. But there are ways to put your expertise on display for the benefit of your audience. For example, whenever someone calls a customer service line for help, or to ask a question, they expect to actually receive help or come away with answers. More often than not, it seems they do not. Not only is it possible to address customer service issues proactively, it is critically important. With a simple shift in thinking and the appropriate planning and training, your organization can become proactive in addressing issues.

There are a lot of benefits to being proactive. No matter how quickly you respond to an inquiry from someone affiliated with your organization—a member, a customer, an employee, the media— there is still a lag between their awareness of the problem and its resolution. By being proactive, you can eliminate issues before people beyond the organization are aware or it becomes a larger issue. Since the high quality of service can be a key element in how people decide whether to choose your organization over another one, less hassle will help to ensure longer, more productive relationships with your audience.

Second, being proactive is less expensive from an operational standpoint. You will always need to be able to respond when something happens, but the more proactive you are, the fewer people you need to respond to.

Very few organizations, it seems, are proactive in addressing issues their audience brings up. Being proactive about your messaging, your processes, and your quality assurance, and making sure that your organization is continuously learning, are all keys to success.

The world needs experts and frequently consults them. Our society is undergoing rapid and significant change. Many of the practical solutions that we have all become accustomed to in life are no longer applicable. Your audience wants you to be an expert—they want you to be good at what you claim to do.

Experts have an edge in problem solving that is demonstrated in the results of their work. They have more knowledge to draw from and a better sense of how to organize and apply that knowledge than someone who is not practiced in a particular area. They perceive and frame issues more efficiently and come more comfortably to a conclusion about how to act. And, there are typically free PR and other self-promotion related benefits to being an expert, self-proclaimed or otherwise.

Obviously, people with many years of experience solving a particular type of problem are bound to know more about that type of problem than would someone who is a newcomer to the issue. Experts have more examples of past problems to compare with and lessons learned from previous attempts to solve a problem that allow them to rule out certain options. It is that experience that provides them the necessary perspective to be helpful to others when needed. And that is why we find it so valuable.

Possessing Expert Tools and Methods

Should we have to commit such significant effort to answer even the most simple of tasks or questions? Is that really what you want to spend your time on? We don't think so. People need someone to guide them through the many choices and challenges that come with making decisions and taking action in their daily life. They want to know that the time and energy they spend, whether in searching online for an answer or climbing a ladder to make a repair in their house, is being well spent.

Developing functionality that substitutes for advice makes you an expert in that area, even though you don't possess the knowledge yourself. You are providing the tool that allows someone to access and understand it and that is no small task. By developing a proprietary method or a technique that provides factual insights that form a basis for judgment, one can make one's expertise more valuable and certainly easier to understand. You make everyone who uses your tool better.

In short, the audience wants expertise. You should be their expert. And if you can't be their expert, you can help them find what they need—and that is just as valuable.

CHAPTER

Be Part of the Best Team

Nobody can be good at everything. But, as we discussed in Chapter 3, your audience expects you to be all things. Many organizations are formed with the belief that they know more, are better suited, or can figure out whatever they need to know to succeed at any level. Why wouldn't they? Nobody wants to go into business to be mediocre or launch an organization that doesn't have an impact. Operating in isolation, however, only serves to limit the contribution you can make to your audience. To meet their expectations, even the experts need to be a part of a team.

That doesn't stop people from claiming they can go it alone. Corporations think that they offer the best product or service—think of the *New York Times* saying they provide "All the News That's Fit to Print" (though we know a print newspaper can only do so much with the available column inches, and the *New York Times* offers only one limited perspective). Nonprofits believe their solution to a particular social issue is the most innovative—the ASPCA says definitively that "We are their voice," though dozens of organizations offer support to abused and neglected animals just like them. Even educational institutions believe they provide the best guidance and support to all who step foot on their campus—knowing full well they can't match the interests or needs of every student, all the time.

Your customer knows, however, that no person can do it all and no organization can go it alone. We don't know of a single person who only watches one channel on television (in fact, a study by Nielsen Media found that the average household watches 15.7 different channels[1]), buys all their clothes from just one store, or gets their washing machine, lawnmower, and car all repaired by the same person. Many people who only care passionately about one issue, be it breast cancer or early childhood education, will contribute to a variety of different groups in those areas of interest, because all do something meaningful.

Moreover, it is not difficult to find evidence of organizations trying to do everything and failing at something. Some of those failures are more spectacular than others, but all of them are the result of the same basic organizational hubris. It is just not possible to be good at everything.

Organizations must bring expertise, discipline, historical perspective and experience if they want to communicate successfully and build a strong, trusting relationship with their audience. If your organization is weak in one or more of those areas, you leave an opening for a competing organization to promote a similar offering (or at least be able to convince the audience they can, long enough to lure them away) and you will lose out. Even if you don't have a competitor, you risk disappointing your audience. For companies this might mean offering an excellent product but poor customer service. There are a lot of nonprofit organizations that can frame a particular social issue in a compelling way but whose execution of certain programmatic elements is a clear weakness. We all have our own examples.

Building the Best Internal Partners

As the role that technology plays in our society changes, so changes everything else.

Technology alters how organizations, from the largest companies in the world to smallest nonprofits, must manage and market themselves. It changes the way people get and share information. Technology changes how we communicate and interact with each other. Technology changes our work—what we produce, how and when it is distributed, and who consumes it. It changes who we are.

In order to adapt and survive, let alone thrive in an environment where technology either dictates or supports almost everything we do, organizations and the people who work for them must change. Organizations need to hire people with different skills and understanding to better reflect the audience they are trying to reach. Employees who have different expectations about how decisions are made and communicated need to be supported and mentored differently than in the past. None of this should be news to you—the changes have been under way for a long time and their impacts are already seen across every department, in every type of organization.

There is, however, a significant difference between recognizing the need for change and actually taking the necessary steps to adjust how your organization thinks and operates. There are lots of places to start, but the team you put in place is certainly the most important. And how you attract and keep the best people, whether they are employees or vendors, partners or volunteers, is where you need to focus your effort.

What do you think when you hear that the Conference Board, a Manhattan-based business membership and research organization, found that almost half of Americans dislike or are not interested in their work?[2] Are we providing our employees with the best possible environment to work in and challenging them in the most compelling ways possible? When the same study suggests that more than 60 percent of the people from Generation Y are dissatisfied with their current jobs, do you start to wonder if your organization is prepared to support this current generation well? And what about the next generation of employees and leaders—are we ready for them?

As Jason Goldberg, CEO of Jobster, an online job placement firm, explained to us,

> People who are growing up on these new technologies are fundamentally different than the people who were in the workforce before, on and off the job. Posting a video on YouTube is second nature and participating in MySpace or Facebook is something that's ingrained in them, from an early age. Also, this digital generation is incredibly comfortable doing things that we never would have thought of five years ago. They'll put their whole life out in the Internet for the world to see. They will post personal messages that they don't mind a hundred other people reading. News feeds on social networking sites like Facebook have basically replaced e-mail for teenagers—just think of what that will mean to our work culture in the future. They go online expecting to find real-time updates about what is going on in their friends' lives and around the world with equal ease.

Technology and the flattening of our world have given people broader opportunities to travel and experience things around the world, and immerse themselves in different customs and cultures.

They have had different, and in many cases better, means of communicating; borders and language do not place the kinds of limits on meeting people halfway around the globe as they once did. Networks and communities are the order of the day. People are looking for jobs they can feel passionate about, not just a paycheck to bring home. All of that is having a dramatic impact on how people think about sending information and interacting with people. As a result, where they spend their time, money, and energy, and what that means to the workforce, needs to be adjusted.

It is not as hard as you think—and you don't have to be a Silicon Valley start-up to change the ways in which your organization operates. Rob Waldron, the former CEO of Jumpstart, asked:

> Is anybody doing the ROI of three-week vacations versus two-week vacations? Is anybody doing the ROI of the employee cafeteria? Is anybody doing the ROI of the CEO giving out awards to top performers? No. But it is within the common understanding that when you have an employee cafeteria, people are sharing information. Sharing information leads to more productivity, and when the CEO stands up and gives out awards and celebrates great behavior, then other people feel good. People feeling good at the workplace is going to lead to better productivity, to better retained employees, and a better work environment.

Jeffrey Hollender, the CEO of Seventh Generation agrees. He told us, "Being nice and being authentic and being environmental or sustainable at treating your employees nice is not an alternative to succeeding under the traditional financial metrics, and where I think most people really miss the boat is not understanding how all of this soft, fuzzy stuff, if done correctly, makes you more effective under the traditional financial metrics." That's easy for Jeffrey Hollender to say, since his whole company operates on these principles. But what about the rest of you?

Sumaya Kazi, co-founder of The CulturalConnect, an online media publishing company, was recognized by *BusinessWeek* as one of the top 10 entrepreneurs under the age of 25. Not surprisingly, earning that designation requires a lot of work—to the tune of two full time jobs (one with Sun Microsystems, the other working to grow CulturalConnect, the organization she founded). She may be an extraordinary case in terms of the hours she works but she is not extraordinary in her desire to demonstrate her true potential and provide a meaningful impact in the work that she does. She told us:

> The types of people I surround myself with are all driven and ambitious individuals that have no boundaries on their ideas for growth and work schedule. I guess that's what "normal" is to me. There are some days where I feel strain—but I think I react differently to it than most people. I don't let things effect me. If I do feel overwhelmed I try to go out and do something fun with friends to get my mind off of it, etc. At the end of the day, it's work and it's not life threatening so I'm not going to stress over it." She added, "I definitely thrive on challenge, the next big idea, and especially the types of people I work around. I don't consider what I do at Sun or at my start-up "work"—I'm very lucky to be a part of very cool work cultures that promote my interests. Also, I'm the type of person that has had this lifestyle since I was a kid, always stacking too much on my plate, so it's very hard for me to say no to cool projects.

The common belief is that the digital generation is motivated to promote their interests on Web sites and through social networks because of ego. But that is not why we do it. As media digitizes, fragments, and moves closer to the audience, the information, experiences, and stuff become more a reflection of the community than a product that is delivered to the audience.

Kill the Complete Game

Let's compare a typical organization to a baseball team. On a ball club, teams have players specialized in almost every position. Nobody is more specialized than the pitcher. There are starting pitchers, long-relief pitchers, middle-relief pitchers, short-relief pitchers, and closers who are hired and paid to do just that job. The closer, for example, is typically brought in to pitch one inning, a couple of dozen pitches at most. His role is to preserve a win for his ball club.

In an organization, you always want to build the strongest possible team. As a part of that team, there are always spots for someone to fill a specific role. Organizations, in other words, are always looking for a closer (or maybe more than one). But there is a problem with this model. In baseball, the closer is only good in one situation—the ninth inning when the game is close and a save is needed. If he pitched the night before, he might not be available or have his best stuff. If he didn't pitch the night before he might take a little while to find his groove when one mistake can cost his team a victory. The closer is great when he is pitching well, but his capabilities are pretty limited. Similarly, as the marketplace changes dramatically, even on a daily basis in some organizations, that specialized employee is only moderately useful.

There is an alternative. Consider Pat Venditte, a student at Creighton University and a pitcher on the college's Division 1 baseball team. Venditte is ambidextrous. He throws left-handed to lefties and right-handed to righties, and effectively. According to the Creighton Department of Athletics, Venditte is one of three known ambidextrous pitchers in college baseball today. He wears a special glove that has two thumb holes and four fingers so he can switch hands at will. In 2006, he pitched both left-handed and right-handed in 22 games. In 12 of those appearances he struck out batters by using both arms including one game where he struck out two batters left-handed before switching and striking out the last batter right-handed—a total of 10 pitches. The *New York Times* wrote, "Venditte is smoothly proficient from both sides. His deliveries are not mirror images of each other: as a right-hander he throws over the top and relatively hard, up to 91 miles an hour, with a tumbling curveball; as a left-hander, he relies on a whip-like sidearm delivery and a biting slider."[3]

How did Venditte become such a valuable player? He worked at it. At the age of three Venditte threw a football left-handed to build strength and muscle memory. He would punt footballs left-footed to develop the leg kick needed for pitching. And how has he become so effective? The coach of the Creighton baseball team has put him in a position to succeed. Venditte is easily the most valuable pitcher on the Creighton ball club. If he continues to improve, he may someday be a major league pitcher.

Organizations need people like Venditte—specialized but with more than one skill and more than one way of delivering. Add to that an ability and commitment to work hard and strengthen additional skills on the job and you have a recipe for success. For an organization to be competitive at what it must acquire the right talent, deploy it properly, and continually evolve to meet changing needs and situations.

Moneyball

In 2003, Michael Lewis analyzed the mathematical methodology used by Billy Beane, the general manager of the Oakland Athletics, in his book, *Moneyball* (New York: W.W. Norton, 2004). Beane challenged the conventional wisdom of baseball that big name, highly athletic hitters and young pitchers with rocket arms were the only way for a baseball team to succeed. His theory had proven itself—the A's routinely have a winning record and make the playoffs despite having player payrolls smaller than the Boston Red Sox, New York Yankees, and nearly every other major league team.

Lewis argues in the book that little-known numbers and statistics matter more that most physical attributes. In reality, the success the A's have enjoyed is probably a combination of luck, careful player choices, and poor decisions by other major league teams in how they choose and invest in players. Still, a new model for how to build teams was born.

The same is true for all organizations. There are several core elements in the practice of hiring employees that don't seem to have ever changed. They include the writing of a resume and cover letter by a prospective employee, most likely following the format outlined in one of the hundreds of books or Web sites on the subject. There is the interview process, where employees are run through a gauntlet of conversations that cover the same basic questions, such as:

- Tell me your greatest accomplishment.
- What was the most difficult thing about the role you played in your last job?
- Give me an example of when you took the time to share a co-worker's achievement with others.
- What steps do you take when you have to make a tough decision?

In some organizations, where you are simply hiring someone to toil away using only basic skills, we are pretty sure this process will work. But innovations in technology and changing audience expectations require organizations to hire—or train—people with different capabilities.

Start with the hiring practices. Does the established process help you find really dynamic people? And short of being a psychologist or behavioral specialist of some kind, do you think you can adequately judge someone's capabilities and organizational fit from a handful of conversations?

Jason Goldberg told us that Jobster takes the approach that finding a job is not a transaction, it's a lifestyle, and furthering a career is not a thing you do just once, it's a thing you do continuously.

> It is ingrained into our being and our culture. How do we show that there are real people here and not just resumes? How do we show that there are real people here and not just job listings? One of the foundations of our site is user-generated content around what it is to work at certain companies. What is the interview experience like? What are the best projects to work on? And through this, we have developed this incredible wealth of knowledge that gets to the heart of the hiring process. It only works because we get the content from real people. It is based on the same notion of we hire people here who are passionate about solving the problem we're trying to solve. It's not just about connecting people via technology. It's about how do we help that job seeker or how do we help that person who's trying to get ahead in their career, or how do we help that company find someone to fill that important role for them? How do we help them solve that challenge they have?

When Brian worked in the White House Office of Presidential Speechwriting, the process of hiring a speechwriter started with identifying and recruiting the best writers, thinkers, and public servants— the people who would best take advantage of the opportunity to serve at the pleasure of the President. Candidates went through rounds of interviews that, if they were successful, end in a meeting where the President or Vice President gets to size you up for himself. The most important aspect of the interview process, however, is a simulated on-the-job testing exercise—the writing of a series of speeches, of varying length and focus, on a deadline similar to what the speechwriters in the White House faced on a regular basis.

As you might imagine, the job of writing with and for the most powerful people in the world is a high-stress job. The topics they address are wide ranging, and as a speechwriter you have to take on the voice of the principal for whom you are writing. You have to quickly master a variety of subjects and styles, input the comments of dozens of advisers, all on a short deadline. But in the end, through this rigorous training exercise, you were more likely to find the person who not only has the qualifications on his resume but who actually fits the role and the culture of the office. The same can be true in your organization.

Your goal should always be to put a team together that can excel in any way they are called upon, in the moment. It is also important to maintain that balance between the present and the future, to ensure your organization is always learning and being challenged. The question Jeffrey Hollender asks is: "How do you intentionally create a process that allows your employees to grow and flourish as people at work in a way that is connected to the purpose or the strategy of the business? Not in a way that is solely defined by what someone wants to do. So someone's development has to be aligned with the strategic objectives of the company." He added, "What has amazed me is, when you realize that you can actually go about helping that blossom in other people, that's where the huge potential is."

We talked to one Major League Baseball team executive who told us,

> We want to put a team on the field every year that we think can reach the post-season. So we do try to put a team on the field every year that we think can reach the post-season, but we do always have our eye out for a three- to five-year plan to make sure that we're covered. Trading prospects is probably the most obvious place where this comes up. If you have a center fielder who you think can be really good, or a relief pitcher who will develop into a star over time, but you can get a number starter for this year, do you trade those other players? Do you give up a possible starting center fielder, or a possible invaluable eighth inning guy, for a guy that's going to be helpful for this year? You probably don't. You never would customize your team around one challenge.

Like in baseball, you need to fill your organization with people who will help in short and long term situations, as starters and closers, and are capable of playing several different positions and roles. They will bring different strengths and weaknesses, complement each others style of play and your style of management. You want the best possible team on the field at all times and when you have that in place, you can feel confident that the rest will work itself out.

You Are Only As Strong As Your Virtual Link

Organizations do not have to offer everything on their own. "To build or buy" has long been a common question among financial officers in corporations and the concept, when applied to partnership, can be extended to all organizations. More importantly, the current media environment expands the pool of partners. You have an opportunity to combine your expertise—share it up and down the line of experience, and maximize the elements that each partner specializes or focuses on.

For example, if you are in the consumer food product business, let's say the cereal business, you should actively partner with the supermarkets, the groups that reach and engage your target audience, and the dieticians/lifestyle managers to understand how best to produce, package, and sell your product. The goal in these partnerships is to enhance the target audience experience so whatever you are offering fits into the lifestyle, the home, and the customer expectations. You might be able to do part of that on your own, but with partners you can accomplish much more.

The 2004 Cone Corporate Citizenship study found that companies are now trying to determine which causes will best benefit society, enhance their brands, and create bottom-line results when looking for a partner. Instead, they should be looking at which partner best enhances their ability to provide a high-quality experience to their audience. Education is the issue that most Americans say is important to them, with health, the environment, poverty, crime, terrorism, youth, and housing/community development also on the list. While companies know that they can adopt one of those issues, perhaps by donating to an organization or in other ways, what they need is to determine is whether their organizational mission supports it. There has to be a core element within the organization that makes real sense, or the partnership will be hollow.

Whether a prospective partner comes from the same space (two media companies aligning to take on a third company, as NBC and NewsCorp did recently to battle YouTube), or from completely different worlds (a corporation and a nonprofit aligning in a cause marketing partnership), there will be differences in culture, values, the ways of approaching problems, and the ways of relating to people. The partnership should extend only to the point where everyone benefits, as a result of the collective action.

One natural opportunity for a partnership is between corporate and nonprofit organizations. Cone's study found that 89 percent of Americans believe that corporations and nonprofits should work together to raise money and awareness for causes. It also found that 76 percent of Americans believe partnerships result in a more positive image of the nonprofit; 79 percent are more likely to buy a product that supports the nonprofit; 76 percent are more likely to tell a friend about the nonprofit; and 70 percent are more likely to donate money to the nonprofit when corporate and non-profit interests are working as one.

Beyond the perceived benefits of a partnership, or the simple financial benefit that comes from the two working together, these types of partnerships can also align in more substantive ways. According to the Cone research, 75 percent of people surveyed felt nonprofits would benefit from having employees of a partner company volunteer and 66 percent would welcome information about a cause or charity on the company's product or packaging. But they can also offer substantive help—in the form of shared research and expertise.

The partnership may occur with a project or focus, or it could be used as a reason to create a new initiative or even a new organization with a socially driven profit motive. The effort may leverage the existing assets of the two organizations, such as relationships with their target audiences, communities, or brands—or it might simply borrow on the expertise and experience of people from both sides. No matter its origin, the partnership can yield cost savings for the nonprofit, improve community relations or public image for the company (and the nonprofit really), lay the foundation for new product or service development, or allow both groups to enter new markets they wouldn't have been able to penetrate on their own.

It is worth noting that nonprofits use the term *partnership* to mean many things, including corporate philanthropy or cause-related marketing. That is not what we are talking about here. Those are necessary and welcome coordinated efforts between organizations. But our focus is on ventures with shared operational involvement and a social focus.

Michael Brown and Alan Khazei explained how City Year began to offer services to corporate partners.

> Companies started coming to us and saying, "Hey, this is great, this model of success that you have. Can you do something for

our employees and companies?" So we started to invite them to participate as part of our citizenship program—much more than just saying "Hey, give us a check." They began hiring us and what they found is it is great for team building. People can be painting a school and you can have people who are on the front line and people who are senior executives working side by side, who otherwise would never talk or rarely; they get to know each other in a different way. You can get a sense of wow, we transformed that school in one day; we can then go solve this business problem. It's more about you building an opportunity, but it is a structured opportunity.

The most successful partnerships between organizations should include some sort of transfer of talent. A company can provide guidance and training to a nonprofit organization for how to operate more efficiently in the marketplace, and a nonprofit can provide the credibility and expertise that only an independent entity can provide. Nonprofit organizations, meanwhile, can provide special training around how to deal with difficult issues.

Corporate partners often don't realize that nonprofits lack management, marketing, and communications expertise and personnel. They identify the organization because of their passion for a particular issue and not necessarily because they have any knowledge of the training required to run an effective organization. Additionally, with limited budgets, nonprofits are often unable to secure the talent they need to fill a particular role. Or, if the nonprofit organization does have the appropriate staff in place, they often don't have time or money to focus on everything they need to do.

Social Capital in Action

How do you know you are doing it right? Start by following what the best organizations do. Fast Company teamed with Monitor Group beginning in 2004 to assess how leading social entrepreneurial organizations achieve success. Each year, they offer what they call Social Capitalist Awards, recognizing strong performance in both social impact and organizational effectiveness. Some of the groups, including three who are represented by interviews in this book—DonorsChoose, Jumpstart, and City Year—have been recognized for their efforts. Their performance is represented by five critical components: social impact, aspiration and growth, entrepreneurship, innovation, and sustainability. What does that all mean? Here's how Fast Company defines these components:

- *Social Impact:* First, we examine the rigor and sophistication of the organization's approach to social change: its understanding of the problem it is trying to address and the solution it is providing, and whether its performance metrics are tightly aligned with the problem it is addressing. Organizations that look for the highest-leverage, root cause solutions and are committed to assessing their progress in "moving the needle" are positioned to have the most significant social impact. Secondly we assess the social impact created by the organization. We look for organizations that can demonstrate that they are having disproportionately large impact on the problems that they address, relative to other organizations in their area or at their organizational age.

- *Aspiration and Growth*: In addition to proving that an organization is having significant impact today, we also look for organizations that dream big, that aim to push their direct and systemic impact out into the world as far and as fast as they can. Having said that, we look for those high aspirations to be backed by a logical, achievable growth plan that recognizes relevant organizational challenges and milestones. An enormous vision that is not in any way believable or achievable is very unlikely to create tremendous impact, and the organization may waste scarce resources in the process.

- *Entrepreneurship*: We define entrepreneurship as "the ability to do a lot with a little." For each applicant, we look for specific evidence that the organization is able to gather and command disproportionately large resources (e.g. financial, human, partnership or intellectual assets), and thinks strategically about which resources it deploys in solving its social problem. We also seek proof that these resources are being used to their maximum potential and efficiency. Finally, we look for indications that the organization is truly entrepreneurial in nature: passionate, ambitious, creative, flexible, focused on constant improvement, and willing to hold individuals accountable for meaningful results.

- *Innovation*: We define innovation as the organization's ability to generate a game-changing or pattern breaking idea—either a new solution to an existing social problem or a startling new business or operational model. We also look for evidence that a culture of innovation exists within the organization—that there are processes for continuously developing significant new ideas, evaluating whether or not the organization should invest in a new idea, and plans in place to carry them out. At the highest level, a Social Capitalist winner is not a one-hit-wonder of innovation, nor does it endlessly pursue new ideas without significant results; it systematically and strategically uses innovation to maximize its social impact against its targeted problem.

- *Sustainability*: Sustainability has two primary dimensions in our assessment. The first establishes that the organization has a strong income strategy to support the organization and its future growth plans. This means reliable, renewable funding sources that are strategically aligned with the mission and business model of the organization. We are purposefully agnostic on the subject of earned revenue. If an organization earns revenue in a way that is fully integrated with its model for creating social impact, that organization gets high marks; if the earned income seems to be an unrelated add-on business, a distraction from the social mission, we're not impressed. In addition to sustainability from a financial perspective, we also look for indications of the general strength of the management team and board and their combined ability to anticipate challenges within the organization and or its operating environment.

- *Customized Approach*: One of the most challenging aspects of our assessment methodology is the need to understand and take into account the unique context and choices of each individual organization and their social mission. *There are no standardized, universally applicable metrics for any of our criteria that would allow an apples-to-apples comparison across all applicants.* Instead, we invest significant effort to develop a sound understanding of each organization and the environment in which it operates. For each organization, the unique challenges and influences of the problem it is tackling, its chosen business model and organizational form, and its relative age or life stage all influence how we define strong performance for that organization.[4]

Fast Company adds, "Increasingly, we're witnessing the blurring of commerce and charity: Companies now tend to their citizenship; nonprofits hitch income-earning solutions to markets. That phenomenon led us this year to assess the most innovative corporate partnerships among our winners—alliances that represent both business value and a choice about what kind of future to create . . . [and] to philanthropic purists who fear that the stain of profit making might corrupt the conscience of social endeavors, the message is clear: Quit thinking small. As ably as nonprofits have created elegant solutions to address complex social problems, business has proven distribution systems, scaling strategies, and technological know-how—all things that nonprofits need to truly succeed globally."[5]

While the focus of the Social Capital Awards is on the work that non-profit organizations are doing to change the world, the same core principles that are rewarded—impact, aspiration and growth, entrepreneurship, innovation, sustainability, and customized approach—should be the feature of any organization, no matter its focus. Too much of the success in our society today is measured in dollars, suggesting that the bottom line outweighs every other metric that a company could produce. What we can assure you of, is that if the other metrics are achieved as well, things like high employee retention and satisfaction, continual growth and innovation in both products and services—the financials will be strong as well.

Getting Out

Partnerships are great and have the potential to change the world—as well as the very organizations that drive the change. Perhaps the greatest challenge in aligning two or more organizations in a true partnership is synching the different values and motivations of the participating groups. As a result, sometimes it just doesn't work out.

A survey by PR Week noted that "When relationships do fall apart, one of the leading causes cited for the failure was that the corporate partner did not fully understand or support the goals of the nonprofit. Seventy-one percent of all respondents say that having a corporation with unrealistic expectations of how the alliance will impact its business was a key concern, while 68 percent add that bad relationships could come when a nonprofit fails to offer a realistic view of what it means to be their partner."[6] In other words, organizations enter partnerships all the time and realize after the fact that it is not working.

Some successful partnerships are the result of chance encounters. Some partnerships are developed because the two organizations involved share a board member or similar important person. After a little while, something may just not seem right. Maybe the differing organizational cultures between the two partners make for a tough integration. Maybe a company is investing millions of dollars without a clear plan of action and the money is simply being invested without return. Maybe the project is efficient and effective, but the mission of the nonprofit has been lost in the process. A true partnership that achieves success means more than just finding a sugar daddy.

The *PR Week* study also found that "One of the biggest problems in these partnerships is that they can suffer when PR opportunities go underutilized on both sides, according to 76 percent of respondents. Failures can also come when the nonprofit does not understand the business objectives of the corporate partner, say 73 percent. Other communication breakdowns include excessive demands of corporations on the time of nonprofit staff, unrealistic expectations of what the partnership will do, unrealistic promises on the part of nonprofits, and poor leadership at nonprofits."[7]

In the best-case scenario, two organizations will align because they share elements of a common mission and a desire to impact that effort. The way in which those organizations approach their mission may be different—a corporation might want to sell more product by promoting a good cause on its packaging while the nonprofit partner might just want awareness of its cause raised to a new level. But their commitment to the product is sound. At the same time, one of the participating groups may be focused on training and motivating its audience, or its stakeholders, while external action is the goal of the other partner.

When it is not working, you have to get out.

The very nature of how we get and share information, experience things, and consume stuff has changed, so naturally the people who created that media need to change as well. Organizations will have to put more money and energy into finding or educating people who create content that can attract and retain valuable audiences. In the digital world, the incremental cost of distribution gets closer and closer to zero, so the value proposition is centered on the content—that information, those experiences, and that stuff— so the ability to create value rests on the people who create content. If you can't bring in the right people to your own organization, find the right partners and collectively provide the value that your audience expects, instead of trying to do things you can't. It's not the normal way that most organizations operate, but it is the way they should.

CHAPTER 10

Be Ahead of Your Audiences

Does your organization stand out?

You probably think, or even know, that your organization is better at whatever you do than the others in your space (hint: you *should* think that). Lots of organizations think that. But is it true, and more importantly, does your audience know that is the case? Can your audience tell the difference between what you offer and what your competition does? Can you differentiate yourself—not only in marketing, but in service and support and ongoing relationship building — from the others in your space?

We are not trying to question your ability or criticize you work. It's a matter of fact that it is getting harder and harder to tell one organization a part from another in many cases. Why is that? Because your audience goes looking for information, experiences, or stuff to answer a very specific question they have, conquer a challenge, or satisfy a curiosity. They don't go looking for brands. They probably aren't knowledgeable enough about what various groups do to tell them apart without first researching. And, just to complicate matters, their pool of available options includes a near-infinite number of possibilities. Distinguishing one provider from another is difficult.

Your ability to be located and to become rooted in the consciousness of your target audience is perhaps the greatest challenge you will face as an organization. Call it your *findability factor.*

Findability is not only about being found on the Internet, having your name and address in the Yellow Pages, or placing a billboard where all can see. Findability is the likelihood that someone encountering your organization can get the relevant, timely, and compelling information they expect throughout their interaction with you. If they do, they are far more likely to remember you and return again. If they don't, that person from your audience will make a judgment about you that puts you at the bottom of their priority list. And when they go out looking for someone to sell them something or to answer their question in the future, they will have plenty of other, better choices to look to for help.

Organizations that support their audience in finding the information they want and need have a lot to gain. Organizations that don't, or can't do that, invite increased competition. Most organizations fail miserably when it comes to findability, because they don't consider the interests of their audience over their own interests. The good news is that it is not that difficult to make yourself more findable.

Achieving Findability

The term *findability* was coined by Peter Morville, a leading information architecture and user experience consultant, following a visit to the McNamara terminal at Detroit Metropolitan Airport. At the time, the airport was new, state-of-the-art. The WorldHub for Northwest Airlines, where Morville was traveling through, boasts 36-foot-high cathedral-like arched ceilings and floor-to-ceiling windows that help shower the ticketing area with warm sunlight. When it opened in 2002, it offered 99 gates, 18 luggage carousels, an 11,500-space parking garage spread across 10 levels (Morville describes it as "the largest single parking structure in the world ever built at one time"), and an automated express tram system to help the 30 million passengers who travel through the Motor City airport each year to traverse the 1.6-kilometer terminal.

Somewhere inside the two-million-square-foot structure, the designers found room for a massive fountain; an 800-foot tunnel connecting concourses that includes a mixed media installation to create a changing experience of sound and light; 475 public restrooms; and hundreds of restaurants and shops. Further, the airport authority featured a 6-foot-by-37-foot directional sign in the center link area displays information on the location of the terminal's assets and recommends the best way to reach the various gates (by foot, moving sidewalk, or using the Express Tram). The terminal was fawned over by design experts, the newspapers, and local officials for its creativity and technological sophistication and had become one of the jewels of the American airport network.

But Morville, who lives in nearby Ann Arbor, Michigan, found the terminal extremely frustrating to navigate. Upon arrival, he set out to find a bathroom and buy a cup of coffee before his flight took off. With nearly an hour before his flight was to board, and only those two quick errands and a walk from one end of the terminal to the other to complete, Morville had tremendous difficulty. What happened? While the airport designers had put their energy into promoting the glossy eating, shopping, people-moving and other features of the terminal they had overlooked the need to clearly label things like bathrooms to help passengers find their way. Morville wrote about how people search, and how they find what they're looking for—or more likely do not find what they are looking for after his trip through the airport, saying "Findability applies broadly across all sorts of physical and virtual environments."[1]

Findability is a combination of usability and information architecture. Usability speaks to the ease with which someone can use something, whether it's a product or a Web site, in either the physical or virtual space, to achieve a particular goal. For example, if the primary function of a Web site is to take online donations and the donate button is hidden in the bottom right corner of the site (where tests show users typically do not look), that site is probably not usable. Similarly, if a water bottle was designed too big for the hand of its target customer, it would not be considered to have good usability.

Information architecture is the practice of organizing and structuring knowledge or data according to how the user might need to receive it. It is most commonly used when talking about how Web sites are structured, so a user knows what link to click on or path to follow. It can also be applied to filing systems or libraries. In findability, there is also a third important dimension—considering how users process the experience they are having with something, and specifically whether their common sense is enough to carry them from beginning to end of their quest for information.

For an organization to have a high level of findability, it has to achieve in three key areas: design, user experience, and service. Peter Morville told us:

> The most important element that's going to make you successful there is—for lack of a better term—user centered design. That means including the user, the customer, in the design process. I don't like the term *user centered design*, because I don't think it exists in the real world. We're always balancing business goals

and strategy with user needs and behavior. And yet it's critical to include the user in the design process. In the case of the airport, I read at that time, in Germany it was a pretty common practice when opening an airport to have a whole bunch of school kids come through to see if they can find their way to the right airplane, and observe the kinds of problems they ran into trying to navigate the airport. So whether you're designing digital or physical products, making sure you do some sort of user testing, ideally with a mix of audiences.

There is not a simple rule that organizations can follow. It is more about adopting a mind-set that isn't drawn to any extreme. More experienced people at organizations will always bring some real strengths, as well as perspective, based on how a group developed. But you must also keep learning and stay open to new ideas and ways of interacting.

We will take up the first two keys here—design and user experience—and leave service to another chapter.

Attractiveness is Not Effective Design

The world is full of bad design. And yet, either because bad design has become so commonplace, or because it can be so effective (and requires less energy then good design), it remains a constant and defining part of our society. The concept is subjective—whether something is good or not—and everyone has an opinion about it. You see it in advertising, architecture, products, and of course on the Internet. Good design, it is argued, is user-centric, considering the needs, wants, and limitations of the person who will become the audience for something. Bad design, by contrast, does not consider the audience and therefore fails to connect.

Tom Chi, a collaborator and writer on the comic strip *OK/Cancel* (www.ok-cancel.com), argues that bad design exists on the Internet because the functionality and underlying purpose of a site outweighs the impact that the look and feel of the page provides. "Whether it's Craigslist or MySpace or IMDB, by being the first in the space they were able to capture the community and the net result was that early success led to later success," Chi wrote on his OK/Cancel Web site. Chi describes this as the "community lock-in" effect, where people will go where other people are, regardless of how the site looks or feels—the more successful the site is, the less important the aesthetics are.

A simple example, according to Chi, is eBay. He wrote, "eBay has huge community lock-in effect, but in some smaller niches they are losing ground to people who specialize in the niche." He cites the growing number of competitor sites that have been created to offer niche services and target a key subset of eBay's large audience. Writing about one such competitor, Blue Nile, which has successfully competed with eBay at selling diamonds, Chi explains, "It's not because their community is larger, but because their user-experience (and aesthetics) have been tailored for this niche buying experience, they can outmaneuver eBay, who must create a generalized (and sometimes ugly) buying experience for all types of goods."[2]

Design, of course, is not just about products and pictures—it extends to experiences as well. JoRoan Lazaro, who was creative director for America Online for three years, said,

> It just really depends organization by organization. In the AOL years early on, design and creativity played a very large part in the organization, because we created brand new things that didn't exist before, some of which became key component parts for the company. We literally designed the service, meaning how you get online, how you use it, as well as products, like instant messenger. They were made, crafted, and built for the express purpose of people's needs. We taught people how to send e-mail, how to communicate across long distances for free using IMs, and conveniently. And that was how many people actually learned how to browse the Internet because it was so early on that it wasn't a common, everyday tool like a phone or a TV.
>
> So in that particular instance, design was integral. I wouldn't have happened without us, whether it was in terms of specifying what the product or the service was going to be, all the way through the visual design, which is how are you going to interact with it and what the branding is like.

Currently, McDonald's is in the early stages of remodeling all of its franchise locations around the world to compete better with the décor of competitors like Panera Bread Company, Starbucks, and others. The goal is to reshape the entire experience that customers have, beginning with the look of their store environments. The shift in focus began with the menu, which now includes healthier items like salads, targeted at women, and apple slices and skim milk for children. Executives soon realized that menu changes also contributed to changing habits of how customers ate—and as *BusinessWeek* reported, "the chain's typical starkly lit, plastic-heavy look" was now "at odds with the contemporary, welcoming image the company wants to present."[3]

The slanted rooflines are gone in place of golden sloping curves. The traditional McDonald's yellow and red colors will remain, but the red will be muted to terra cotta, and olive and sage green will be added to the mix. The restaurants will have less plastic and more brick and wood, with modern lighting, framed photographs or other art on the walls, and music catering to different types of customers.

The most dramatic of the changes will come in the dining areas, where three different sections will support three different, distinct personalities of patrons: a "linger" zone will offer comfortable armchairs, sofas, and Wi-Fi connections; the "grab and go" zone will feature tall counters with bar stools as well as plasma TVs for customers who eat alone; and the "flexible" zone will offer families comfortable fabric booths and flexible seating while keeping them away from other diners. Even Ronald McDonald is being given a more modern look to help customers better relate to him.[4]

What motivated McDonald's to make these changes? Revenue was a major factor, of course. Sales in 2004 totaled nearly $19.1 billion worldwide but niche establishments have been effective at peeling away customers from breakfast and lunch—meals where McDonald's used to dominate when they were virtually the only fast-food game in town. Experience also played a key role. With more than 31,000 franchise locations in 119 countries it is not hard to locate a McDonald's. But as our society evolves and user expectations change, customers no longer believes that McDonald's can offer the dining experience they are looking for, and the company has to adapt. A wholesale change in the way McDonald's operates, including the integration of a whole new design for the company, is underway. The response from those who have been to redesigned locations has been positive. Though their locations are ubiquitous, these changes will surely make for McDonald's findability rating to once again be on the rise.

While McDonald's will heavily promote its new design as a way of attracting customers away from places like Starbucks, other organizations deliberately present designs for their marketing and store locations to reach a crowd specifically because they have no interest in Starbucks. Or so argues Robert Scoble, co-author of *Naked Conversations* (New York: Wiley, 2006), who termed the phenomenon *anti-marketing design*. In a March 2006 post on his blog, Scoble wrote that bad design for Web sites has its virtues, namely that it gives organizations a contrast with those that do good design.

> Why does anti-marketing design work? Well, for one, big companies will never do a site that doesn't look pretty. Why? Because of the prevailing belief that great brands need to be beautiful. Look at what corporate branding experts study. Apple. Target. BMW. Everything those guys do is beautiful. Aesthetic. Crafted by committees of ad marketing department experts.[5]

There are plenty of organizations who design their stores, Web sites, and marketing materials to cater to an audience that has a desire to get in and out without any consideration for style. Markus Frind, the CEO of Plentyoffish.com, has deliberately underdesigned the Web site for his free-dating business so users are not distracted as they seek out a good relationship match. He argued in a post on his blog, Paradigm Shift, that this concept applies online as well as off-line and that users are most focused on product and not design. He wrote, "Users don't want to be distracted by useless graphics, colors, features, etc. When you buy spoons from a place like Wal-Mart, you just pick them out of a big box of spoons. They don't come with a mountain of packaging, they don't come with manuals, and most of all they don't come plastered with pretty graphics and a 'beautiful layout.'"[6]

In the design community, the discussion about good design and who it is targeted to has been tied to a discussion of class. A panel at the 2007 South by Southwest (SXSW) interactive festival in Austin, Texas, posited that "Just as Apple, BMW, and the *New York Times* market high-end products to elite customers, Wal-Mart, Fox News, and World Wrestling Entertainment target their working-class customers very . . . differently," and asked, "Is there a design class system?"

There is absolutely a difference in how design is applied to different products or issues based on the educational or economic status of the target audience. There is nothing inherently wrong with this practice of targeting information based on what the audience knows or is accustomed to. After all, the purpose of marketing is to sell products, build brand, and sway people's perspectives about an issue. The more closely aligned the design of an organization's materials is with the experiences of the audience being targeted, the more likely they are to resonate and be effective. The tension comes if designers deliberately alter their work with the belief that what the audience is capable of is limited. Those who do so are unfairly stereotyping the audience and limiting the ability of their own designs to truly engage an audience.

Designers of products, stores, Web sites, advertisements, or anything else, who deliberately keep their creations simple and focused, are trying to put an emphasis on the functionality of what they are designing—trying to get people in and out of a store quickly (instead of creating an environment where they must linger to truly understand a product and be motivated to purchase) or help them find the answer to their question without delay. Remember, most people go looking for information, experiences, or stuff to answer a very specific question they have, conquer a challenge, or satisfy a curiosity. Effective design can help a user meet those needs and build trust between an organization and its audience. And depending on the brand and the user, what constitutes effective design can be very different.

User Experience

There is more than how a store looks or an organization markets itself that is required to achieve a level of trust with an audience. In other words, design has limits. Where design leaves off is where user experience begins.

User experience is a measure of how organizations match their operational objectives with the needs of their audience, in practice. A good user experience is unique to each organization. There is no single way to deliver what the customer expects, develop a process around that, and make the necessary changes over time—but there are standards you can set, and follow.

Organizations that create a good user experience for their audience begin with a clear understanding of what they want to do, and why. We have no doubt that every small business owner dreams of making money and supporting her lifestyle while working as her own boss—but that wasn't the original focus when she started selling cupcakes from her kitchen or first designed a new toy in her basement late one evening. The same is true for nonprofit organizations or academic institutions. These groups began operating with the fundamentals of business in mind, and a social mission, be it around education or service, competing for attention at the very core of what they do.

Frank Kern, who helps lead global marketing for Starbucks told us that their customer comes in with a certain user experience in mind, and it is up to each store location to match their desire.

> Our customer expects a really high-quality beverage, a really consistent execution, all the things that you would want in any retail establishment, but most of all they want a comfortable environment. Cleanliness, quiet, all those elements would be part of it. Whether you call it the third-place experience or the Starbucks experience, it comes down to people having a desire for "their space," and their comfortable place that they want to go and spend time. We refer to it as the "third-place" experience: It's not work, it's not home. It's that place that you go to use however you see fit. And I think that's what our customers want of us. That's what our customers expect from us.
>
> And I also think that our customers, just from a brand perspective, sort of look to us to always be providing something new, something unique, something innovative within that space, whether it's a new form of entertainment, whether it's a new product or new merchandise—whatever it would happen to be. I think there's some type of expectation level that "When I go to Starbucks, there's always going to be some new, interesting, innovative element that will be unique for me to see and enjoy in my space."

Creating a good user experience takes time and focus. The most successful organizations test, solicit feedback (and are sure to listen), learn from that feedback, and modify their practices to improve on mistakes. When successful, a good user experience creates a positive return in customer loyalty and organizational revenue, but it is not just a practice—it's a way of life for successful organizations.

Michael Brown and Alan Khazei from City Year have improved their user experience over the past 20 years and explained the impact to us this way:

> What we've seen is that if people spend a year, full-time, deeply immersed in active service with a diverse group of their peers, people who otherwise would never meet, people who come from all walks of life, doing meaningful work, that is transforming, and it enables them to be much more active citizens and leaders for the rest of their life.
>
> That's why we believe in national service. We actually think that if this idea can get to scale, if there were a million people a year in AmeriCorps, for example, that, more than anything else, would fundamentally change our country, and if there were millions around the world doing it, because you would release that kind of justice and that kind of energy, more than anything else, that's what we believe in.
>
> We've actually seen it. We did a study two years ago and found that our Corps members volunteer at much higher rates, and they lead other people into service. They contribute to causes at much higher rates. 90 percent said they made and maintained a friendship with somebody fundamentally different that they otherwise wouldn't have known. 80 percent go on to further education. They are leaders in all sectors. They have started charter schools, they are working in government, working in other nonprofits; some have started their own nonprofits.

User experience, of course, is very different online, but the principles remain the same. In a store, some customers want to browse, while others want to find their item, get the best price, pay, and be on their way. You can often tell what type of shopper a customer is by his body language. The ones who have a desire to browse the merchandise in the hope that they will find something that feels, smells, or looks just right for them will walk a little slower, peruse all the aisles, and avoid asking for help right away. The customers who are on a mission to find the specific pair of shoes that matches an outfit or the tool that will allow them to complete the project will move quickly to a specific area or seek out an employee for assistance almost immediately. From the moment they walk into a store, each of your customers is bombarded with the sights and sounds that either help them find what they want or cause them distraction, and even confusion. A user's experience begins when they approach the store, and it doesn't end until the final transaction is complete, sometimes long after they leave the store.

On a Web site, you can't tell what kind of shopper is entering your site. The only way to match the shopping patterns on a Web site to the customer is by offering different shopping experiences for each type of shopper you wish to serve, and then measuring to see if your options resulted in transactions. According to usability expert, Jakob Nielsen, there are thousands of lessons that you can follow to make sure that whatever you build online can be easily used by a variety of audiences. Is it easy to move around the store? Are my customers able to find what they want? How can I speed up transactions at the checkout counter? In a brick-and-mortar enterprise, the problem would be so obvious, no one could ignore it. Online, you might spend hours looking for something before realizing it is simply not there.

Online and off-line users have different expectations for what their user experience will be like. Off-line, the generally accepted belief is that if you purchase the wrong product you can simply return to the store and get an exchange. Online, because you have never met your sales associate, nor encountered what you purchase in a physical environment, the user is taking more of a risk. Providing your customer with confidence that they are not buying the wrong product, a defective product, or other disappointment can be achieved through attention to user experience. For example, when offering a variety of choices, offer the opportunity to compare them side-by-side instead of forcing users to seek out (and worse, remember) what the different features are to consider. Since customers are used to being able to get an opinion or assistance from a human being in an off-line shopping experience, create the same opportunity online for those who seek it out.

Good user experience off-line is about being able to respond quickly to any type of customer who walks into the store. Even if you can't satisfy what that customer wants—because you don't have the product they are looking for or the answer to their questions—how you respond and choose to act is important.

Being ahead means being useful. It also means being visible, and therefore findable. That doesn't mean that you should be alone, that you must stick your head out and try something risky that has only a small potential for reward. Success is a collaborative effort between you and your customers, not just a response to their demands or an invitation to try new things that have no place in your existing structure. When you discover what the right balance is, you will be able to move forward quickly enough that you keep an advantage over your competition and prudently enough that your customers come along with you and success is assured. How you do that, is what we tackle next.

CHAPTER 11

Be Second to Your Competitors

There is a common belief that to be successful, you have to be alone—you have to stand out. Is that true? We don't think so.

Former Vanderbilt and UCLA football coach Henry "Red" Sanders is credited with introducing the saying, "Winning isn't everything, it's the only thing," into the American lexicon. Legendary coach Vince Lombardi popularized the mantra in the 1960s as coach of the Green Bay Packers. Jack Welch made sure the business world was aware as well, writing a book entitled *Winning* (New York: HarperCollins, 2005), and going around offering the theory that "In the end, winning companies are the only thing that sustains societies like ours."[1]

On this point, *BusinessWeek* wrote in 2006: "Everyone likes to win. Beneath all the talk about teamwork and balance, all the books on being kind and cultivating emotional intelligence, people still crave to be the best. Call it passion, drive. In the world of competition, few battlegrounds are more intense than the one with the self. The hunger to reach the top, regardless of the obstacles that stand in your way, remains a fundamental force in the success—and, at times, the dark side—of the human race."[2] Second place is not acceptable. If you aren't at the head of the pack you are permanently behind. If you don't win, every time, you are a loser all the time.

We have idolized characters like Gordon Gecko, putting the ruthless business tycoon in the 1987 movie *Wall Street* on a pedestal for business students to emulate. We cheer reality TV shows like *Survivor*, which invites scheming and dishonesty in the name of competition, yet we are somehow surprised when our leaders are caught with their hand in the cookie jar. Donald Trump has created an entire industry around *The Apprentice,* a glorified gladiator battle masked as a job interview—and executive coaches are now using the show as a model for how organizations should run their teams!

Our world is obsessed with winning, and organizational leaders have come to believe that being first or finishing first is the only way to operate. This is the norm in business and in everything else. But, in the previous chapter we noted how infinite choices exist for audiences, which makes it increasingly difficult to be unique. In the robust media environment that we are in, it is impossible to be alone (in the user's mind), so the best option is to be a part of the crowd, but at the same time to distinguish yourself, to stand out within that crowd.

Winning is absolutely important, but it must not be the sole focus of an organization. Developing a strategy that winning only emphasizes is not going to get you or your organization the kind of long-term, measurable success that you desire. The obsessive quest for victory creates a strategic blind spot that puts the ultimate finish ahead of the natural improvements and other innovations an organization needs. That blind spot will weaken your organization. Though it may not be obvious can easily be exploited by your competition.

Times have changed and the definition of success has changed as well. Nobody wins all the time, and trying to do so is not a sustainable way to run an organization. The goal must be to build an effort that has an impact that you, and your audience, view as important. Moreover, there isn't as much belief that one person or one organization can handle a big issue on their own. We want the wisdom of crowds or the wiki-fication of everything to help us through tough times.

Even Rupert Murdoch, who controls one of the largest media empires in the world, acknowledges that media companies don't control the conversation anymore, at least not to the extent that they once did. He wrote in *Forbes,* "The big hits of the past were often, if not exactly flukes, then at least the beneficiaries of limited options." He added that when three networks divided up the American population, or when only one newspaper could claim a monopoly in their home city, life was a lot easier for media executives. "All that has changed," he writes. Companies who realize this and "adapt to the expectations of the networked consumer can look forword to a new golden age of media," one Murdoch notes will be filled with "relentless experimentation and innovation, accelerating change, and—for those who embrace the new ways in which consumers are connecting with each other—enormous potential."[3]

There are many ways to measure a successful organization and a whole host of strategies for achieving success by those or any terms. The most important thing is to be positioned to succeed at any time. In some cases that means preparing early, anticipating the challenges that might come up. As the speed at which information travels, both online and off, increases, being well positioned also means being ready to respond quickly and to pivot if needed. It is not about claiming the ultimate prize—it's about keeping up, and not falling behind.

The Myth of the First-Mover Advantage

The concept of the first-mover advantage is simple: By being the first to enter a new market, an organization gains an advantage over its potential competitors. The concept is not really new at all—it has been applied to everything from business to the military for as long as competition has existed. Being the first-mover in a space can help when staking out a particular geography or demographic target, or when trying to break into a new market or define an issue for the first time. In some cases, the first-mover literally creates their market space.

The importance of being a first mover varies, however. In the pre–Internet bubble days, the first mover got all the funding from Silicon Valley or Wall Street, so it was seen as a significant strategic advantage. The goal was to find the hot technology that would chase all the other technology start-ups away and make millions in the process. Today, post-bubble, almost any good idea can get funded for at least an initial start-up phase. The goal for investors now is to pit the best ideas against each other in the marketplace to see what rises above the rest.

The same is true for politics. In campaigns, the first mover usually gets the attention in the press and the buzz among the voters. Being the first to stake out a position on health care, education reform, or a key foreign policy issue can lead to significant fundraising advantages and put a candidate on the fast track to becoming the party nominee. At the same time, being a first-mover in politics means starting almost two years before the first primary voting occurs, raising and spending an extraordinary amount of money, and increasingly leads to early favorites getting overexposed in the eyes of voters. The first-mover advantage used to be the ticket to victory. It leaves the door open for a candidate who gains momentum down the stretch, or seem fresh at the right time, to steal the prize. You don't see many striving to be a first-mover in politics any more. Finishing first is what matters most.

The thought has always been that if you get out in front you can lead the pack or even define the terms that all who follow must abide by. That is not always the case. In the past, the pace of technological evolution was moderate, so first-movers had good conditions to create a dominant position that was long lasting. Competitors might have had to wait years before the playing field changed significantly enough to mount a serious challenge. Today, technology is evolving very rapidly, so organizations are provided never-ending opportunities to innovate, and first movers must defend against an almost constantly evolving playing field.

The position of the first mover today is not as strong as some previous first movers might have enjoyed. Because technology is evolving so quickly, an organization's time at the top could be brief—it often isn't able to leverage its short-lived advantage into a long-term relationship with an audience or a significant financial windfall. The value of the first mover shifts mostly because people learn from experience when the advantage is useful and when it is not. Many of the companies that were funded in the pre–Internet bubble days flamed out and their investors lost money. This time around, investors are much more cautious and interested in finding the best company to fund, not the first one that comes to them. Along those lines, the audience's interest has shifted whether an organization has first-mover status to whether an organization offers the right product or service to meet their needs.

This is not an attack on winning, or on moving quickly to take advantage of opportunities. Rather, it's a plea to organizations to think about how to build a long-term strategy for how to manage a successful organization. Winning is great—it creates opportunities for new investment, builds your following, increases your brand recognition, and brings more opportunities to be part of better networks, which can lead to better opportunities in the future. But winning can also lull people into false complacency or overconfidence. If your organization is a first-mover, remember that being first is not always a sustainable advantage and you will encounter many challenges as you go forward.

First movers fail all the time. It is unlikely that you are the only person who has thought of a particular idea for an organization or offering. Nonprofits are routinely guilty of this, launching a whole new organization to offer one tiny variation on a well-worn concept. If you are first into the marketplace, chances are either it's a bad idea, someone else has thought of it and is working on it too, or someone else will immediately recognize what you're doing and enter closely behind with a similar concept—and the benefits of having watched you go first. Sometimes the first-mover is very successful and simply fails to spend the time or energy focused on keeping that advantage. And in those rare situations where the first-mover is and remains a success—well there isn't much we can do beyond congratulate them, and harbor a bit of jealousy. We can only hope to have that kind of good fortune.

Why Being Second Is Sometimes Better

For the majority of us who won't see the kind of sustained first-mover success that legends are made up, we argue that sitting in second can often be the best position of all.

Think of yourself as a race car driver, competing for a season-ending championship. If you have the fastest car on the track every week, you can get out ahead and stay there. But being the fastest car week-in and week-out is very hard to do. Beyond the investment of time and resources, there is luck, not to mention your fellow drivers to deal with.

So you think about a long-term strategy. When you don't have the fastest car, you position yourself in the best place to be when those ahead of you falter (and they often do). You watch and learn what works for them and try to integrate the best practices into your vehicle, hoping one day you might be the fastest. On race day, sometimes you yield to the faster driver behind you, and other times, when the conditions and the field are more favorable, you do the passing.

This is the core concept behind keeping up and not falling behind. More often than not, first movers are overtaken by a late-arriving competitor who has identified the better opportunity and moved in to capitalize. Seth Godin argues that the advantage comes from finding the right fit for a service in a particular market or with a particular audience. He writes:

> There are a million markets. Markets of one, or markets of small groups, or markets of cohorts that communicate. If you're an eBay user, my guess is that eBay was the first auction site you used. If you use Windows, my guess is that you never used [the programming language CPM. And if you are a Starbucks junkie, my guess is that you don't live near a Peets.
>
> What happens: The market often belongs to the first person who brings you the right story on the right day. Yes, you must be first (and right) in *that* market or *this* market. But that doesn't mean you have to be first (and right) in the universe.[4]

This is who you want to be.

Being firmly in second place is the best place to be in terms of positioning yourself for long-term success. You are able to look ahead and see all the mistakes the first mover has made while trying to engage your target audience for the first time. At the same time, you have the luxury of trying something different based on what you learned from their example. You must still innovate quickly enough to remain ahead of your competition, the people who are in third, or fourth or fifth place behind you with the same desire to move up that you have. But you can pick the right time to drive the market, build loyalty with your customers, and succeed in meeting your goals (be they profit, loyalty, or simply defining the conversation).

Your goal should not always be to finish first, but to lead by innovating and improving on what those who have come before you have done. If you succeed, you will change the space you are in and have to explore ways to move again. And if you do it well, you will end up being the most successful in your space anyway.

Whoever Has the Most Doesn't Necessarily Win

It is natural for an organization to want to grow, to reach more people, to be in every market, and to succeed on every front. Why not? If you could provide the same service to an audience 10 times the size of the one you currently reach, would you want to? If you were given the chance to sell your product in a thousand stores instead of just two or three, wouldn't you jump at the chance? Of course you would. It is part of we call the *winning* syndrome.

To put your organization in a strong position to succeed, you must know what you are good at and what you are not. That means you might make a deliberate choice not to grow larger, and instead focus on getting better. Organizations that make the choice to stay focused on doing one or two things really well, instead of trying to do a dozen and falling short, have more than enough room for success and a lower margin for failure. A lot of organizations start off being focused and niche, They find a product, a service, or an idea that they can offer to a certain audience and they build a successful operation around it. If they hold on to their core vision they can replicate that success over and over. If they let the winning syndrome, that constant quest for more and bigger gains, get the best of them, they try to grow too far, or too fast, and end up straying from their original mission and dilute their offering.

Competing in every market and for the attention of every audience is extremely difficult. Don't do it. You don't have to. There is no expectation from your audience that you will be good at everything. That's not why they sought out your products or services in the first place and it is not why you have been successful in maintaining a strong relationship with them over time.

Take Starbucks as an example. The global coffee chain began as a place where people could hang out, read the paper, and enjoy a cup of coffee, all the while escaping from the real world for a bit. Starbucks offered a much-needed change of scenery from what people would get at work or home—what Howard Schultz the founder and chairman, called the *third place*. The global audience embraced this alternative lifestyle that Starbucks had created and the company was able to expand rapidly, becoming a coffee and business phenomenon.

But by early 2007, all was not well at Starbucks. Despite continued financial success and a very public plan to grow to 40,000 stores worldwide in the next five years, Schultz was concerned about the Starbucks experience. As he should have been. He wrote in a memo to his senior staff on February 14, 2007, "Over the past ten years, in order to achieve the growth, development, and scale necessary to go from less than 1,000 stores to 13,000 stores and beyond, we have had to make a series of decisions that, in retrospect, have led to the watering down of the Starbucks experience, and what some might call the commoditization of our brand." He cited several examples, including:

> When we went to automatic espresso machines, we solved a major problem in terms of speed of service and efficiency. At the same time, we overlooked the fact that we would remove much of the romance and theatre that was in play with the use of the La Marzocca machines. . . .
>
> Clearly we have had to streamline store design to gain efficiencies of scale and to make sure we had the ROI on sales to investment ratios that would satisfy the financial side of our business. However, one of the results has been stores that no longer have the soul of the past and reflect a chain of stores vs. the warm feeling of a neighborhood store. Some people even call our stores sterile, cookie cutter, no longer reflecting the passion our partners feel about our coffee.

Anyone who has visited a Starbucks in the past several years has seen some evidence of how Starbucks has strayed from its original focus. Starbucks still offers coffee and basic pastries but now also sells breakfast and lunch, music, books, and even housewares—home espresso machines, dishes, and the like. It launched an entertainment division in Los Angeles that is working to produce motion pictures like *Akeelah and the Bee*, its first theatrical release whose DVDs were sold in stores.

Some of the expanded offerings, most notably the music, are reasonable extensions of the coffeehouse experience. Frank Kern, the vice president of global marketing at Starbucks, explained how it came about naturally: "Our music endeavor, Hear Music, actually began from a barista who would come in with his CDs and play his favorite songs in the store. And it eventually evolved."

He added that anything within the coffeehouse experience was likely to be considered:

> We are very mindful of [the customer's experience, because], at the core, we're a coffeehouse. So I think we're comfortable in expanding the brand into those areas that still accentuate the coffeehouse experience. And I think music, books, for instance, would fall within that. I think it's interesting, though, even when

we promote or offer a book for sale—like since we offered Mitch Albom's book at the end of last year, with the proceeds going to benefit Jumpstart for Young Children, and now we have a new book with an emerging author from Sierra Leone, with the proceeds going to benefit UNICEF, that we're currently selling in our stores—we are offering up, perhaps, artists or authors that the general public wouldn't necessarily be exposed to.

But clearly, some things that Starbucks offers are not adding to the coffeehouse experience, which is why Howard Schultz is so nervous. And he should be. Organizations, whether they are a global coffee chain or a tiny nonprofit organization, face the same challenge. There is a desire to compete, and win, in every market and with every audience. Push too hard and you can easily lose your focus. Let down your guard and you may never recover.

How do you strike that balance between pushing for a victory while still keeping your organization focused and innovative? Jeffrey Hollender, CEO of Seventh Generation, told us:

> We are a company that has these huge aspirations and desires to make a positive contribution to the world, and you know, that attracts other people if it's done in an honest, authentic way. More recently, we have really tried to be even more intentional about that. And the thinking that we have applied to that particular question is: What is the essence of this company? You know, who are we really? And how do we understand that essence in our customers so that, not by chance but by intention, we can create sort of mutual value?
>
> And you know, it takes lots of forms. It is not just about our customers. It is about our whole stakeholder group and value. We think about the retailers we do business with this way, we think about the manufacturers we deal with. When we hire an agency to represent us, we really want to understand who they are and where they're going to see if there is alignment with who we are and where we're going. If we are partners on that journey together, it creates a very different possibility. If we are valued not just because we're a client or we sell a product, but we are really seen as people trying to move the whole conversation forward or the bar up, that creates a very different kind of

relationship. And I think it can happen by itself, but it doesn't necessarily happen by itself, and it really is an effective tool to think about who you want to do business with.

There are traditional metrics of success, like profit or loss. There are also metrics about social impact and how they relate to your industry as a whole. Many organizations, including some of the world's largest and most influential, have begun realizing the benefits of measuring success in more than dollars and cents. Smart leaders realize that good works go hand in hand with profit, and that continual renewal and innovation spur on further success. But few organizations truly understand how to achieve meaningful change and drive lasting success, instead becoming all too easily distracted by the narrow definition of success that has existed up till now.

You can't win them all. So choose carefully and position your organization to take advantage of the new tools for communicating to be more prepared than ever before. Ask yourself, does this opportunity serve to further our original mission or meet our goals? If not, don't do it. Focus on having the impact that you, and your audience, view as important. Recognize that the most important thing to do is to position yourself to succeed. And that means keeping up, and not falling too far behind. Being first, does not mean you can't be distinctive or successful. You can more clearly display the attributes that your audience looks for and work to sustain a relationship with them that will benefit you, and your audience, in the long run.

CHAPTER

12

Be Fresh

In the highly competitive, fragmented world in which we now live, being fresh is a necessity. Innovation is a must. The ability to innovate is what keeps your organization at the top of its field The faster and better you innovate, the more likely you are to remain a leader and set the standard that the others will follow.

Being fresh is important to almost every aspect of what you do— the delivery of information (is it updated regularly?), the creation of experiences (is it the same ride with new characters?), or the development and marketing of good stuff (is that a new color?). There are so many opportunities for your audience to look elsewhere to have their questions answered or their needs met. Perhaps even more than being able to demonstrate expertise or quality service at the start, organizations must ensure that the information, experiences, and stuff they deliver are relevant and timely.

Most people think that to stay fresh you have to introduce something new. It does not. Fresh does not mean new. Being fresh may be about surprise or change. Freshness can come from improving on, leveraging, and extending old and still-popular elements of what you do, or from producing new ideas. Sameness has its place. The role of familiarity should not be underestimated as a way to get attention. Nostalgia is an important tool—it draws on the memories people have of (hopefully good) experiences from the past and allows them to associate those (hopefully good) feelings within the present context.

To remain fresh, you should have a schedule and make updating your offering a regular event. You should make a commitment, to promise your audience that you will not take your relationship with them for granted by allowing it to grow stale. In other words, make freshness an inherent quality of your operation. Relevance and timeliness are the critical factors in a fragmented world, and that standard can be met in a number of ways. The notion of *new* has changed. Fresh is what you need to be.

Am I Getting Stale?

The United States is in the midst of the most entrepreneurial era in its history, with more than 500,000 Americans involved in launching their own companies each year and an estimated 10 to 15 percent of all working adults engaged in some kind of entrepreneurial activity.[1] Among these entrepreneurs, it is the innovators who matter most. Innovators spot gaps in the marketplace, whether it is a product, service, or idea, and are quick to fill them with their own initiatives and efforts. There is often a focus on research and development, building a strong team, and leveraging investment for long-term good. You may be one of them, and if you are—congratulations.

It is equally important to have innovators within an existing organization—people who constantly push their colleagues and the boundaries of what is possible. Innovation can be about adding a little additional creativity and focus into the work—and coming out with bigger and better ideas. It is about experimenting and testing. Again, you may be one of them, in this case an innovator within an existing organization. If you are—congratulations and consider your organization very lucky.

How do you know when you need to innovate? The answer is, you don't ever know for sure. You should be constantly reviewing and evolving what you do to improve and learn while balancing this with continued delivery of consistently high quality products and services at the same time. In most organizations constant evolution is a major challenge, both organizationally and in terms of available talent and resources. And continuing to provide high value to your audience while pushing new boundaries, as an additional challenge. If you aren't able to push the boundaries all the time, you should position your organization to respond quickly as new innovation occurs so that you are never caught flat-footed.

The March of Dimes was founded in 1938 to raise money for polio research and to care for those suffering from the disease.

Originally named the National Foundation for Infantile Paralysis, the group was launched by President Franklin D. Roosevelt, whose resolve to prevent the disease from limiting his ability to govern the nation helped to grow the group into one of the most influential charities in the country.

In 1955, University of Pittsburgh researcher Dr. Jonas Salk announced to the world that a polio vaccine had been developed, in no small measure because of the support that March of Dimes had advocated for and helped to secure. Having successfully completed its mission, March of Dimes decided in 1958 to use its charitable infrastructure to serve mothers and babies with a new mission: to prevent premature birth, birth defects and infant mortality. The organization accomplishes this with programs of research, community services, education, and advocacy. It is now one of the few charitable organizations in the world that achieved its original mission and has gone on to reinvent itself.

The March of Dimes had a clear mission, and the discovery of a vaccine to prevent polio was a clear sign that its mission had to change. It had the option of closing—and for many organizations that is the best option, instead of continuing to push a mission that has lost its core purpose. Unfortunately, few organizations acknowledge that the best option is sometimes to change or close. However, the most effective way to learn if or when your efforts need to change is to listen—to your audience, to the space you operate in, and to yourself.

Some key indicators:

- *You wake up one day and find yourself competing with groups you have never heard of before.* The growth of technology has made the cost and hassle of starting and promoting a new organization much more manageable. Almost anyone can start a company, their own nonprofit, or similar group. *Time* magazine estimated that there are more than 1 million 501c(3) charities in the United States, up nearly 70 percent from the 614,000 that existed a decade ago, tackling everything from education to disaster relief, job development, the environment, and AIDS.[2] The growth is fueled by the growing influence of baby boomers with a social entrepreneurship mind-set who have time to give back to their communities; by the learnings from September 11 and Hurricane Katrina that government needs help solving our nation's problems; and by the greater numbers of wealthy individuals with the funds to launch their own nonprofits.

Everyone has an idea and most of them think they can take the world by storm. If new organizations are coming into your space and you haven't heard of them, watch out. They have found a way to jump into your space with a new idea, a different application of technology, or something that has attracted some interest in the audience. There might not be anything wrong with what you are doing, but rather someone has brought innovation to your doorstep. You earn no points for status quo thinking, no matter how successful you are.

- *You are under increasing pressure to lower your prices.* Chris Anderson wrote in *The Long Tail* that the new technology and the flattening of our society would give consumers control of the market and lower costs within niche product areas. He used the music business as an example, writing: "Imagine if prices declined the further you went down the tail, with popularity (the market) effectively dictating pricing. All it would take is for the labels to lower the wholesale price for the vast majority of their content not in heavy rotation; even a two- or three-tiered pricing structure could work wonders. And because so much of that content is not available in record stores, the risk of channel conflict is greatly diminished.

  The lesson: Pull consumers down the tail with lower prices."[3] Consumers expect to get their information, experiences, and stuff at lower or no cost. Competing organizations often feed into that, lowering prices to undercut another seller. But no one likes to compete strictly on price, particularly when you offer the best item or service for your audience. But more players in each space will mean more battles on cost. It will be necessary to realign your offering, not just to compete on dollars, but to exceed expectations and capitalize where others fall short.

- *Your audience asks for changes you cannot or do not want to make.* When your audience moves forward without you, take that as a not-so-subtle sign that what you are doing may no longer be relevant or competitive. It happens all the time. Your audience says, "I want it this way," or "You need to be doing this or I won't support you" and you have to decide whether to honor that demand or let your competitor have their support. Your instinct is to say no because you doubt you could ever recover the costs of the change, or the shift in focus to your mission. But when your competitors have leapt ahead of you in features and benefits, or offer a service that you hadn't conceived of, you must either catch up or leap ahead of them with innovations of your own. If not, you will fall behind.

- *Your competitors are leaving the market.* In the short term, this sounds great. Your competitors drop out, and you pick up the audience that they leave behind. But movement in today's fractured world is so quick that market opportunities, no matter the space, disappear and change so rapidly that what you are picking up may not be the right audience, but instead the audience that hasn't caught on quite yet. When your competitors change their focus or begin to highlight other aspects of their work and you don't, you will quickly feel like the last person standing on a sinking ship without access to a life preserver. Nobody walks away from an opportunity to grow and expand their business or mission. Vibrant markets encourage competition, now more than ever.

Nobody wants to admit that their organization has lost momentum or that the changing times have put them in a position where they can no longer be effective. It can sometimes take months, even years, for the signs to clearly develop and the lessons to be learned. Waiting that long, however, can spell disaster for your organization. The only recourse is to focus on innovation to do things to remain fresh.

Getting to Fresh

Tom Kelley, co-author of *The Art of Innovation* (New York: Currency, 2001) and a principal at IDEO, a Silicon valley–based design firm, tells this story about how innovation unfolds, often quickly:

> [A] crew from ABC News came in and said, "We want to see innovation happen." They gave us four days to reinvent a product category that turned out to be grocery-shopping carts.
>
> We went through all the steps that we normally go through in a real project, but we did them incredibly quickly. So we went

through the "understand" phase figuring out what the current market is in the first day. We then went through the "observe" phase, which involved getting away from our desks, and getting out into the real world to watch people grocery shopping.

Then we went into the "visualize" phase, where we started prototyping. Some of those first prototype carts really looked pretty messy, and even a little ugly because they were all done in a day. We're talking about foam core and wire, the cheapest, quickest materials we could find.

The next step was to evaluate and refine. We had a pretty broad range of prototypes. In the "refine" stage, we said, "Okay, let's narrow it down to the stuff that we think people are interested in." In the "implement" stage, we built a finished model good enough to clearly communicate the ideas of the new shopping cart.[4]

Everyone talks about innovation, but few organizations are able to truly pull it off. Some people associate it with age—only the young can innovate. Salon.com noted that "Steve Jobs and Steve Wozniak were in their 20s when they pieced together the forerunner of the Apple computer. So was Tim Berners-Lee when he created the first hyperlinked structures that led to the World Wide Web. By their late 20s, Jerry Yang and David Filo had created the Yahoo! search engine and left the Ph.D. program at Stanford to run the company. Jeff Bezos—who was a little slower to get into the game—founded Amazon.com at age 31."[5] But age is not what drives innovation. Think about it. Facebook founder Mark Zuckerberg is still only 23 years old. It's a state of mind and an acceptance of the challenge at hand.

What does it take to truly innovate? No fear, for starters. Many of the limitations that organizations have are put there by the organization itself. Ever hear one of your colleagues say "We have never done it that way" or "Can you give me some examples of how this has worked before?" as a way to buy time or provide an easy escape from trying something new? There are obviously risks for falling short, but the risks of not innovating, particularly as technology continues to advance and expectations among audiences continue to rise, are even greater.

We are surrounded by examples of the need to iterate and grow and develop, from the auto industry in America whose business model has come to an end, to the oil industry where British Petroleum (BP) is saying they are "beyond petroleum." BP has not figured out how to do that yet but they have identified where they have to go to remain competitive, and that will serve to drive innovation internally, and across their industry, in response. In some ways organizations need to have some foundational beliefs to drive that long-term change. You need to believe that things are going to keep changing, and that what worked yesterday doesn't tell you anything about what will work tomorrow.

Look at your product portfolio. Do you think anything you are selling today you will still be selling in the same way three to five years from now? Look at your programs and initiatives. Will your audience and impact be the same in a year, let alone 10 years? Whatever packaging you are using won't be right in the future. Whatever ingredients define your success today will have changed in the future. Jeffrey Hollender adds:

> One of the biggest changes that we look at is, for twenty years our business has been selling products that were not as bad as everyone else's products. We're good because we're less bad. That's no longer good enough. We now need to define what is really good. We can—the whole paradigm that has defined product development for us for twenty years is no longer valid going forward. And the challenge for businesses is deciding what system you put in place to detect that, and then how do you redesign what you're doing to change as the world changes?

So what can you do? Here are a few suggestions:

Be a Part of Your Own Audience

When you launched your organization, you were probably one of the few, if not the only person who believed that you could make an impact with your work. You were your first investor and first customer—and you should always be your best.

Over time your audience will grow, your team will expand, and your offering will evolve and change. Your focus will shift to serving that audience and away from being a part of it. But you must remain a member of your own audience and demand innovation the same way a customer would or you won't be able to keep fresh.

Consider how Steve Jobs, the co-founder and CEO of Apple computer and visionary leader, lives his brand. Like all technologists, Job believes that Apple products are better than the competitions. But he takes it to another level. He keeps Apple's management structure unusually flat, especially for a company its size. He leads, or provides input on, the development of all new projects. In fact, there is just one committee in the whole of Apple responsible for setting prices. "I can't think of a comparable company that does no-zero-market research with its customers before releasing a product," wrote Lev Grossman in *Time* Magazine. "Ironically, Jobs' personal style could not be more at odds with the brand he has created. If the motto for Apple's consumers is "think different," the motto for Apple employees is "think like Steve."[6]

Steve Jobs wears an iPod, carries an iPhone, and demands the same of his team that every Apple customer does—and he gets it. You should be able to as well.

Understand What Role Technology Really Plays

Technology plays such a big role in the distribution of information and creation of experiences—for both organizations and their audience—that it is easy to give it more than its share of the credit for the success of a project.

Many of Brian's clients call to ask how they can be just like the most innovative organization from another space—how they can emulate Howard Dean's dynamic online fundraising and mass audience engagement from the 2004 presidential campaign, only in a consumer package goods setting, for example. When Howard Dean ran for President during the 2004 cycle, the Internet was widely credited by the media and many political observers as being the key factor in his success as a candidate. The Dean campaign did raise tens of millions of dollars online, recruit and send e-mails to hundreds of thousands of supporters, and host a vibrant and engaging discussion on its blog. But the technology that powered all of those activities—a database, a content management system, an enterprise server, and the like—were not the keys to his success. His campaign had a message that resonated with Americans and a media clamoring for a juicy political story. Yes, his use of the Internet was fresh and new to the political space but it was not the sole reason he flourished.

Others want to build platforms that feature the same capabilities as MySpace or Facebook, hoping that they will be able to attract the same energy and enthusiasm that those networks have enjoyed. Most organizations, however, fail to realize how those networks align their functionality with a certain audience, or a particular area of interest, like music or college life, which doesn't easily apply to others. The technology is innovative, for sure, but the success of these organizations is driven by far more. So instead of looking at technology alone as the reason that an organization grows its size and influence, look at the factors that technology helped to elevate.

Always Be Curious

There is a famous line in the David Mamet play *Glengarry Glen Ross* when a character says, "Only one thing counts in this life—get them to sign on the line which is dotted!" adding "A-B-C. A—Always, B—Be, C—Closing. Always be closing." Today, the A-B-C should be redefined to read "A—Always, B—Be, C—Curious." Your organization's ability to innovate should be driven by the curiosity to continue exploring your audience's changing expectations, not the satisfaction that you can expand your offering or monetize your relationship with them.

You have to acknowledge that you may not completely understand the impact you have on your space all the time and be curious about what your competitors are doing, what it means to your offering, and how your audience is responding. Looking at what your competition is doing will help you to innovate and stay fresh. Keeping on top of what your competitors are doing means you'll find out when they make a move into a certain area. If they get to the audience before you do, there's a good chance you'll end up the loser. Organize some sort of competitive-intelligence-gathering system that will help you keep track of what they're doing. Find something that another organization is doing successfully and finds their own spin on how to do it as well, or better. Bookmark all of your competitors' Web sites and load them a few times per week. It is important to know what they are up to and when.

Listen to Your Audience

Many organizations think they know better than their audience and choose to talk instead of listening. But that is a mistake. The opportunity for you and your organization to monitor and engage your audience is, and will always be, important.

The toymakers at Hasbro observe thousands of children and adults playing games in a lab they call GameWorks at the division's headquarters and also talk with prospective customers about how they want to spend leisure time—to understand better where games might fit into their lives. And now, as new technologies become available, they also do online surveys of customers. In the fashion world, trend spotters still track fashion shows in New York, Paris, and Milan, but also comb through style Web sites, from Style.com to *New York Magazine's* nymag.com, to see the trends in real time. Monitoring runway trends has become increasingly important for mass retailers, according to the *Wall Street Journal,* because consumers have become more fashion savvy and demanding. Retailers compete to grab a bigger slice of the . . . fashion market with "cheap chic" looks.[7]

It will take some time and effort to figure out how to harness the millions of opinions and ideas that come in through the Internet, but recognizing the importance of listening is key.

There's no substitute for keeping your eyes and ears open to improve your awareness of the environment around you. But if you want your audience to keep coming back, you have to let them know you are listening and will be there to fulfill their changing requirements. The audience knows what it wants, so ask them. You see your work from one point of view and your audience sees it from a different one. Your perspective is important. Their experience is more important. You should take feedback very seriously and try to incorporate suggestions into your plans. Dig deeper into what drives customers' actions, and thus find rich opportunities for innovation. Market researchers can use many tools, from metaphor elicitation to product attribute evaluations, to get at the whys of customer behavior.

Cycles Are Important

Our society and the technology that powers it change regularly and rapidly. The assumption made by many people is that new ideas fuel change. In reality, much of what is considered new is simply an improvement on something that has already existed. Sometimes the original idea or tool wasn't as well formulated. Other times it was ahead of where the audience was at the time. New ideas, and innovative thinking, comes in waves, so understanding and building on the lessons of the past is a key component to staying fresh. Cycles are important.

A big part of managing cycles, of course, is keeping a schedule. Schedules don't mean you can't do things differently. Newspapers have schedules and their stories are different every day. Sports teams have a schedule but the outcomes change constantly. The movie industry pays attention to the seasons, as do fashion designers and retailers, but that doesn't limit their creativity or experimentation. So, you should have a schedule, too. Your goal should be to focus on what drives new thinking for your organization so that you can align the expectations of your internal production and your audiences with the need to remain fresh. Keep yourself fresh by creating a schedule and building in time to drive change.

To the audience, cycles just happen. A style of fashion that you wore a decade ago is all of a sudden interesting again. A game that you played as a child is updated with modern characters or functionalities. The process we once went through to complete a task becomes simpler, seemingly overnight. But we know that doesn't just happen—in fact, as organizations, we control it.

Take the game Monopoly as an example. When the original game was released in 1935, the board featured streets in Atlantic City, which was a glamorous tourist destination at the time—but today Atlantic City is far from the top tourist destination it once was. Last year, designers and marketers selected destinations in 22 U.S. cities and asked customers to cast online votes on which they preferred. In three weeks, Hasbro received three million votes, which were used to design a Monopoly Here and Now board. Times Square in New York received the largest number of votes, so it replaced Boardwalk. Las Vegas Boulevard replaced Pacific Avenue. On a recent visit to FAO Schwartz, Brian noticed that there were close to thirty different versions of the Monopoly game on sale—the Here and Now Version, but also editions branded with movie and television characters (like *Star Wars* and *The Simpsons*), and sports franchises (Yankees, Mets, the NBA, and NASCAR all had versions) to cite just a few.

According to the *Wall Street Journal,* this innovation is part of the strategy that Hasbro uses to keep the company competitive.

> Every Friday at lunch, game designers, marketing managers and other employees at Hasbro's games division gather in the cafeteria to play board games. Some compete over Scrabble, Sorry, Clue or more than a dozen other famous games invented

decades ago and still manufactured at a factory here. Others play games sold by competitors, or they enjoy their own childhood favorites no longer on store shelves. . . . These lunchtime games have a business purpose. They are part of Hasbro's efforts to find ways to update classics and create new games.[8]

[Reprinted by permission of The Wall Street Journal, *Copyright © 2007 Dow Jones & Company, Inc. All Rights Reserved Worldwide. License number 1770790398600.]*

So, as games have taken on a renewed importance in family life—driven partly by the desire to spend time disconnected from many of the technology-driven distractions of daily life—Hasbro has innovated and kept its games fresh. And being fresh has worked: Sales in Hasbro's games unit rose 11 percent last year.

Staying fresh is a matter of keeping knowledge of your ideas, designs, processes, techniques, or any other unique component of your creation moving and changing at all times. Tom Peters, said that "Nearly 100 percent of innovation . . . is inspired not by 'market analysis' but by people who are supremely pissed off at the way things are. I happen to believe that only pissed-off people change the world, either in small ways or large ways."[9]

So get pissed off, and stay relevant. Keep things fresh.

CHAPTER

13

Be Geographically Relevant

Geography guides choice. Geography is what aligns certain customers to certain stores, determines what community will benefit most from the services an organization offers, and dictates how a marketing message is targeted.

Technology has made geography easier to access and understand—on the Web and through mobile devices, for everyone from corporations to average folks sitting in front of a computer at their home or library. How? Geography relates experience to the physical world, its inhabitants, and the interactions between them. It gives you a perspective on how big or small things are and how far we are from them.

Adding a geographic component to your analysis of a situation helps to provide clarity and context that might not exist from within a conference room or on a spreadsheet. In short, geography is about relevance. And you have to be geographically relevant to be relevant at all.

In today's flatter, leaner organizations, one of the ways that your organization can improve productivity is by making sure that your people collaborate and cooperate across every traditional boundary. Traditionally, geography has presented a challenge. But today, technology allows geographic information services and communities of users to develop, without borders or boundaries.

In the past two decades, geography has evolved from just the study of the earth and its features or just the political and economic landscape of our times into perhaps the most the important factor in organizational operations worldwide. Geography plays a role in every organizational plan and decision an organization makes. Politically, socially, economically, and culturally it either contributes to the decision on how to act or is the result of that action. Geography has always mattered and today it matters even more.

"The old role of geography is that constraint choice—you only had access to what was available in your geography," Chris Anderson, calls it the *tyranny* of geography. He wrote:

> Because the cost of traditional distribution required concentrated demand, you only basically had a broad choice in concentrated populations—in other words, cities. You can have any national cuisine you want in Manhattan but only Chinese or Italian in your little town. The tyranny of geography has been the requirement to concentrate—to find the sufficient number of people within a five-mile range to deliver whatever you are offering.

According to Anderson, the Internet gives you access to a global market. In the process it both breaks down geographic barriers and creates a new challenge on the local level. Technology is bridging the divide between the global Internet, which provides access to the entire world, and your local community, where your audience lives and works every day. "The Internet drives demand to local merchants simply by revealing who they are, what they do, and allowing anyone to patronize them and for them to maximize their visibility in the local community," Anderson says.

Where an individual, a family, or even a business is located—in what geography they exist—plays an important role in how they function and the choices they make. In particular, most localities feature a sense of community as a result of their geography. Location can also play an important role in the timing and mechanics of decision making. For example, weather patterns dictate when people travel, how they purchase, what media they consume, and even the charitable donations they make. And location plays an important role in determining how people get and share information.

A very basic example is that rural customers are less likely to have access to a wide range of retail locations so they might be more likely to utilize mail or telephone services. In politics, many urban neighborhoods have lower penetration of traditional telephone lines, combined with having housing located more closely together (including in apartment buildings), so canvassing becomes a critical element of an outreach strategy. By contrast, candidates might use advertising and mailers to reach more suburban residents whose homes they might not be able to reach as efficiently in person.

Your local world is about geography. You are most likely to see, do business with, interact with, and learn from the people who live in your neighborhood, city, state, or even country, more than those who are half a world away. The Web has opened borders and made an individual computer a gateway to a global customer base, but what you sell and how you sell it do not necessarily relate to all who can find it. Local is also about culture and experience—and of course language. You are connected to the people with whom you share experiences, those whose lives are similar to yours or whose access to culture and media mirror your own.

Geography Is Not Flat

Technology helps to flatten our economy and bring users from opposite ends of the world together into the same experience. Thanks to the availability of a global, Web-enabled platform, multiple forms of sharing knowledge and work have been created, with few limitations for time, distance, geography and language. But user experience and customer expectations are different around the world, and they always will be. The execution of a global strategy cannot ignore the importance of geography.

"The simple definition of globalization is the interweaving of markets, technology, information systems, and telecommunications systems in a way that is shrinking the world from a size medium to a size small, and enabling each of us to reach around the world farther, faster, deeper, and cheaper than ever before, and enabling the world to reach into each of us farther, faster, deeper, cheaper than ever before," wrote Thomas Friedman, famed *New York Times* columnist, in his book, *The World is Flat*. Friedman explains how globalization represents the increasing interconnection of societies in terms of their economic, political and cultural aspects. In other words, it goes beyond networks and the Web. Globalization means that borders become less relevant. It means that virtually anything we do has the potential to be shared and participated in by people from all over the world. And it means that how we operate as a society has to change.

Friedman offers some of the potential benefits of globalization. He notes how companies like Wal-Mart are able to streamline sales, distribution, and shipping to bring low-cost products to consumers around the world. He explains how a doctor in the United States can get help reviewing the results of MRI scans from a technician in India, allowing him to deliver a diagnosis to more patients at less cost.

But globalization has both positive and negative implications. Nobody actually wants to live in a global village, at least not all the time. We want access to the resources and perspectives from the other side of the world, without the feeling that they are coming from the other side of the world. Besides the fact that there isn't time to be connected to everyone in the world, for most audiences there simply isn't that much interest. The global village provides innumerable resources and the possibility to get information, experiences, or stuff to or from anyone at any time. But when you look at what the majority of people choose to do, the result is often a narrower focus on the things that matter most to them. And what matters to them is what is local.

Ethan Zuckerman, founder of Global Voices, an international blog collaboration project, wrote the following on his blog:

> I had a meeting yesterday morning with friends who run a direct marketing company in Williamstown, MA. Their offices are across the street . . . Walking me out to my truck, my friend said, "I can walk to work. I can walk to my lawyer. I can walk to my accountant. I can walk to my parent's house. Hard to get better than that."
>
> That used to be my life . . .
>
> My life now couldn't be much more different. I live over 150 miles from my "office" [at the Berkman Center for Internet & Society at Harvard Law School] and I consider myself lucky if I make it in to work once a week. About half of the time, I'm on the road—the other half of the time, I work in my home office, a reclaimed landing at the top of a flight of stairs to the attic. I keep binoculars on my desk so I can watch the porcupines climb the trees and the insomniac owls.
>
> This time around, my coworkers are all over the world. We had a meeting today over IRC [a back-channel communications tool], the medium we use for almost all our realtime professional interactions. My colleagues were in Hong Kong, Oakland, Port of Spain, the Hague and Montreal. One woke up to make the

meeting, another went to bed as soon as we logged off. Weeks
will go by where I don't actually speak to any of the people I
work with, but it's rare that ten minutes pass without an IM, an
e-mail or blogpost.

Part of me—a big part—thinks that businesses can't and
shouldn't work this way. If we're going to trust each other, rely
on each other's judgment, read each other's moods, we need
to know each other. The reason Global Voices holds an annual
meeting isn't primarily to make decisions or plan strategy—it's
so we have an excuse to wander through strange cities together,
share cab rides, ethnic food and rounds of drinks. We get to
know each other at an express pace, squeezing in a year's worth
of water cooler conversations in an hour-long walk through a
flea market or a cab ride to the airport.

I miss working with my neighbors. When I find myself talking to the cat too often, I head to Williamstown and work at
the coffeeshop where there's a good chance that I know half
a dozen of the other laptop-toters camped out at cafe tables.
I wonder sometimes if it's time to turn from global to local
again, rent a corner of a mill and start working with the people
I live with.

But working this new way means that I get to work with some
of the most remarkable people on the globe, and that none of
them have to leave their homes, their families and their lives
so we can work together. Remarkable people pass through
the Berkshires every day, and some even settle down and stay
a while, but it's hard to imagine a physical space anywhere in
the world where I could share my office with Tunisian human
rights activists, Tanzanian linguists, Bahraini journalists and
Trinidadian radio producers. (London, maybe, or New York.
But I bet it's rarer than you think.)[1]

Over time, the audience will need to learn how to appreciate the
benefits that a global culture with many languages and new customs
provides.

- Corporations are changing their production management,
  information and service functions, and communications
  efforts, and must help to educate their audience about what
  that means for their capabilities and limitations.

- Nonprofit organizations are expanding the audience for their services and looking for new and better ways to have a measurable impact on society. They must also consider how funding must change and new ways for impact to be measured.
- Academic institutions have always taught a broader curriculum than just what exists around their campus, but increasingly welcoming perspectives and participation from students from beyond their borders increases the reach and influence of their teachings.
- And while entertainment and sports have welcomed athletes, performers, and fans from other countries for some time, increasingly the rules and policies that govern these institutions need to change to reflect the global sensibilities of all involved.

Driving that greater appreciation will be the organizations, and the people like you who run them, and what changes they make to the ways in which they operate.

Think Globally, Act Locally

Does globalization mean the end of geography? The opposite is actually true. As technological and economic forces flatten many of the connections in our world, geography takes on even greater importance in understanding how organizations operate. How much does geography matter?

The Internet gives you access to a global market, with virtual commerce, but its usage is mostly for local activities. According to comScore, Inc., 63 percent of U.S. Internet users (or approximately 109 million people) perform local searches online.[2] Similarly, Ask Jeeves estimates that roughly 20 percent of the Web searches it handles are local in nature, such as the query "San Francisco plumber." Another 10 percent are implicitly local, such as the query "plumber," since the consumer presumably is loo king for a plumber near a specific location, such as his home or business.[3]

Why? Chris Anderson explains:

> There's more variety in your community than you know about. The Internet can serve as a way to solve that information problem. That's why even a dry cleaner needs a Web site. The

dry cleaner needs a Web site because you have a generation that goes to Google to find everything! If the dry cleaner is not visible on Google, the Google generation who believe that if it isn't on Google then it doesn't exist, won't come to it! So in a weird way, although you could be next door to the dry cleaner, if you're not connected via the Internet, that connection doesn't happen.

The rise of the Web and the expanding reach of technology over the past two decades has helped to bring people from all over the globe into a series of inter-connected online communities. As the audience online has grown, the volume of information and the varying perspectives have risen as well. Geography has given way to networks—understanding and tapping the ways that people and culture are connected. While the challenges that geography creates—transportation, permission (to access), and time—are being reduced, new ones like language and connectedness arise. People have different needs, different goals. People manipulate given structures to meet their desires. We are faced with a digital environment that has no single unifying perspective or direction. That is by intent—the Web is not owned by any one person or group and should not be directed as such. But it also makes it nearly impossible at some level to navigate.

It is a major challenge for organizations to connect with, or at the very least function with an eye toward, the global audience and still retain local focus and values. There are new technological solutions every day designed to improve on how to find and share information on the Web. These include reputation systems, folksonomy, recommendations—specific services like Angie's List, a subscription based community engine for local services, and applications like Digg.com and del.icio.us—which give the user the ability to convert information into whatever they want. These all provide value but they barely scratch the surface of what is needed. And none offer a true human understanding that reflects certain users' needs.

The proper mix of these attributes reveals a strategy that many now refer to as *glocalization*. Glocalization is the internationalization of a global product adapted to fit the local norms of a particular region. Deborah Sontag wrote in the *New York Times:*

When MTV began to establish channels abroad in the late 1980s, critics viewed the expansion as quintessential cultural imperialism that would homogenize youth culture worldwide. Early on, though, MTV learned that it made better business sense to be "glocal"—their motto is "think global, act local"—than to impose a wholly American cultural product. Young people, wherever they were, would watch international acts for only so long before they wanted to see something of their own. So each of MTV's international channels developed local talent and its own personality: MTV Indonesia has a call to prayer, MTV Italy has cooking shows, MTV Brazil is, visually speaking, extremely colorful and, sartorially speaking, quite bare.[4]

Having our information be glocalized means making it accessible and organized in a local context, letting the individual who receives and processes that information assign its relevance and context (not having it forced on them). Glocalization is about making global information available to local social contexts and giving people the flexibility to find, organize, share, and create information in a locally meaningful fashion that is globally accessible.

"Language is expressed in writing with a series of symbols," William Safire wrote in his "On Language" column in the *New York Times Sunday Magazine* on March 5, 2000.[5] "When people cannot agree what the symbols stand for, all is confusion." Media and technology, of course, easily transcend this problem by using translators and algorithms that adjust to whatever region the IP address of a user dictates. That is why an entry in the Google search box in Israel appears from the right side, but in the United States it appears from the left.

Over the past two or three decades, as digital technology has risen in importance, English has become the lingua franca of the global network—the standard for oral and written communication across national frontiers. French, Spanish, Arabic, German, Russian, and other languages are spoken all over the world and, have become regional languages that have only limited impact on the economic and social structure of our society. But online, they have increasing influence as communities that share a common language form and promote a dialogue.

Information is meaningless to someone else if they can't repurpose it to make sense of it in their own context. It is for this reason that technology is not enough.

Tapping the Community

Smaller organizations can narrow their focus on a particular locality and adapt a pilot of their program to meet a specific need. They will, however, almost certainly encounter some difficulty when their idea is proven successful on a local level and they seek to expand it. Typically, these organizations have been successful simply replicating their offering in other markets—the same look and feel of their chain restaurant or clothing store or the same program in a local school or community center. But of late, audiences have resisted the commoditization of their experiences. They are looking for local and unique, even from the largest of organizations. The goal should be to create local opportunities for your audience to engage—not a single one, but many. It is necessary to understand how individuals, and the groups they are a part of, relate to each other in order to meet individual localized needs. Reputation systems emerge to help localize the social structure, to indicate trust, respect, and relations. Reputation is not a universal structure, but one deeply embedded in particular cultures.

Technology and experience are both critical factors in this process. Success comes from a constantly shifting, multidirectional, complex flow of information, with the information evolving as it flows.

Organizations need to pay attention to how different cultural contexts interpret the technology and support them in their variable interpretations. We need to create flexible infrastructures and build the unexpected connections that will permit creative reuse. Technology needs to support social and cultural practices rather than determining culture.

Take the mass (aka big M) media, for example. To succeed, the 1,500 or so daily American newspapers that are not the *New York Times,* the *Wall Street Journal,* or *USA Today* (the major papers that have become the national newspapers of sorts) must excel at coverage of local issues. Only a daily newspaper can provide the link that connects national and international events with local readers' interests.

A single wire service is no longer enough for most newspapers because it is no longer enough for most newspaper readers—they seek out information through dozens of sources a day, some from mainstream media and others from the blogosphere or through social networks. Readers take notice; they value this level of news. They want to understand how their lives, and the lives of their fellow residents, intersect with global and national events. Politics is local. So are business, news, sports. But *local* has been redefined. You can be in one area geographically and still be very connected to what is happening on the other side of the globe through the news.

Shayne Bowman and Chris Willis, media consultants and futurists, explain the impact of the Internet on local news this way:

> The Internet is a unique phenomenon that has delivered not just technological innovations but become a conduit for change, accelerating the rate, diversity and circulation of ideas. It affects nearly everything from culture to competition . . . First, it enables nearly limitless distribution of content for little or no cost. Second, it has potentially put everyone on the planet into the media business, including the sources, businesses, governments and communities newspapers cover. Add other ingredients—easy-to-use, open-source publishing tools, a generation who finds it more natural to instant message someone than to call, a greater demand for niche information, and a rapidly growing shift of advertising dollars to online media—and you have a recipe for radical change in the news media landscape.[8]

Resources don't always allow for it. So what's the alternative? Tapping the community. "The place I start is the falling cost for people to get together, share information, and collaborate, and therefore know something in common that would be very hard to know alone," said Jay Rosen, a professor of journalism at New York University and founder of the open-source journalism experiment, Assignment Zero.

> I think the falling cost for like-minded people to share information, pool their knowledge, collaborate, and make stuff that's good is a very dramatic sort of social change that takes

a long time to unwind and move this way through society. And we're starting to see it now. So if it's possible to do, it's possible to bring this kind of horizontal knowledge into being, into products, into services . . . into a kick-ass investigative story, a campaign for this, and a product like that. If it's possible to do that, this is very important. What that means is we are not in the same relationship of dependence that we were in with big media organizations. And that people can do more things for themselves.

When you consider the potential for open source software or open call productions to democratize the creation and sharing of media, let alone the development of new products and services, you see the potential that participation across borders creates. Most of the examples to date of when an organization has adopted a shift towards this perspective, they do them entirely in the spirit of fad acceptance—hey look for a new way to do the same thing they've always done. Real, meaningful change will require you to commit to collaboration across borders, without boundaries.

Making Sure Geography Matters

The new world of the Internet, with lowered costs of participation, more efficient peer-to-peer communication, and a very potent ability to share data and knowledge, makes all kinds of things possible now that just weren't before. The organizations that believe their long-standing rituals and behaviors represent the mainstream, or even the appropriate way to operate, are putting themselves at a big disadvantage. Those organizations can't see what is changing, what is different, and where they should be looking to adapt in order to survive. Those organizations can't invent or create new ways to operate and engage the audience. But you can.

Organizations are undergoing radical changes as a result of the globalization of our society. These changes require organizations to be more flexible and increasingly networked to help them compete (or sustain themselves) in a global marketplace. It's not just products; ideas, education, culture, and media have all been impacted by the global nature of our society. Globalization results in new similarities, standardization, homogenization, concentration, and coordination on a worldwide basis.

Organizations have to keep evolving if they are to survive. To do that, you must structure your team to be lean, innovative, and competitive—and you must also make sure they are tapped into the world and the local community, so that the changes and differences that result from being connected to people all over the globe are integrated into what you do at local and global levels. To do this, make sure that geography matters . . . in the decisions you make in all other areas of your organization.

CHAPTER

14

Be a Public Failure

You are going to fail. Not completely, not all the time—but it will happen.

According to the Small Business Administration, 50 percent of small businesses fail within the first year and 95 percent of small businesses fail within five years.[1] And major organizations fail often on individual projects, major initiatives and big ideas. Countless non-profit organizations fizzle after just a few years of operation, unable to raise funds to operate their programs. Sports teams languish in mediocrity for decades, sometimes even centuries. It happens, we can't avoid it.

But failure has changed. The visibility of failure in the new media environment is more common, because everything moves so quickly, changes constantly, and reaches so many people. More than ever, you are going to fail in full public view now, for everyone to see. Failures are broadcast around the world. Entire reality shows are written around the prospect that a contestant or character will fail. Failures are documented on the Internet and archived forever in blogs and on YouTube. The impact of failure, in many cases, is more dramatic as well, because the amplification of even the most minor of mistakes. Once you fail, everyone knows.

Failure sucks. We're not going to tell you otherwise. Losing is no fun. But failing is a part of being organic. It is part of establishing a real, trusting relationship with your audience—letting them know that you aren't, and don't claim to be, untouchable and inhuman. And failing in full public view is becoming a bigger part of that world. So embrace it.

Failure creates a powerful opportunity to learn and grow so that you don't make the same mistakes in the future. The question is, how will you know what to do and what not to do when faced with a similar challenge in the future?

Change Blindness

One of the primary reasons that organizations fail is because they are unable to innovate. They fall behind their competitors or fall out of touch with their audience and never recover. But for most organizations, it is not a failure to innovate as much as it is a failure to notice the need to innovate at all—a strategic blind spot, if you will.

It reminds us of the story of the boiling frog. If you place a frog in a pot of boiling water, it will jump out, uninterested in being burned or boiled. But if you place that same frog in cold water that is slowly heated, it will never jump out. It won't know that the heat is rising until it is too late.

People, it seems, are like frogs. Researchers believe that we aren't able to see the change occurring around us because we need to focus on the present situation to survive. If we noticed everything around us, it would be too distracting. So what we actually see is very different from what we think we see. The phenomenon is known as *change blindness.*

Daniel Simons, a professor of visual cognition and human performance at the University of Illinois at Urbana-Champaign, and Daniel Levin, an associate professor of cognitive neuroscience at Vanderbilt University, are two of the scientists who have studied this phenomenon. In one experiment, they read to participants a description of changes in four different short film scenes, ranging from one actor alternating between wearing and not wearing a scarf to a change in actors. The participants were then shown both the pre-change and post-change views and the changes were pointed out to them. The participants recorded whether they thought they would have noticed the change, as well as their confidence in their response. Nearly 83 percent of participants insisted with reasonable confidence that they would be able to detect the changes, even though only around 11 percent of participants in previous studies using the same clips actually detected the changes.[2]

We would love to say that if you act in a certain way, make certain choices, or hire the right people, you will be able to avoid change blindness or failing all together. But it's not possible.

Responding to Failure

Recognizing and responding to failure has never been easy. Who responds? What should they say? Who are you talking to?

The best defense in any failure begins long before the moment of truth. Put together a strong and thoughtful process, practice it, refine it, update it over time, and make sure everyone in the organization understands what their role is. Start by explaining what happened. In a lot of situations your team, your audience, journalists, neither know nor understand all the nuances of your organization and the facts related to your failure. But that doesn't mean they won't make assumptions or judgments—all the more reason to have a plan for how to respond ahead of time. Introduce them to your organization and make sure they know the environment in which you are operating so they can understand your failure in the appropriate context.

In late 2006 and early 2007, Jason Goldberg, the CEO of Jobster, became, with help from the news media, the poster child for why CEOs should not blog. First the two local papers, the *Seattle Times* and the *Seattle Post-Intelligencer (PI)* (Jobster's headquarters is located in Seattle), started to chase rumors about some key departures and layoffs at the startup, reading into his blog posts for information. John Cook at the *PI* wrote, "It certainly appears that layoffs are coming, especially when a CEO is using phrases such as 'optimizing the business' and 'tough choices.' Stay tuned."[3] The *New York Times* picked up the story as well, saying of Goldberg, "Some executives, like Jonathan I. Schwartz of Sun Microsystems, pull [blogging] off with aplomb. Others, like Jason Goldberg of the online recruiting company Jobster, have had more difficulty."[4]

In fact Goldberg, and Jobster, had a plan for how to push information about their annual review, and the prospect that the company might need to downsize to increase profitability. While most CEOs would hide behind a press release or a spokesperson, or not say anything at all when such a situation arose, Goldberg went the opposite way—blogging openly about the situation and later submitting to questioning from the general public online. He wrote in one post:

> Why would a CEO be so public with his thoughts and open himself to so much public scrutiny and criticism? Answer: Shouldn't we actually ask ourselves: "Why not?"
>
> Why am I so comfortable blogging here right alongside the right hand column on this blog which has feed after feed of public comments and criticisms? Answer: transparency. Embrace it. Don't run from it.
>
> Why would a relatively young company with millions of dollars in the bank, real revenues, and hundreds of customers (over 100 new customers signed in just the past 2 months alone) be undergoing a strategic review of how best to build long term value while driving towards near term profitability? Answer: isn't the better question why wouldn't we be?
>
> What will 2007 bring for jobster? Answer: the answer to a lot of the questions everyone is speculating about as well as a whole slew of surprises which I'm sure that even the closest watchers won't expect. We've got some pretty big tricks up our sleeves for early 2007 (or at least we like to think so . . . Time will tell).
>
> What will 2007 bring for online job search?
>
> Answer: more efficient ways than ever to connect individuals with people, information, and opportunities to help further their careers.
>
> Why don't I listen to my PR folks when then tell me to stop blogging?
>
> Answer: 'cause I'm different and I hate being handled.
>
> Here's to progress all around in 2007.[5]

Sure, at times Goldberg's blogging has been awkward—at first he had denied there was any trouble at the company, only to later change tune, but he explained that his obfuscation was a necessary measure designed to give the employees of Jobster first knowledge of the impending changes. Goldberg posted a "Confessions of a CEO Blogger"[6] video he put together to show he is still committed to failing in full public view.

It is important to take responsibility and apologize for errors in judgment, mistakes, and the like—and, most importantly, to begin to explain what will be done to prevent future events.

And there as an additional benefit to Goldberg's public failure—thousands of people, prospective clients and partners, became newly aware of Jobster and its offerings.

When JetBlue fumbled the customer service and public relations challenge that followed their colossal management failure during the Valentine's Day storm of 2007, most people, including myself thought the airline was doomed. *BusinessWeek* crossed out their name on the cover of their first-ever ranking of "client pleasing brands."[7] You see it all the time: A company screws up, the press jumps all over them, customers start gravitating to a competitor—and a few months later a little notice appears in the media saying that the company filed for bankruptcy.

But this failure was different. The very same issue that led to JetBlue's troubles during the storm—its small size and relatively thin management structure—played a key role in its recovery. If JetBlue had acted like most companies and issued a press statement or used a PR flak to offer an apology to customers, it would have fallen flat. When David Neeleman, JetBlue's founder and CEO, went on a personal apology tour through the media and talked directly to customers online (through the JetBlue Web site and even on YouTube) it came across as genuine, sincere, and personal. Watching the video, it is obvious that Mr. Neeleman hadn't slept in days and was taking the responsibility and stress of the crisis very personally. It is nice to know that a CEO wasn't shielding himself from tough times when customers were up in arms.

Second, they took swift and decisive action. Lots of companies promise to fix problems when a crisis hits. Usually the investigation into what went wrong takes a few months. Then a few more months pass before any real changes are announced. The public forgets what really caused the problem and the impact that the changes a company makes are hardly noticeable. Not at JetBlue. Their new Customer Bill of Rights was issued within days of the crisis, while emotions were still high over the delays and inconveniences. In today's fast-moving media environment, where news travels very quickly and the attention span of the average person is very short, JetBlue was able to put into place a plan for real change while the audience was still paying attention.

The way JetBlue responded to this very public failure—in the media, to customers, online, by making the necessary changes to its structure and policies quickly—probably saved the airline. We all know that weather will always cause problems for airline companies. We all probably gave up on most of the major airlines long ago when it comes to supporting us as customers when these situations hit. But JetBlue has earned itself at least one more chance to prove that its model, and customer-focused philosophy, can and does work.

The Right Way to Fail

As long as you are going to fail, you might as well do it right—and fast. An organization that fails badly usually ends up realizing long-term, even catastrophic failures. Think Enron or WorldCom. One that fails well can contain failure and turn it into a positive. Think JetBlue. Failing fast and well allows you to mitigate what long-term impact that failure has on your organization and audience.

What are some of the ways that you can fail well? Try launching products quickly, instead of waiting to make sure they are perfect before release. Anyone who has ever launched a Web site knows that it will never be perfect, nor will your audience notice or care much if it isn't, presuming you set their expectations appropriately. The same is true for a service, or really anything. By releasing an offering early and committing to a process of reviewing and improving, you can learn how to make critical adjustments over time. If you hold on to something in the hopes that you can get all the bugs out, you will surely run into problems that are more challenging to fix or explain away down the line.

Failing as a community is important. It is not uncommon to find an organization that considers its team to be the authority on a certain subject, though everyone else knows that isn't the case. No matter how large or how accomplished your organization is, other voices in the conversation can be helpful. The *New York Times* reported that the government of Denmark has established the idea of user-driven innovation as a matter of public policy, inviting citizens to test products and make suggestions for how they could be improved upon. In the same article, Eric von Hippel, a professor at the Massachusetts Institute of Technology's Sloan School of Management and the author of *Democratizing Innovation,* noted that in one of his studies 82 percent of new capabilities for scientific instruments like electron microscopes were developed by users.[8]

Being candid about your shortcomings will only help to build goodwill with your audience. Don Tapscott, author of *The Naked*

Corporation (New York: Free Press, 2003), explains in the introduction to his book:

> People and institutions that interact with firms are gaining unprecedented access to all sorts of information about corporate behavior, operations, and performance. Armed with new tools to find information about matters that affect their interests, stakeholders now scrutinize the firm as never before, inform others, and organize collective responses. The corporation is becoming naked. Customers can evaluate the worth of products and services at levels not possible before. Employees share formerly secret information about corporate strategy, management, and challenges. To collaborate effectively, companies and their business partners have no choice but to share intimate knowledge with one another. Powerful institutional investors today own or manage most wealth, and they are developing x-ray vision. Finally, in a world of instant communications, whistleblowers, inquisitive media, and googling, citizens and communities routinely put firms under the microscope.

There is no need to wait until your audience figures out your weak areas on its own. Develop a proactive approach to communicating the ongoing values of your organization, as well as your challenges, so that you can draw on the reserve of goodwill that you build up by being transparent when those challenges present themselves.

Asking lots of questions will help you to avoid some of the most common failures. You aren't the first person to run an organization, and in most cases you aren't even the first person to run an organization like yours. You definitely aren't the first person to fail, so there are important lessons that others who have come before you can offer.

Ed Schmults, the CEO of FAO Schwartz, told us, "I think, at least most good companies ask customers questions. The question is: Are they asking the right questions and are they interpreting the answers correctly? Like Sony in the late 1970s, it said, 'Do you need a little device that you can carry and listen to your music?' Ninety percent of people would have said no and they wouldn't have made that investment. But maybe if they'd asked, 'Wouldn't it be great if you could have your own personal music with you as you were outside walking your dog?' The answer would have certainly be 'Oh yeah, that's great, how could I do that?' and it would have justified the investment they made—that changed a generation of technology."

We talk a lot about context and understanding the user's perspective when considering how you should position your organization and what activities to pursue. The best opportunity for gaining information and understanding from your audience is to admit that you don't know, and to Ed Schmults' point, to ask the right questions. Smart organizations, and leaders, will admit they don't know before they make a mistake—and get the information that helps them to avoid a fall. All organizations should have the confidence to admit when they are wrong after a crisis and use smart questions and good listening to redeem themselves with their audience.

Redemption is a Good Narrative

There are two ways to go after you fail: up or down. Every one of us will have days when we just want to give up. The stress will be high, the cost of failure will just seem to be too great. No matter how impossible something might seem, however, push ahead. Learning from failure and rebounding stronger than before is a hallmark of successful organizations.

To capitalize on failure, your organization has to have a philosophy that embraces failure and a process for turning tough times around. The organizational leadership—staff, board, other key stakeholders—all need to be open and able to probe failures and analyze the root causes. If you start playing the blame game the whole organization loses. Create an environment where the entire organization, staff, volunteers, and customers alike, are encouraged to help identify failures and offer solutions. And don't wait—you should own up to and begin to assess the reasons behind a failure immediately after it happens so the learnings can be applied and the change begin immediately.

Business 2.0 quoted Douglas Merrill, a Google vice president for engineering, saying that "Fundamentally, everything we do is an experiment. The thing with experimentation is that you have to get data and then be brutally honest when you're assessing it." The article added that "when introducing new features, Google has remained true to a 'fail fast' strategy: launch, listen, improve, launch again."[10]

Success, no matter how you define it, depends on integrity and values as well as outcomes and impacts. There is a certain amount of luck and timing involved as well. Rather than stress about avoiding failure, you are better off determining which elements of your organizational success you can control and which elements you cannot.

When an organization fails it often because it is trying new things, explores new ideas. It is stretching itself beyond the comfort zone. Organizations should create a culture where failure is allowed and mistakes are encouraged (even promoted) as long as they contribute to growth and future learning and keep their audience engaged through the failures and challenges as well as through the successes.

Be Connected and Coordinated

To be successful, you need your team and a network. You must work hard and deliver on the information, experiences, and stuff that your audience expects. Times have changed, and will continue to change, so while the premium today is on having a leader with vision and demonstrable passion for your organization, you must always remain approachable and connected, grounded and accessible. It is from these attributes that your audience will find the ability to engage, trust, and follow you.

The poet, George Santayana, famously wrote that, "Those who ignore history are doomed to repeat it." In some ways that is still true. The same fundamental concepts that drove economic expansion in the past are still relevant today. Audience expectations of the organizations they belong to haven't really changed—maybe audiences have a better focus on how to explain what they want or are more easily able to express it. But there are many who believe that a new model must be created in order to maximize the opportunity that this new economic reality creates. Truly, the more some things change, the more some things can stay the same.

The Because Effect

It is easy to become confused about what is new and what hasn't changed with the flurry of theories, articles, and examples flooding the conversation every day. Instead of chasing the newest and hottest trend all the time, remember what motivated you in the first place. There was and will always be some foundational elements that created the opportunity for your organization to launch. And there is, and will always be, a series of resulting activities that spring from that foundation.

Doc Searls, a PR and advertising veteran and research fellow with groups like the Center for Information Technology and Society at the University of California in Santa Barbara and the Berkman Center for the Internet and Society at Harvard University, calls this the *because effect.* He wrote on his blog, "This is what you get when your new business isn't just about inventing and controlling technologies and standards, but about taking advantage of the new opportunities opened up by fresh new technologies and standards. For example, making money *because of* blogging, or RSS, or desktop Linux, or whatever—rather than just *with* those things. The *because effect* is a kind of jujitsu. While other people look to make money *with* something, you're finding ways of making money *because of* something."[1]

This because effect has always been a driving force in how organizations are created and managed. And the reach goes well beyond the relatively small number of examples that Searls cited. For example, television was invented so that advertisers would have a way to sell products to a larger, more mainstream audience—but entertainment companies were able to make money *because* the television was invented. The government has programs focused on public safety, health, and education all across the country, but nonprofit organizations like Jumpstart and City Year launched and are able to grow and change the lives of more and more people across the country *because* AmeriCorps was launched to provide funding and support to local, state, and national service programs that help meet critical societal needs.

The innovation economy and the success of organizations created in the next decade—along with those who refocus to adapt to the changing times—will be driven by this because effect. No single piece of technology, not even something like TiVo or the iPod, will shift the way that we think about our lives. No solitary event, not a tsunami or a horrific terrorist attack, will dramatically alter how we act on a day-to-day basis. But every day, every hour it seems, a new way to learn, to share, to communicate, or to act is being rolled out. More and more of these will succeed, and more of the audience will choose to engage, because technology has lowered the barriers for entry and made it possible for people to do things they never imagined before. The because effect will drive much of what we do going forward.

Relationships Are the Foundation for Long-Term Value

With our intellectual and emotional marketplace flooded with opportunities, and our time increasingly feeling limited, the thing that will define success for organizations will be the same as it has always been: value.

That is true for all of us and everyone in our audiences. Naturally, everyone will have a slightly different answer when asked what they value. We are all different. What any person finds valuable depends on their circumstance in life, and over time those perspectives will change as well. It is part of the natural order of events. Of course, for marketers and representatives of organizations looking to find and engage a target audience or sell a product, all these different opinions make for quite a challenge.

Carl Shapiro and Hal Varian, two business professors at the University of California at Berkeley, classify things like a newspaper subscription or a ticket to a baseball game as *experience goods*. The challenge to selling an experience good, they argue, is that people only find its value through using it—and once you read a paper or attend an event, the knowledge and the value has decreased. They write that "[t]he tension is between giving away your information—to let people know what you have to offer—and charging them for it to recover your costs."[2] They note that most media producers overcome the experience goods problem through branding and reputation.

Branding and reputation are powerful attributes for an organization to have in their arsenal, but they also take time to create. More important, perhaps, is having a strong relationship between you and your audience. At the core of any good brand, and any good brand relationship, is trust, and that trust comes from value. That value might reside in how you present the information—to some there is a need for content to be filtered, organized, and prioritized, which is why newspapers continue to be popular. For others, the important element of information is opinion, which is why blogs have grown in popularity as an alternative to traditional news coverage for many. When you look at how people make decisions about what information to consume, share, and, most importantly, pay for, you can trace it back to the value that the offering provides to the particular audience.

Stephen Cassidy from UNICEF, who is a former CNN producer, thinks part of the problem is how organizations communicate with their audience. He thinks organizations don't give their audience enough respect or credit. He told us:

> We make that case, we put information out there, which is factual, believable, and credible, and we hope the audience appreciates it. I happen to believe that the audience is smart. I know a popular phrase when I was working in the television business was this sort of disparaging reference to somebody by the name of "Joe Six-pack." And colleagues that I had would refer to Joe Six-pack and they would think that somehow Joe Six-pack was not smart, that Joe Six-pack needed to be led, and could be led.
>
> I don't believe that. I'm Joe Six-pack. You're Joe Six-pack. Everybody's Joe Six-pack. And I don't think I'm dumb, I think I'm pretty smart. And I think most people think that they're pretty smart, and that they make pretty good choices. The vast majority of the people on the planet are doing okay, making good choices, and given an opportunity to make a good choice, I think people choose well rather than badly, more often than not. So with that as a premise, I think that if I give people information that they didn't have before, when they then are at a moment of tipping point or decision, they'll do the right thing.

With so many technologies available for people to get and share information, the information itself does not have as much value to most people as it once did. The thing that makes the difference is the ability to personalize the information to someone's particular interests. Technology has also given people access to products they would never have imagined being available. The thing that makes the difference is the uniqueness of the product. Organizations have also sought ways to differentiate themselves from their competition. What has always worked, and will continue to, is providing value to the audience, which helps create and maintain strong and lasting relationships with them and vice versa.

Technology Is Just Technology; Information Is Just Information

In the information age, many see technology as the solution for a host of organizational challenges including the mechanism for providing value. Having trouble raising money for your nonprofit organization? Put in a customer relationship management (CRM) program and personalize your e-mails. Are sales at your small business lagging? Build a Web site and post some glossy pictures of your product, or stock photos of people who represent your audience. It is true that additional promotion online will help to raise awareness among your target audience, and being more organized will maximize the time you spend on a certain activity. Technology creates efficiencies and efficiency has many benefits. But technology, and the efficiency that it provides, won't compel someone to donate or make a purchase. Technology by itself does not create value.

Technology is just technology. Technology allows an organization, which has the same amount of time as its competitors, to make the information it needs more easily accessible. Technology can keep track of inventory across a network of stores. It can help you track donor behavior in real time so you can see if your message is resonating. It can give your audience unique control over their user experience. So yes, technology saves people time. And yes, when you create that kind of efficiency in an organization you create opportunities for people to provide the added value that will be critical in pushing someone to engage. Retailers can spend their energy creating unique offerings of the hottest styles for each particular audience segment. Fund raisers can spend their time doing research on a particular donor or crafting a letter that will touch the recipient in a personal way. It is the combination of the technology, the best use of that technology and the value that the organization adds, increases the likelihood someone will engage.

Tom Friedman wrote in *The World is Flat* that "every new product—from software to widgets—goes through a cycle that begins with basic research, then applied research, then incubation, then development, then testing, then manufacturing, then deployment, then support, then continuation engineering, in order to add improvements."[3] And, thanks to globalization, "it is now possible for more people than ever to collaborate and compete in real time with more other people on more different kinds of work from more different corners of the planet and on a more equal footing than at any pervious time in the history of the world—using computers, e-mail, networks, teleconferencing, and dynamic new software."[4] The result is flattening of the world's information and power structure and the lowering of production and distribution costs everywhere. Chris Anderson added in his book, *The Long Tail,* that "When you can dramatically lower the costs of connecting supply and demand, it changes not just the numbers, but the entire nature of the market."[5]

Technological advances are changing business models, diminishing the importance of scale and increasing the benefits seen in things like outsourcing, partnering, and alliances with specialty firms (with their own economies of scale). Organizations are able to keep costs down and maximize profits. Sometimes, however, technology can make things worse. Greater access, new tools, and more data do not solve anything by themselves.

Information has certain critical characteristics that make it valuable to an organization as well. Information is timely—when it needs to be available, it can be, even in real time. And the same information feeds analysis long after its initial creation. Information can also actionable, but it must be accessible to be so. That means the right users must be able to get the information when and where they need it. If they do, the information is relevant to them. If that information is not available, it loses relevance quickly.

Information, like technology, is not valuable on its own. It must be accessible, usable, and relevant. It must help organizations and users form new knowledge to make decisions, make changes. It must be able to be presented in a way that users can share it, talk about it, and get value from it.

Rules Are Rules

The cover of *Fortune* magazine on July 11, 2006, showed a picture of Jack Welch, the former CEO of General Electric and one of the titans of American business, with a red circle around it and a stripe through it. The headline read "Sorry, Jack! Welch's Rules for Winning Don't Work Anymore (But We've Got 7 New Ones That Do)." The article began: "Once upon a time, there was a route to success that corporate America agreed on. But in today's fast-changing landscape, that old formula is getting tired." It went on to outline how the old thinking about business is no longer applicable, thanks in part to the increasingly important role that technology is playing in our society.[6]

In an information age, the application of a single way of thinking is unlikely to be the only pathway to success. Jack Welch is wrong in believing that only his rules apply. *Fortune* magazine is wrong as well. The old rules of business do not apply in the same ways that they used to. The constant in the business world (and really any world) is that you have to constantly adapt and change. Technology is evolving and customer expectations change all the time. But there are some things about business and life that have always remained unchanged.

What are some of those things? Customer service. Innovation. Strategic thinking. Leadership. Management. Those fundamental principles have existed since business began. They continue today with the growth and increasing influence of the Internet as well. The organizations that understand and can integrate those principles into their operations thrive. They have adapted over time to reflect what changes in audience expectations mean as a result of technology advancement, and they have been successful because of it. Those who continue operating the way they always have are not as fortunate.

The definition of those things, of course, varies greatly from your perspective to that provided by your audience. Lisa Poulson offered insights from the audience's perspective:

> I get to choose. Am I going to get what I already know I want? Do I want to browse on Amazon.com for what they might have for me? Or am I going to the bookstore? I get to decide. When I'm buying plane tickets, I generally start online, and if something goes wrong I just call. And I could say, "I started this reservation online, something went wrong, can you please help me?" So I always have that option available for me.
>
> To me, what e-commerce is about is the convenience and the shipping. That is why I use Amazon.com. This year, I was probably only home for twenty days between October 31 and December 31 because of travel for work. I bought every single Christmas present from some hotel in some part of the world because I did not have any time to go to any stores. And there's

no way that I have time to go stand in line at the UPS store and ship stuff. I hate doing that! There's nothing I would rather not do than go to the post office or the UPS store or go to FedEx and spend the time getting bubble wrap. So for me, Amazon. com is about shipping.

Lisa is not alone. Consider a Forrester Research Poll from 2000 about why people shop online. They offered the following reasons:[7]

- I like that I can shop online whenever I want—84 percent.
- It's easy to buy products online—79 percent.
- I'm always willing to try new things—58 percent.
- I'm always pressed for time—43 percent.
- It's easier to keep track of what I purchased online—43 percent.

Not surprisingly, the greatest obstacles to buying online are the inability to touch or feel a product online, like you are able to when you are physically in a store; learning, or relearning how to find products in an online environment (where there are no aisles or signage like a brick and mortar location), trust and security, fulfillment— the fact that in most cases you have to wait a couple of days to get the product you just ordered, as opposed to carrying it out of the store with you; and, of course, customer service—no friendly salesperson to help answer your questions.

If you surveyed the audience again today, do you think the answers would be any different? What people look for in an online experience is really no different than what they look for from an offline retail operation. Advances in technology and increased comfort with the Internet over time will focus and amplify those expectations, but it won't change them dramatically.

Still, organizations routinely lose site of these basic offerings that audiences value most. You can easily become consumed with the prospect of success, defined by profit or by mass audience adoption of an idea or offering. But, audience loyalty, profit, international acclaim, and other success metrics you seek will follow when the information, experiences, and stuff that you produce are sound.

Lisa Poulson added this:

Let's say I want to buy a pair of diamond earrings. I feel more comfortable going to a store that was personally recommended by a friend of mine where there was a relationship with the jeweler and where my friend, whom I trust, trusted the jeweler. And I could go in and say, "I need to spend $20,000 on a pair of diamond earrings, and I want to go to someone that I know someone else that I trust, trusts." And then I want to open a relationship with that person. I'm never going to buy a pair of diamond earrings online. I need that personal connection.

Sooner or later, we are going to have to get to a place where the communities online create the same kind of trust and intimacy and connection that offline communities do. Then we can buy diamond earrings, opera tickets, and pick out political candidates all online if we want. We aren't there yet.

David Gale, executive vice president, New Media, at MTV Networks, explained how the movie industry is adapting as well. "Everybody loves a four quadrant movie," says Gale, referring to a film that resonates with male, female, old and young audiences at the same time. "It's great when you have them—they're rare to get, they're usually expensive to get, now more than ever. What's happening now, though, is that because there are so many methods of distribution and ways to access content, you can get those audiences more specifically. You can target them with advertising, distribution, and marketing so that you know where to spend your money. You know what you've got, you know how much you should spend, you know what the size of your audience is, and you know what 'successful' will be in that specific niche. And that's just becoming easier to do with new technologies, so that you could have so many more channels, and you can have it all."

Organizations have expanded to national and global markets while achieving efficiencies in the supply chain. You can walk into one of a hundred chain stores in any country around the world and get the same outfit you could get a mile from your home. You can see a blockbuster Hollywood movie in any major capital around the world, as well.

In many cases, audiences are also finding their experience as a customer diminished. Audiences are looking for quality, service, and personality. The organization that can provide a more tailored offering, more personalized attention to its different groups of customers, will distinguish itself.

This change won't be realized simply because an organization makes some obvious changes in policies or procedures. The new information economy requires wholesale differences in the way organizations are managed and marketed. As Seth Godin noted, "You don't win an Olympic gold medal with a few weeks of intensive training. There's no such thing as an overnight opera sensation. Every great company, every great brand, and every great career has been built in exactly the same way: bit by bit, step by step. If every element of an organization gets a little bit better every day, then the organization will become unstoppable."[8] And in many ways, they are going to have to be rebuilt again.

Change Doesn't Happen All At Once

Jim Collins, the author of *Built to Last* (New York: HarperBusiness, 1994) and *Good to Great* (2001), has worked with hundreds of CEOs and social sector organizations to build dynamic organizations. But the turnaround that Collins talks about doesn't happen overnight. He wrote:

> Picture an egg. Day after day, it sits there. No one pays attention to it. No one notices it. Certainly no one takes a picture of it or puts it on the cover of a celebrity-focused business magazine. Then one day, the shell cracks and out jumps a chicken. All of a sudden, the major magazines and newspapers jump on the story: "Stunning Turnaround at Egg!" and "The Chick Who Led the Breakthrough at Egg!" From the outside, the story always reads like an overnight sensation—as if the egg had suddenly and radically altered itself into a chicken.
>
> It's a silly analogy—but then our conventional way of looking at change is no less silly. Everyone looks for the "miracle moment" when "change happens." But ask the good-to-great executives when change happened. They cannot pinpoint a single key event that exemplified their successful transition."[9]

We are now in the middle (or arguably just at the beginning) of a major shift in the way the global economy operates. This revolution was launched by the creation and adoption of new technology, and continues to expand because of the same forces. But it is fueled by the information, experiences, and stuff.

To be successful, organizations need to know what each customer needs, and not only deliver data and information to them, but do so in the format(s) they demand across all possible touch points (phone, e-mail, in person, proactive notification, any time of day, etc.). If you start from scratch, you can build the type of system you want. If you are trying to change an existing organization to adapt, it might be more complicated.

CHAPTER

Be a Steward

Organizations and their leaders demonstrate at least two very dramatic responses to this rapidly changing environment. One is that the organizations, companies, nonprofits, educational institutions, networks, hold their ground and say, "We're right, we're going to hold on to the way we have always done things, and we're going to tell the audience that our way is the way they should get their information or buy their stuff." And on the other side, you have organizations throwing up their hands and saying, "The audience is in control. There's nothing we can do," and ceding nearly complete control over how the company operates and communicates to the audience.

There is a happy middle ground. It is possible to treat every member of your audience like she is the most important person to your organization. This is especially true in the new media environment where technology facilitates your ability to deliver specific, tailored, and personalized information, experiences, and stuff to nearly everyone – on terms they help to dictate. It's a good idea, too. Your audience expects it. The success of your organizational mission demands it. And when done properly, the results are obvious.

The starting point is putting the information, experiences, and stuff that your organization excels at in the center of what you do. If the media doesn't rule, the rest will fall flat.

From there, think about how you can segment and personalize what you provide to the audience that you want. Consider how to align what you offer to what your audience really wants—not once, but continuously. And explore ways to build relationships with your audience that last forever, rather than achieve a single transaction that you can only count for an instant.

The key ingredient is trust. Your audience has to trust that you are working on their behalf, with their interests in mind. And you have to trust that when you do, they will respond the way you want. It's a tough thing for an organization to do, but it works.

We'll call this process *stewardship*. Organizations must look past the short-term gain and put the audience first. No longer should you focus on simply making a sale or getting a donation. Instead, invest in growing the relationship with each person in your audience. These relationships will be more natural to all involved and will pay off for you in the long term. Think of how you would expect to be treated if you were your own audience (hint: you are). Tending to the relationship makes your audience want to buy, or become members, or show their support, however it is you choose to quantify it.

Organizations need to be stewards of their relationships with their audience. Everyone in the organization has a responsibility for managing the relationship, and everyone in the organization understands they have a role. That also brings with it responsibilities about how you act—the information you put out to your audience must respect their values, their privacy, and the trust they have put in you. You will make decisions that run afoul from time to time, but your commitment to delivering that type of relationship to your audience will be repaid in long-term trust.

This potential exists because the cost of communication and the costs of personalization have dramatically decreased. The integration of new technologies means that people can get the information they want, when and how they want it. More than just realizing that they have they lost some of the control over their audience they once enjoyed, organizations must embrace the relationship they have with their customer and work twice as hard to make sure the information customers are using to form their opinions comes from the organization. Customers want help, they want to be led—and organizations can, and should, fill that need. You must be their steward.

Trust Is More than Just a Buzzword

We all know what trust is.

Trust is a core element of the strategic operation of an organization. It forms the foundation for effective communication—internally with your team, and when engaging your audience. It allows you to find, and keep, the best employees and volunteers, the ones who show the most passion. When you have earned the trust of your audience, they will share extraordinary amounts of information with you and help you to succeed on their behalf.

But how do you earn it? Trust is not something that simply exists from the beginning, something we can assume or take for granted. Trust is an emotional skill, an active and dynamic part of our lives that we build and sustain every day with our actions. When you make a promise, you have to keep it. When you say something, you have to follow up and show that you are serious. Trust must be built and sustained.

Without trust, the machinery of organizations would grind to a halt. We're all more apt to make a purchase when we trust the company selling the product or service. When you have a physical store and someone walks in, you can build trust through your conversation with them. From the moment they walk in you answer their questions and make idle chat and develop a rapport with them. Online, that give-and-take isn't there, so you need to do other things to establish trust. Online you can reveal more about yourself than you might think. Most of us tend to think we should appear to be larger than we actually are. But if you are a one-person company, why not say so?

Without trust, nobody would be able to sell anything. The information we produce would be worthless. We would have no audience. Trust makes everything more efficient. Trust allows an organization to go more directly to the heart of an issue, without having to reintroduce or requalify itself with the audience each time. If they trust you, they will listen. If they don't, you have no shot.

Trust has to be earned. And in many cases, your audience will have to learn how to trust you. That may mean that over time, they will have to see you continually demonstrate behavior that engenders trust in them. More likely, it will mean they literally have to be taught what your organization is all about and why you should be trusted. You can do this by providing the rationale, background, and thought processes behind the decisions you make. Actions alone are not enough.

Trust alone, however, is not always enough. Even when organizations do their best to build and demonstrate trust with their audience, many people will be unwilling to return the feeling. How your organization is perceived and what level of trust people feel has to do with your actions as well as what others in your space do. If you run a newspaper and people think that journalists are dishonest because of one reporter's misdeeds, all your reporters are going to fight an uphill battle to get credibility with an audience. If you raise money for a nonprofit organization and another organization gets in trouble for mishandling funds, you are going to have to go above and beyond what you would normally have to do so that your audience knows you won't make the same mistake.

To build (or regain) trust, recognize what is going on, acknowledge problems as they exist, raise the bar on performance so the issue is eliminated, and learn from the change so that the trust is not breached again. Transparency isn't only about sharing the good. It's okay to say what you don't do well. Being honest about things you don't do so well will just make me trust you more when you tell me the things you *can* do well. Without trust, stewardship cannot happen.

Stewardship

Organizations want, and need, to build a strong, loyal audience, and to find ways to tap that audience for support, whether financial (through purchases) or in the form of buzz. Moreover, as the audience changes, the challenges of reaching and engaging your audience change as well. What worked a few years, even days, ago might not work anymore.

Audience expectations continue to rise as a result of changes in technology that allow people to have more information and more access than ever before. We all know that our audience, not the press, not the investors, is the lifeblood of our success—yet we haven't been able to demonstrate that in our management or marketing. Recently, major marketers have begun launching audience-centric campaigns, everything from the Dove "Real Beauty" campaign to the user-generated Super Bowl advertising by Doritos, to the American Cancer Society's presence in Second Life, the virtual world. There are multiple channels for everything now, and the key challenge is to create the right experiences at the right time in the right way for your audience.

The stakes are high when it comes to customer experiences. According to a 2004 IBM customer study, 59 percent of customers who have multichannel interactions will stop doing business with a brand after just one bad experience. Conversely, 79 percent of consumers will commit to a deeper product or service relation-ship with a brand after a satisfying experience.[1] Building meaningful experiences is a daunting challenge in this environment, particularly given the growing number of channels and continuing complexity of tracking a specific audience.

The key to engaging your audience remains, however, under-standing their needs and expectations. By doing so, organizations can understand what the most important interactions are and how to recreate them time and time again. The customer decides which interactions are important. That deserves emphasizing: The *customer* determines the importance of an interaction.

When your organization acts as an appropriate steward, you build up good will with the audience, create a trusting relationship, and build up a tolerance for the inevitable challenge that will come in the future.

The obvious outcome of persistent stewardship is that you improve the performance of all aspects of your operation. Your audi-ence invests more time, more energy, and more resources in you because they feel a part of something meaningful. The more subtle outcome is the creation of a community within, and made up of, your organization and your audience, that can be directed to other, related efforts as needed.

The Rise of Social Leadership

For most companies, operating in the current media environment requires a pretty significant change in perspective and potentially some serious investment of time and resources. The effort it takes to make those changes provides reasons enough to keep most organi-zations from acting. But the real changes that need to be made can happen over time, and even the smallest of efforts can have a dra-matic impact.

The perspective that is needed when an organization must change is similar to the perspective required when it was just being started.

Consider the new class of leaders that has emerged, often referred to as social entrepreneurs. We talked about them earlier, in the con-text of the Social Capital Awards that Fast Company hands out each year. Social entrepreneurs recognize a social problem and use entre-preneurial principles to organize, create, and manage a venture to institute social change. Most companies can't justify a shift away from their core business objectives to tackle a social problem. Many non-profit organizations, educational institutions, and other groups are quite comfortable with the success they have had and the prospects of continued profit or growth in the near future. Success, however, can be about more than just replicating what has worked in the past. It should be about continual renewal and change, evolving opportunities, and pushing the entire environment you are in to align with your organization's values.

To do this, we need a new role in the leadership of organizations—the social CEO (or social executive director, social president of a college or university). You see, social entrepreneurs set out to find what is not working and solve the problem by changing the system, identifying new opportunities and solutions, and persuading entire societies to take new leaps. They aren't satisfied with the status quo of their industry or their organization. They are personally committed to, and believe their audience is interested in, making institutional changes and not just achieving personal or organizational success.

Entrepreneurs have always worked to change the face of business. They are the risk-takers who are able to pursue a small innovation in a market so that other companies can replicate their model in a different vertical or scale. Similarly, social entrepreneurs act as the change agents for society, seizing opportunities that others miss and improving systems, inventing new approaches, and creating solutions to change society for the better. While a business entrepreneur might create entirely new industries, a social entrepreneur comes up with new solutions to social problems and then implements them on a large scale. Organizations must combine business and social entrepreneurship to succeed in today's marketplace.

Organizations must find a way to balance serving the needs of their community, environment, customers, vendors, employees, and stakeholders. One concept that relates to this is a double bottom line: one part financial profit and one part contribution to society. Like Seventh Generation, companies that offer alternative employee health care programs, gym, day care, educational opportunities, flextime and/or telecommuting, financial counseling services, a chance to make monetary donations, and paid opportunities for employees to contribute time and skills to charitable community programs are successful. You see this in the tech space in particular, with Microsoft and Google among the giants. Embracing your company's social responsibility means applying the same sustainable practices to your suppliers and setting those expectations for employees outside the company as well as working with your partners to improve their values and performance as well. It is a change in the very lifestyle and life cycle of a company, not just a new program or initiative.

Jim Berk, the chief executive officer of Participant Productions, explains stewardship this way:

> At the heart of it we're a company which aspires to be the leading provider of entertainment that inspires and compels social change. And at the heart of the thesis of the company, or the vision for the company when we founded it, is the belief that in order to inspire, you have to develop an emotional connection that has relevance, as opposed to the use of, let's say, guilt or anger. Those tend to fade away, whereas if you are inspired it's a behavioral change that occurs that then leads to a change that is permanent, that has some legacy attached to it.
>
> The other piece of it for us is that it's entertainment and it's media which actually does more to evoke emotions or an emotional connection. And it's that emotional connection that we believe is critical to establish with the client, the customer, the audience, in order to have a lasting impression that then gets taken with you in terms of the way that you look at a situation. And actually you see it in terms of the entire industry, a movement in terms of product marketing and what's going on in the industry now. It's all about establishing an emotional connection, as opposed to going to low fare or low price or this type of thing, which tend to be a singular emotion that passes.

Ricky Strauss, Participant's president adds:

> For Participant the idea is to create the most compelling, entertaining movies and television shows and ultimately publishing and digital and broadband. But the most important thing is that our movies actually bring audiences in so that a lot of people are seeing these movies and experiencing these stories so that more people that are inspired by them can then do something to make a difference. What we're going to expect from our audience over time is that people come to understand

what Participant means and what the value is of being part of a Participant experience. As far as expectations on how we change the world, I think that has to be fluid because every movie's going to have a very different kind of campaign.

Participant Productions represents this concept we have been talking about throughout the book, how the organization's, passion for providing its audience a sustainable and inspiring offering are a part of the company DNA.

From its founding, Participant has been structured with this in mind, and now Participant's founder and chairman, Jeff Skoll has taken the same principle and applied it to managing not-for-profit ventures and investment funds with the same values and practices. Skoll created a foundation that gives early funding to small nonprofits that are ready to grow their impact and he runs an investment group that looks at supporting people who manage social change initiatives in different ways and funds them without any interest in return, just to enhance a particular business model or behavior that they'd like to see expanded. Skoll was motivated by the fact that strong, impactful organizations need a funding source and level or organization that would ensure success.

Of course, Skoll and Participant Productions, didn't set out to remake philanthropy or Hollywood, but they are on their way to doing both.

As we have explained, it is not only possible to treat every member of your audience like she is the most important person to your organization, it is imperative. Everything you do contributes to the perception that your audiences holds of you—so operate wisely. Your audience knows that the technology they carry every day, use every minute, and hear about non-stop makes it possible for them to get information, experiences, and stuff the way they want it. They also know that this technology is more invasive and disruptive than almost anything we have experienced as a society to date. Other organizations working to engage your audience, so you must also. How you communicate, and what type of experience you create, will differentiate you from others. This is not simply compliance or commitment, and its certainly not about competition. Stewardship is about the opportunity to create a new kind of relationship with your audience, one that recognizes the changing nature of our world and grows along with it.

As we have said throughout the book, organizations are confused and in some cases struggling in the wake of massive technological advancements and societal change. The path to success is to deliver the information, experiences, and stuff that meet your audience's expectations and distinguish your organization from others in your space. Doing this right is a form of stewardship, as well as a sound combination of business and social enterprise, and our recommended model for the future.

CHAPTER

Be Measurable

We talk in this book about how media is virtually anything that we create, consume, and share in our daily lives. It is the information, experiences, and stuff that define our daily interaction with brands, causes, organizations, and each other.

By now, we hope you are convinced that adopting and communicating through a mediacentric strategy must be a key part of what your organization does and how you engage your audience. Gone are the days of broadcast-style communications where an organization used a single message or venue to reach its broad audience, and walked away with the assurance that their efforts met the intended target audience in the intended way. Instead, we now live within a communication ecosystem where many different channels exist and virtually anyone—organization or individual—can deliver information, experiences, and stuff on terms that they dictate.

As members of the audience, we all have opportunities to create, consume, or share information like never before. As organizational leaders, we all have an obligation to adapt and change with the times.

We understand that for some, the thought of abandoning or even changing ever so slightly the well-established methods of operating and communicating requires more than just a solid theory and compelling stories. Some companies need to see a demonstrated ROI before putting resources into new things. Even if our arguments over the last two-hundred pages resonate for those people, something more is required to make the leap.

What is missing? Numbers. Some kind of measurement is needed to show, with certainty, that a communications effort, whether it uses a commercial, an e-mail, a podcast, a shout across the room, a creative mailer, a brand tattoo, or all of them combined, actually resulted in a sale, compelled someone to make a donation, increased awareness, or drove a key action. Every organization has a slightly different definition of what success looks like, but every single one has a definition for sure.

But, there is a problem.

There is no certainty in communications. We are not scientists or mathematicians, but even without a masters degree in statistics or a PhD in human psychology, we can say with confidence that determining the exact reasoning behind why someone makes the choices they do is not possible with any certainty. You can measure your activities – how many commercials you ran, how many impressions you bought, how many newspapers your article appeared in, or how many emails you sent – and you can measure the resulting actions— how many viewers your show received, how many click-throughs your online ads prompted, how many people bought your book, and how long someone spent on your Web site—but you cannot apply a metric to what your audience was thinking when they engaged with your offering or why they responded as they did.

We know that we can move people with our messages, can reach them with our technology, and can account for the actions they take, in far greater detail than at any point in our history. Newer forms of media are designed to allow us to more clearly measure these actions and target communications based on behavior. But we can't say why a person took a certain action, what particular piece of information finally pushed them over the edge, or when that moment of recognition occurred in their brain. To be successful, you need to define goals in terms of things that might be measured.

Consider this. You are making a pot of soup, from scratch. You have dozens of ingredients: broth, different vegetables, spices, and so on. One by one you start to add the ingredients until the moment— just after adding the carrots—that the pot boils over and spills. Naturally, you blame the carrots. They were the last item you added to the soup, so they must have been responsible for everything boiling over, right? No. Stop to think about it for a moment. All the ingredients share some responsibility for the soup boiling over. And the same is true for media. All the interactions your audience has with little "m" media – the ones you direct and the ones beyond your control – all contribute to a person's experience.

We understand and value analytics: having a way to measure and assess the impact of your efforts is absolutely critical. But we don't believe there is, nor can we create a magic bullet solution to confirm that any activity is better than another. We don't endorse any particular tool, or system, or algorithm for determining that impact. There are too many factors and most of them well beyond our control. It's about having the right mix. So when people come to you selling a tool that they claim can determine with certainty whether your strategy is a success or a formula that assesses which of your activities will be worthwhile, in the future, don't be fooled.

So how do we measure success, and demonstrate that success is contingent on adopting this way of thinking?

The end starts with the beginning.

What does this mean? There is a very basic four-step order of operations that every organization must follow, right from the start of their efforts, before any bit of communication is created or pushed out to your audience. If you don't follow this order of operations you will encounter challenges, many of which you won't be able to overcome.

What is the order of operations?

1. Define and articulate your goals in a way that lends itself to measurement.
2. Outline strategies that help you to achieve your goals.
3. Identify tactics that can help you execute your strategy.
4. Assign the necessary (or available) resources to manage your tactics.

That's it. Goals. Strategies. Tactics. Then resources. It's no more complicated than that. Why are we spending time explaining something that seems common sense? Maybe you think you have already done this? Most organizations that we have ever worked with—and we are talking Fortune 100 brands, major nonprofit organizations, some of the most successful groups by anyone's standards—have tried to short-circuit this process and run into problems. Some tried to skip a step (going straight from goals to tactics without considering the overall strategy) while others determined the resources they had available to spend on a campaign first, before they knew what they were trying to accomplish.

If you can follow this basic order of operations, then you have put yourself in place to achieve meaningful and measurable success for your organization. If you can't, you should learn how.

Putting media at the center of your decision making, operations, and communication is not the only key to your success; it's just one piece of the puzzle. Our recommendations are based on an assessment of this moment in our history, and the result of the convergence of continual technological advancement, improvements in statistical technique, and societal change. We know that the purchase decisions, loyalties, actions, and sensibilities of your audience are made up of a combination of factors, to which you can only contribute a very tiny fraction.

The details of how you do this are not complicated, but they will take some time to explain and experimentation. They change depending on the audience you are trying to reach and the tools you choose to employ. Advances in technology, our changing society and how your audience embraces or responds to those actors, plays a role as well. We will continue this discussion and explain how to walk through each of these four steps and measure progress along the way. We will also look at what the future of media and communications looks like, how it is applied—and measured—and what role we will all play in shaping that future.

With that, we invite you to log on to www.themediarules.com and read the remainder of this chapter and join us for a conversation about media rules!

Notes

Chapter 1   The Media That Matters

1. Dale Peskin, "Connected to the News by a Generation of Wired Witnesses," iFOCOS, April 23, 2007. http://ifocos.org/2007/04/23/connected-to-the-news-by-a-generation-of-wired-witnesses/

Chapter 3   Be All Things

1. Tim Borg, "How to Give Your Customers What They Really Want," Careermag.com, October 2, 2006. http://www.careermag.com/articles/default.asp?Display=377
2. James Allen, Frederick F. Reichheld, and Barney Hamilton, "The Three 'Ds' of Customer Experience," Harvard Business School's *Working Knowledge for Business Leaders,* November 7, 2005; reprinted from *Harvard Management Update,* 10:10 (October 2005). http://hbswk.hbs.edu/archive/5075.html

Chapter 4   Be Organic

1. Jeffrey Hollender, CEO letter: "Why a CR Report? The Limitations and Possibilities of Sustainability Reporting," 2006. http://www.seventhgen.com/printpage.php?fkid=54&tid=446
2. Jane Lampman, "Trend-Watcher Sees Moral Transformation of Capitalism," *Christian Science Monitor,* October 3, 2005. http://www.csmonitor.com/2005/1003/p13s01-wmgn.html
3. Kelly Faville, "Civic-Minded Millennials Prepared to Reward or Punish Companies Based on Commitment to Social Causes," Cone Inc. press release, October 24, 2006. http://www.coneinc.com/Pages/pr_45.html

4. "New Survey Reveals That Marketers are Overlooking the Missing Link—Boomer-To-Friend (B2F) Connections," PR Newswire, March 19, 2007. http://www.prnewswire.com/cgi-bin/stories .pl?ACCT=ind_focus.story&STORY=/www/story/03-19-2007/ 0004548570&EDATE=MON+Mar+19+2007+09:00+AM
5. Seventh Generation Corporate Responsibility Report, "Our New Home," http://www.seventhgen.com/about_us/corporate/our_ new_home.html
6. Jeffrey Hollender, "They're Changing It," The Inspired Protagonist, August 1, 2006. http://www.inspiredprotagonist.com/ blog/they_re_changing_it
7. John Mackey, "Conscious Capitalism: Creating a New Paradigm for Business," Whole Foods Market: John Mackey's Blog, November 9, 2006. http://www.wholefoods.com/blogs/jm/ archives/2006/11/conscious_capit.html

Chapter 5   Be a Guide

1. David Sifry, "The State of the Live Web, April 2007," Sifry's Alerts, April 5, 2007. http://www.sifry.com/alerts/archives/000493. html
2. David Kiley, "Mass Customization Maybe Offers Too Many Choices," *BusinessWeek,* June 8, 2005. http://www.businessweek. com/the_thread/brandnewday/archives/2005/06/mass_cus- tomizat.html
3. Poping Lin, "When Product Variety Backfires: Q&A with John Gourville," Harvard Business School's *Working Knowledge for Business Leaders,* September 6, 2005. http://hbswk.hbs.edu/ item/4980.html
4. Chris Anderson, *The Long Tail: Why the Future of Business Is Selling Less of More* (New York: Hyperion, 2006).
5. Chris Anderson, "Anheuser-Busch and the Long Tail of Beer," *The Long Tail: A Public Diary on Themes Around a Book,* February 2, 2007. http://www.longtail.com/the_long_tail/ 2007/02/anheuserbusch_a.html
6. Seth Godin, "Starting Over with Customer Service," Seth Godin's Blog, February 21, 2007. http://sethgodin.typepad.com/ seths_blog/2007/02/starting_over_w.html

7. A. Bernstein, "Edward Arnold, 93; Designer Set Newspaper Industry Standards," the *Los Angeles Times,* February 16, 2007.
8. Jakob Nielsen, "Amazon: No Longer the Role Model for E-Commerce Design," Jakob Nielsen's Alertbox, July 27, 2005. http://www.useit.com/alertbox/20050725.html

Chapter 6   Be Choosy

1. Richard Branson, "Learn How to Say No (Even if You're Known as 'Dr. Yes')," *Business 2.0,* http://money.cnn.com/popups/2006/biz2/how to succeed/4.html
2. Julie Bosman, "Chevy Tries a Write-Your-Own-Ad Approach, and the Potshots Fly," *New York Times,* April 4, 2006. http://www.nytimes.com/2006/04/04/business/media/04adco.html?ex=1301803200&en=280e20c8ba110565&ei=5088&partner=rssnyt&emc=rss
3. "Web Attack," *BusinessWeek,* April 16, 2007. http://www.businessweek.com/magazine/content/07_16/b4030068.htm?chan=top+news_top+news+index_top+story
4. "We Weren't Just Airborne Yesterday," Southwest.com, May 2, 2007. http://www.southwest.com/about_swa/airborne.html
5. "Herb Kelleher on the Record, Part 3," *BusinessWeek,* December 24, 2003. http://www.businessweek.com/bwdaily/dnflash/dec2003/nf20031224_2773_db062.htm

Chapter 7   Be a Fighter

1. Steve Petersen, "When Customers Attack," Bivings Report, March 12, 2007. http://www.bivingsreport.com/2007/when-customers-attack/
2. Jeff Jarvis, "Dell Lies. Dell Sucks," BuzzMachine, June 21, 2005. http://www.buzzmachine.com/archives/2005_06_21.html#009911
3. Susan Carey and Darren Everson, "Lessons on the Fly: JetBlue's New Tactics," *Wall Street Journal Online,* February 27, 2007. http://online.wsj.com/article/SB117254453821320226.html?mod=todays_us_marketplace
4. Dominic Jones, "Starbucks Answers Activists on YouTube," IR Web Report, January 8, 2007. http://www.irwebreport.com/daily/2007/01/08/starbucks-answers-activists-on-youtube/

Chapter 8   Be an Expert

1. "Food Consumption," USDA Economic Research Service, May 25, 2007. http://www.ers.usda.gov/Briefing/Consumption/

2. Orrin, "Energy Tip #21: Veggie for a Week," TerraPass, November 28, 2006. www.terrapass.com/terrablog/posts/2006/11/energy-tip-21-veggie-for-a-week.html

3. "Turkey," *New York Magazine*, 2007. http://nymag.com/nymetro/food/homeent/14995/

4. "Maine Lobster Buying Guide," LobsterAnywhere.com. http://www.lobsteranywhere.com/cgi-bin/category/articles

5. Clay Shirky, "Larry Sanger, Citizendium, and the Problem of Expertise," Corante, September 18, 2006. http://many.corante.com/archives/2006/09/18/larry_sanger_citizendium_and_the_problem_of_expertise.php

6. Seth Godin, *Everyone's An Expert (About Something)*, (Squidoo LLC, 2005). http://sethgodin.typepad.com/seths_blog/files/_everyoneisanexpert2.pdf

7. Kathy Sierra, "How to Be an Expert," Creating Passionate Users, March 3, 2006. http://headrush.typepad.com/creating_passionate_users/2006/03/how_to_be_an_ex.html

8. David E. Williams, "'Grammar Girl' A Quick and Dirty Success," CNN.com, January 25, 2007. http://www.cnn.com/2007/TECH/internet/01/22/grammar.girl/index.html

9. Rob Hof, "eBay's Search for Sellers," *BusinessWeek*, June 17, 2004. http://www.businessweek.com/technology/content/jun2004/tc20040617_6618_tc024.htm

10. Joe Wilcox, "Moseying Up to Apple's Genius Bar," CNET News.com, May 16, 2001. http://news.com.com/2100-1040-257742.html

11. Jerry Useem, "Apple: America's Best Retailer," CNNMoney.com, March 8, 2007. http://money.cnn.com/magazines/fortune/fortune_archive/2007/03/19/8402321/index.htm

Chapter 9   Be Part of the Best Team

1. Center for Media Research, "Average US Household Watches 15.7 TV Channels a Week," Research Brief, June 22, 2007. http://www.centerformediaresearch.com/cfmr_brief.cfm?fnl=070330

2. Patricia Kitchen, "Change@Work: Steps to a New Career," *Newsday*, March 4, 2007. http://www.newsday.com/about/ nybzcov045115684mar04,0,7798544.column

3. Alan Schwarz, "Throwing Batters Curves Before Throwing a Pitch," *New York Times*, April 6, 2007, p. A1. http://www.nytimes .com/2007/04/06/sports/baseball/06pitcher.html?adxnnl=1&a dxnnlx=1175885610-v9MDdRsFH06qlfywiOn5gg

4. Tammy Hobbs Miracky and Amy Lieb, "43 Entrepreneurs Who Are Changing the World," *Fast Company*, 2007. http://www. fastcompany.com/social/2007/method/index.html

5. Cheryl Dahle, "A More Powerful Path," *Fast Company*, 11 (December/ January 2007). http://www.fastcompany.com/magazine/111/ open_socap-intro.html

6. Barkley Evergreen Partners, "PR Week Cause Survey 2005." http://www.barkleyus.com/press_clip/show/32

7. Ibid.

Chapter 10   Be Ahead of Your Audiences

1. Peter Morville, "The Age of Findability," BoxesAndArrows, April 29, 2002. http://www.boxesandarrows.com/view/the_age_of_ findability

2. Tom Chi, "The Role of Aesthetics in Design," OK/Cancel, March 27, 2006. http://www.ok-cancel.com/archives/article/2006/03/ the-role-of-aesthetics-in-design.html

3. "Mickey D's McMakeover," *BusinessWeek*, May 15, 2006. http:// www.businessweek.com/magazine/content/06_20/b3984065. htm

4. Kenneth Hein, "McDonald's Serves Up New Store Design," *BrandWeek*, January 11, 2006. http://www.brandweek.com/bw/ news/recent_display.jsp?vnu_content_id=1001841837

5. Robert Scoble, "The role of anti-marketing design", Scobelizer, March 4, 2006. http://scobleizer.com/2006/03/04/the-role-of- anti-marketing-design/

6. Markus Frind, "Are Designers Clued In?", The Paradigm Shift, June 4, 2006. http://plentyoffish.wordpress.com/2006/06/04/ are-designers-clued-in/

Chapter 11   Be Second to Your Competitors

1. Knowledge@Wharton, "Want to Win? Here's Some Practical Advice from Jack Welch," June 1, 2005. http://knowledge.wharton.upenn.edu/article.cfm?articleid=1209&CFID=3913090&CFTOKEN=48152877&jsessionid=a8301f91ede31b015055

2. Diane Brady, "Yes, Winning Is Still the Only Thing," *BusinessWeek*, August 21, 2006. http://www.businessweek.com/magazine/content/06_34/b3998403.htm?chan=top+news_top+news

3. Rupert Murdoch, "Special Report: Mixed Media," *Forbes*, May 7, 2007. http://www.forbes.com/free_forbes/2007/0507/138.html

4. Seth Godin, "Is There a First Mover Advantage?" Seth Godin's Blog, March 6, 2006. http://sethgodin.typepad.com/seths_blog/2006/03/is_there_a_firs.html

Chapter 12   Be Fresh

1. Innovators Matter Most by Robert E. Litan, *Wall Street Journal*, February 24, 2007 http://online.wsj.com/article/SB117228425986518145-search.html?KEYWORDS=litan&COLLECTION=wsjie/6month

2. Laura Koss-Feder, "An Investment with Meaning," *Time*, March 29, 2007. http://www.time.com/time/magazine/article/0,9171,1604868,00.html

3. Chris Anderson, *Wired* magazine. http://www.wired.com/wired/archive/12.10/tail_pr.html

4. Information Outlook, 6:1 (January 2002). http://www.sla.org/content/Shop/Information/infoonline/2002/jan02/kelly.cfm

5. Colin Stewart, "The Art of Innovation," Salon.com, November 8, 2000. http://archive.salon.com/tech/feature/2000/11/28/art/index1.html

6. Lev Grossman, "Apple's New Calling: The iPhone," *Time*, January 9, 2007/http://www.time.com/time/nation/article/0,8599,1575410-1,00.html

7. Vanessa O'Connell, "How Fashion Makes Its Way from the Runway to the Rack," http://online.wsj.com/article/SB117089461212701622.html?mod=todays_us_personal_journal

8. Carol Hymowitz, "All Companies Need Innovation; Hasbro Finds a New Magic," February 26, 2007. http://online.wsj.

com/article/SB117244992317418824.html?mod=todays_us_
marketplace

9. Tom Peters, "The Brand Called You," in Jim Collins, Mark
    Vamos, and David Lidsky, *Fast Company's Greatest Hits: Ten Years
    of the Most Innovative Ideas in Business.* New York: Portfolio,
    2006.

Chapter 13   Be Geographically Relevant

1. Ethan Zuckerman, "Where I Work These Days," on his "My
    Heart's in Accra" blog web site, April 20, 2007. http://www.
    ethanzuckerman.com/blog/?p=1394
2. comScore Networks press release, September 28, 2006. http://
    www.comscore.com/press/release.asp?press=1017
3. http://online.wsj.com/article/SB110027449364072612.html
4. Deborah Sontag, "POP: I want my Hyphenated-Identity MTV,"
    June 19, 2005. http://select.nytimes.com/search/restricted/ar
    ticle?res=F30E16F7345C0C7A8DDDAF0894DD40482
5. William Safire, "On Language," the *New York Times Sunday Maga-
    zine,* March 5, 2005. http://select.nytimes.com/search/restricted/
    article?res=FA0E17F6395D0C768CDDAA0894D8404482
6. Shayne Bowman and Chris Willis, "Nieman Reports: The
    Future Is Here, But Do News Media Companies See It?"
    December 22, 2005. http://www.hypergene.net/blog/weblog
    .php?id=P327

Chapter 14   Be a Public Failure

1. Robert Longley, "Why Small Businesses Fail: SBA," http://
    usgovinfo.about.com/od/smallbusiness/a/whybusfail.htm
2. Zach Stambor, "Right Before Our Eyes," *Monitor on Psychology,*
    37:9 (October 2006), at APA Online. http://www.apa.org/
    monitor/oct06/eyes.html
3. John Cook, "Facing Threats, Jobster Targets Profitability in
    2007," *Seattle Post-Intelligencer,* December 26, 2006. http://blog.
    seattlepi.nwsource.com/venture/archives/109958.asp
4. Damon Darlin, "A Boss Takes to his Blog to Deny, Then Con-
    firm," *New York Times,* January 22, 2007.
5. Jason Goldberg, "Questions and Answers," Jobster Blog,
    December 29, 2006. http://jobster.blogs.com/blog_dot_jobster_
    dot_com/2006/12/questions_and_a.html

6. http://jobster.blogs.com/blog_dot_jobster_dot_com/2007/01/confessions_of_.html

7. "Customer Service Champs," *BusinessWeek,* March 5, 2007. http://www.businessweek.com/magazine/content/07_10/b4024001.htm?chan=top+news_top+news+index_top+story

8. Michael Fitzgerald, "How to Improve It? Ask Those Who Use It," *New York Times,* March 25, 2007. http://www.nytimes.com/2007/03/25/business/yourmoney/25Proto.html?ex=1175486400&en=009a2fceac64cd2b&ei=5070&emc=eta1

9. Don Tapscott, *The Naked Corporation* (New York: Free Press, 2003).

10. Tom McNichol, "A Startup's Best Friend? Failure," *Business 2.0,* April 4, 2007. http://money.cnn.com/magazines/business2/business2_archive/2007/03/01/8401031/index.htm

Chapter 15   Be Connected and Confident

1. Doc Searls, "Disrupting the VC Business and Exploring the Because Effect," Doc Searls IT Garage, January 25, 2006. http://www.itgarage.com/node/736

2. Carl Shapiro and Hal Varian, *Information Rules: A Strategic Guide to the Network Economy* (Boston: Harvard Business School Press, 1998), 6.

3. Thomas Friedman, *The World is Flat* (New York: Farrar, Straus, and Giroux, 2005), 29.

4. Ibid., 8.

5. Chris Anderson, *The Long Tail,* page 26.

6. Betsy Morris, *Fortune,* July 11, 2006. http://money.cnn.com/2006/07/10/Magazines/fortune/rules.fortune.index.htm

7. Ron Maggiore, "Applying Old Rules in a New Technology Age," June 25, 2002. http://www.marketingprofs.com/login/join.asp?adref=rdblk&source=/2/maggiore1.asp

8. Seth Godin, "Slowly I Turned . . . Step by Step . . . Inch by Inch . . .," *Fast Company,* Issue 70, April 2003, page 72.

9. Jim Collins, "Good to Great: Web-Exclusive Interview," Fastcompany.com, Issue 41. September 2001, page 90.

Chapter 16   Be a Steward

1. IBM Global Business Services, *Advocacy in the Customer Focused Enterprise* (New York: IBM Global Services, 2006). http://static.scribd.com/docs/1axtgs5h8y46x.pdf

Bibliography

Alinsky, Saul. *Reville for Radicals*. New York: Vintage, 989.
———. *Rules for Radicals*. New York: Vintage, 1989.
Anderson, Chris. *The Long Tail: Why the Future of Busir ess Is Selling Less of More*. New York: Hyperion, 2006.
Collins, Jim. *Good To Great: Why Some Companies Ma̅e The Leap and Others Don't*. New York: HarperBusiness, 2001.
Collins, Jim, and Jerry Porras. *Built to Last: Successful F̅abits of Visionary Companies*. New York: HarperBusiness, 1994.
Levitt, Steven, and Stephen J. Dubner. *Freakonomics: A̅ Rogue Economist Explores the Hidden Side of Everything*. New York: V̅illiam Morrow, 2006.
Friedman, Thomas L. *The World Is Flat: A Brief History of the 21st Century*. New York: Farrar, Straus and Giroux, 2006.
Gabler, Neil. *Walt Disney: The Triumph of the American I̅nagination*. New York: Knopf, 2006.
———. *Life: The Movie: How Entertainment Conque̅ed Reality*. New York: Vintage, 2000.
Gladwell, Malcolm. *The Tipping Point: How Little T̅ings Can Make A Big Difference*. New York: Back Bay Books, 2002.
Godin, Seth. *Small is the New Big and 183 Other F̅iffs, Rants, and Remarkable Business Ideas*. New York: Portfolio, 200̅.
Heath, Chip, and Dan Heath. *Made to Stick: Why So̅ne Ideas Survive and Others Die*. New York: Random House, 2007.
Jenkins, Henry *Convergence Culture: Where Old and N̅ew Media Colide* (New York: New York University Press, 2006)
———. *Fans, Bloggers, and Gamers: Media Consumers in a Digital Age* (New York: New York University Press 2006)
Lessig, Lawrence. *The Future of Ideas: The Fate of th̅e Commons in a Connected World*. New York: Vintage, 2002.

McLuhan, Marshall. *Understanding Media: The Extensions of Man.* Cambridge, MA: MIT Press, 1994.

Moggridge, Bill. *Designing Interactions.* Cambridge, MA: MIT Press, 2006.

Ogilvy, David. *Confessions of an Advertising Man.* London: Southbank Publishing, 2004.

————. *Ogilvy on Advertising.* London: Prion Books, 2003.

Pink, Daniel. *A Whole New Mind: Why Right Brainers will Rule the Future.* New York: Riverhead Trade, 2006.

Postman, Neil. *Amusing Ourselves to Death: Public Discourse in the Age of Show Business.* New York: Penguin, 1986.

————. *Technopoly: The Surrender of Culture to Technology.* New York: Vintage, 1993.

Radford, Benjamin. *Media Mythmakers: How Journalists, Activists, and Advertisers Mislead Us.* New York: Prometheus Books, 2003.

Rheingold, Howard. *Smart Mobs: The Next Social Revolution.* Basic Books, 2003.

Reichheld, Fred. *The Ultimate Question: Driving True Profits and Good Grow.* Boston, MA: Harvard Business School Press, 2006.

Schwartz, Barry. *The Paradox of Choice: Why More is Less.* New York: Harper Perennial, 2005.

Scoble, Robert and Shel Israel. *Naked Conversations: How Blogs Are Changing the Way Businesses Talk with Customers.* New York: Wiley, 2006.

Shenk, David. *Data Smog: Surviving the Information Glut.* New York: Harper, 1998.

Surowiecki, James. *The Wisdom of Crowds.* New York: Anchor, 2005.

Tapscott, Donald. *Growing Up Digital: The Rise of the Net Generation.* New York: McGraw-Hill, 2006 (New Ed edition).

————. *The Digital Economy: Promise and Peril in the Age of Networked Intelligence.* New York: McGraw-Hill, 2007.

————. *The Naked Corporation: How The Age of Transparency Will Revolutionize Business.* New York: Free Press, 2003.

————. *Wikinomics: How Mass Collaboration Changes Everything.* New York: Portfolio, 2006.

Turkle, Sherry. *Life on the Screen: Identity in the Age of the Internet.* New York: Simon & Schuster, 1997.

Underhill, Pac. *Why We Buy: The Science of Shopping.* New York: Simon & Shuster, 2000.

Weber, Larry. *Marketing to the Social Web: How Digital Customer Communities Build Your Business.* (New York: Wiley, 2007.)

Weinberger, David, *The Clue Train Manifesto.* New York: et al. Perseus Books Group, 2001.

————. *Small Pieces Loosely Joined: A Theory of the Web.* New York: Perseus Books Group, 2003.

Everything is Miscellaneous: The Power of the New Digital Disorder (New York: Henry Holt Company 2007)

Wipperfurth, Alex *Brand Hijack: Marketing without Marketing.* New York: Portfolio, 2006.

Index